W9-BZF-920

WILLIAM CRAWFORD GORGAS

HIS LIFE AND WORK

Dr. Gorgas in 1920, the year of his death.

William Crawford Gorgas

His Life and Work

By
Marie D. Gorgas
and
Burton J. Hendrick

Garden City New York
Doubleday, Page and Company
1924

PRINTED IN THE UNITED STATES
AT
THE COUNTRY LIFE PRESS, GARDEN CITY, N. Y.
First Edition

CONTENTS

LIST OF ILLUSTRATIONS

WILLIAM CRAWFORD GORGAS

HIS LIFE AND WORK

WILLIAM CRAWFORD GORGAS

CHAPTER I

EARLY DAYS AT FORT BROWN

AT EVERY stage of his career William Crawford Gorgas seemed to confront the gaunt spectre of yellow fever. It was an important influence even in the love story of the doctor's life. The manner in which the conqueror of the disease fought his first battle—a battle that determined his future course, on both the personal and professional side—may best be described in the words of Mrs. Gorgas:

"One warm, sunshiny day on the Mexican border in the month of August, 1882, I saw William Crawford Gorgas for the first time. May Vernou, daughter of Captain Vernou of the Nineteenth Infantry, and I were riding horseback within the confines of the old army post of Fort Brown, Texas, on the banks of the Rio Grande. Near by lay the historic battlefields of Palo Alto and Resaca de la Palma, the favourite destination of our rides in normal times. On that particular day our ride was limited to the post, because we were quarantined against the neighbouring town of Brownsville on account of the yellow-fever epidemic then raging. At the time I was visiting my sister, Mrs. Lyster, the wife of Colonel William J. Lyster, in command of the post.

"During the course of our ride we repeatedly encountered Captain Hewitt of the Nineteenth Infantry, who was driving his spirited horse and smart trap about the post. By his side was seated a strange young officer about whose identity we girls were most curious. Captain Hewitt was a great tease. Several times in passing he stopped his horse as if he desired to speak to us, and to introduce the young officer with him. Then as we also stopped, ready to engage in conversation, he would suddenly whip up his animal and drive rapidly away, leaving us in a state of mingled embarrassment and indignation. This happened several times, until our dignity asserted itself, and thereafter we scorned to notice the trap and its occupants. Thus my meeting with Dr. Gorgas, the captain's companion, was postponed for a few hours.

"For some months previous there had been many cases of fever in Matamoras, the squalid Mexican city across the river from Brownsville, where we went to shop, and remained to watch roulette and the *baile* to the music of 'La Golondrina,' 'La Paloma,' and 'Siempre.' In Brownsville there were a number of fever cases, and a few in the fort. At first it was supposed to be dengue, or break-bone fever, the symptoms of which are similar to those of yellow fever. The severity of the cases and the large number of deaths had made the civilians and the army authorities uneasy. Colonel Joseph Smith, medical director of the Southern Department, had come to Fort Brown to investigate the situation, and to take the necessary precautions to safeguard the health of the troops and check the spread of the disease. He did not long remain in doubt as to the nature of the epidemic. Yellow fever was rampant.

"The cause of yellow fever and the manner in which it was transmitted were unknown at this time. We did not dream that the annoying mosquito which abounded at Fort Brown and the little towns adjacent on both sides of the Rio Grande was the carrier of the disease. Some supposed that it was borne by the breeze—the yellow-fever breeze, as it was called. This was true in a measure, inasmuch as the breeze carries the mosquito. Strange ideas prevailed, not only as to the origin of yellow fever, but also with regard to specifics against it. Oranges and bananas, asserted to be a cause, were in consequence almost entirely tabooed. Whisky and mustard seed were believed by the majority to be infallible as a specific. 'What quantities of mustard seed that fellow —— —— must have swallowed!'

wrote an officer. 'He believed it a specific, and I know that he kept full of mustard seed all summer.'

"So great was the terror inspired by yellow fever that when a person died he was buried with all possible haste—innocently enough the medical profession thought this a safeguard against contagion.

"During this reign of terror Dr. Gorgas, undaunted by difficulties, arrived at Brown a few days before the greater portion of the garrison moved out to camp. He himself never had had yellow fever, nor had he even seen a case. This was yellow fever's first encounter with one who became its most implacable foe, and whose life was to be concentrated on its extermination.

"The official message from the chief surgeon of the department preceding the arrival of Dr. Gorgas was directed to Major Happersett, the post surgeon:

"'I am sending you the most progressive young surgeon under my command.'

"Dr. Gorgas was an advance guard of a large number of medical personnel sent to take care of nearly twenty-three hundred cases of yellow fever. He found the people outside the post more scared than those within.

"'I had considerable difficulty in getting to my station,' he wrote, 'as they had quarantined in every direction. I write now more as a matter of form than with any hope that this will reach you, as our mails are being stopped. I was detained to-day in San Antonio, and spent most of it with Willy Aubrey. At Laredo, where there was another delay of a day, I was entertained by Major Carraher, and saw most of my old friends there. The town has grown so, I should scarcely recognize it. About sixty miles from Laredo I took the stage, and staged it about two hundred miles to this post.

"'The fort is pleasantly situated, the prettiest I have seen in the department. I have quarters with one of the bachelors, Lieutenant[1] Crowder, in the second story of one of the barracks buildings—about the most comfortable place in the post. We have a mess in the building—eight of us. The garrison consists of six companies of the Nineteenth Infantry and one of the Eighth Cavalry, which gives us about twenty officers. There are some half-dozen officers' families in the post. For the last week we have been strictly quarantined against the town, so that I can say nothing about Brownsville so far. A brick wall separates us from the town. I find my immediate superior pleasant and kind—Dr. Happersett by name.

"'They all did the square thing by me when I left Duncan, rather looking upon me as a lamb sent to be slaughtered. All sorts of yellow-fever specifics were

[1]General Enoch Crowder, now American Ambassador to Cuba.

given me, mostly whisky, brandy, and cigars. I came by ambulance as far as the Junction—thirty-five miles—accompanied by Dr. Bedal and Kelso, just to say good-bye; so that altogether I left with flying colours.'

"Dr. Gorgas was ordered to give necessary attention to C Company and I Troop. Sick call for these organizations and also for the casuals at the post was conducted at the main hospital, which Dr. Gorgas was permitted to visit for this purpose only. He had strict orders not to visit the yellow-fever ward of the hospital, nor to place himself in any kind of contact with yellow-fever patients. This order he disobeyed. The story of his disobedience and its result, General—then Lieutenant—Crowder tells.

"'It all came through a professional zeal on Gorgas's part, which even strict military orders could not curb. Captain Hennessey was commanding officer of the attenuated garrison left behind, and I was adjutant, quartermaster, ordnance officer, signal officer, etc.—a kind of military Pooh Bah, as there was no other officer of junior rank present to share these duties with me. The post hospital was always on our rounds. It was on one of these inspection trips that we caught Gorgas *in flagrante delicto*. Gorgas had received strict orders to stay away from the infected wards and parts of the garrison. Arriving at the hospital on one of these inspection trips, we were received, not by Lieutenant Gorgas, but by his hospital steward. Asked where the acting post surgeon was, the steward sought to evade a direct answer. Two or three repetitions of the question having failed to break down a loyalty which Gorgas invariably inspired among his subordinates, Captain Hennessey brushed by him into the yellow-fever ward. Failing to find Gorgas there, he went further in this inspection, and passing down the dead room, he saw through an open window Gorgas dissecting the latest yellow-fever victim, with Dr. Melou witnessing the post-mortem.

"'Upon being addressed through the window, Gorgas's attention was diverted from his absorbing task, and in the manner of one receiving a guest in his own quarters, he replied: "Good morning, Captain! Will you come in?" Which of course was the last thing either of us thought of doing. He was directed to come outside, and upon his appearance before us was asked as to his orders and his disobedience of them. He replied unequivocally to both questions, and was ordered to remain where he was. We proceeded to the administration building, prepared a formal order of arrest, and notified department headquarters at San Antonio and Colonel Charles A. Smith, headquarters at the chief quarantine camp some fifteen miles down the river.

"'My part was limited to serving upon Gorgas

formal written order of arrest, and to giving him directions to take up his quarters in the infected part of the garrison. The quarters designated were next to those occupied by the family of Colonel Lyster.

"'Gorgas changed his residence promptly, and on the same day orders were received from headquarters at San Antonio and from the quarantine camp releasing Gorgas from arrest; but he remained a resident in the infected part of the garrison, giving attention from that time on to yellow-fever patients, until stricken himself.'

"From their Brownsville days General Crowder and Dr. Gorgas remained fast friends, and during the World War there was the closest affiliation between the office of the Provost-marshal and that of the Surgeon-general.

"On the night of his arrival and drive around the post with Captain Hewitt, Dr. Gorgas called on Colonel and Mrs. Lyster and on me. In that warm climate it was the custom to spend the evening on the galleries, and we were sitting there chatting in the cool darkness when he came. I could not see the young officer's features distinctly, but I was pleasantly impressed by the musical tones of his voice and his soft Southern accent.

"A few days later, after most of the troops had gone to camp, Colonel Lyster remaining in command of Brown, I was taken in the early morning hours

Dr. Gorgas in 1882, while at Fort Brown, Texas. Here he himself contracted yellow fever and so became immune to the disease.

with a severe chill, which my brother and sister rightly feared might be the first symptoms of yellow fever. Dr. Gorgas was sent for, and as promptly came. I saw his face distinctly for the first time about four o'clock in the morning.

"The chill had passed, and I was restless, with a high fever. Colonel Lyster was fanning me, and my sister relates that no sooner had Dr. Gorgas entered the room than I, taking the fan from my brother, handed it to the Doctor, saying: 'You fan me!' I have no recollection of this.

"Yellow fever is not a lingering illness. The patient is usually convalescent or dead within a week of the time he is stricken. On the fourth or fifth day of my sickness I was apparently in the last stages of the disease. I even had the fatal 'black vomit,' and all hopes of my recovery had been abandoned.

"The cemetery at Fort Brown was on an island in the Rio Grande. Communication with the post was by means of rowboats. That there might be no delay in burial, an open grave was kept constantly in readiness for the next victim.

"On the morning of the day my life was despaired of, the only son of Major and Mrs. Witherell, a lad about eighteen years old, had died of the fever, and the two medical officers, Dr. Gorgas and Dr. Melou (a contract doctor from Brownsville), not only attended the sick and dying but also conducted the services for the dead. Accordingly, on this morning they accompanied the body of young Witherell to the cemetery, and there performed the rites of burial.

"Dr. Melou, pointing to the open grave awaiting the next victim, said to Dr. Gorgas:

"'This is Miss Doughty's grave. Will you read the burial service for her this afternoon?'

"'Yes,' replied Dr. Gorgas, 'I will read her burial service.'

"He did not. To the amazement of all, I began to recover, but due to the severity of my case and some heart complications I was unable to sit up until the fifteenth day.

"Two days after the time set for my burial by Dr. Melou yellow fever made its first and last attack on its mortal enemy. Dr. Gorgas was himself stricken with the disease, and had a severe case, but he was over the worst by the eighth day. Thus it came to pass that we were convalescent at the same time.

"Dr. Gorgas's quarters being adjacent to those of Colonel Lyster, in the days of convalescence we saw each other frequently, and our little romance blossomed, though slowly, being beset with difficulties.

"These weeks and the ones following were replete with stirring events. Our quarters became a veritable hospital, with every one sick except Colonel and

Mrs. Lyster and the Mexican cook. Mrs. Smith, wife of the superintendent of the cemetery, hearing of the plight of our household, offered her services as nurse, which offer was gratefully accepted.

"Mrs. Smith included in her administrations the 'Gorgeous Doctor,' as she called the young lieutenant. Most of his meals she prepared, and carried over to him herself. Endowed with a romantic disposition and an artistic temperament, Mrs. Smith beautified the Doctor's tray from time to time with a rose which she had the audacity to tell him I had sent. The young surgeon, not being sure of my name, and having been told by Captain Hewitt that I was sensitive about the pronunciation of the name 'Doughty,' sent his appreciative thanks to 'Miss Tea-and-Toast' each time a rose was received. This name later became known in the regiment, thanks to Mrs. Smith, and it clung to me for some time.

"A few weeks later we went out to camp about two miles from the post. Captain Weenie and many others had died. Our camp was fairly comfortable, but scarcely were we settled when Colonel Lyster and his daughter Aileen developed mild cases of fever, and the Mexican cook, considered immune, had quite a severe case.

"The strain of Colonel Lyster's illness and all that Mrs. Lyster had passed through began to tell on her health. We dreaded the lonely nights.

Fearful shrieks coming from drunken Mexicans across the Rio Grande; the barking and howling of dogs and alarming noises of all kinds were most depressing. Sometimes we wondered whether our courage would endure. Smuggling we knew was going on to a tremendous extent, and desperate characters were lurking about ready to take advantage of unusual circumstances. Now and then the beautiful strains of 'La Golondrina,' 'La Paloma,' and 'Siempre' floated across to us, sung in a tender romantic way by some young Mexican with a charming voice. We tried to delude ourselves with the belief that where there was such ardent love of music and so much chivalry, dark deeds could not flourish. Dr. Gorgas and Dr. Melou came out almost daily to see the invalids. Their visits cheered us. Letters from headquarters at Yturria, fifteen miles out, were anxiously awaited, but no cases of yellow fever developed there.

"It was difficult to get supplies at camp, and the isolation was trying. As soon as the invalids had sufficiently recovered, we went back to the post. Quarantine was still in force, and we saw few people. Dr. Gorgas dropped in with increasing frequency. The nights were chilly, and it was pleasant to gather around the fire and listen to Colonel Lyster read to us from Dickens or Thackeray. Often Dr. Gorgas read. Mrs. Lyster and I enjoyed the reading, but frequently the two officers strayed into discussions of the Mexican and Civil wars. Battles were their particular delight, and sometimes when the engagement waxed hottest I slipped away.

"I was surprised when one night Dr. Gorgas asked me to take a row with him on the lagoon next day, and to visit the cemetery. Mrs. Smith was visibly glad to see us, and invited us to walk over to see my grave—or, rather, the grave that was to have been mine, but in which now lay a pretty Miss Reynolds. It gave me a queer, chilly sensation to look at the spot where I came so near being buried.

"It was Mrs. Lyster who first noticed heart complications in the young doctor. In communicating her suspicions to me, she said: 'It is true, he doesn't seem to have much to say to you, but he looks at you all the time. And then—those apples!'

"This last remark referred to a very large gunny-sack of apples Dr. Gorgas had sent me the day before. Apples sold at a premium, and were worth at the very least a dollar and a half a dozen. We heard that the Doctor was not well off, and such extravagance on the part of an impecunious young man denoted interest, to say the least—according to Mrs. Lyster. Quite accustomed to Mrs. Lyster's mode of reasoning, however, I was not impressed.

"The troops returned from Camp Yturria to remain only a short time. The Nineteenth Infantry, of which my brother-in-law was colonel, was ordered to Fort Clark, Texas. Before the garrison left for Clark, a farewell hop was given at the handsome administration building on the banks of the Rio Grande. The dance seems strange to me now, after so many deaths had occurred in the garrison; but it was evidently the reaction from the long, dreary months of strain and anxiety.

"Dr. Gorgas was not a good dancer, in spite of the instruction he had received at Clark. We sat out a dance on the broad gallery, and discussed Henry George and the single tax, Herbert Spencer, and kindred topics. It was rather a one-sided discussion. I listened, much mystified in mind as to whether Herbert Spencer was the Spenser who wrote the 'Faerie Queene.' I thought it very old-fashioned and quaint of the Doctor to ask me for a flower and a bit of ribbon. He was to remain at Brown. In fact, he was there for two years, living in the same quarters with Lieutenant Enoch Crowder. They ran a mess, and had an excellent coloured cook. 'We live in the most delightful style,' he wrote me some months later. 'Scott, Crowder, and I have Molly, Captain Williams's old Southern cook, as the presiding genius of our mess, with another equally prepossessing darky as assistant. If you and the Lysters were only next door where you used to be, we would ask you over to judge for yourselves. Dr. Melou always asks for Miss Tea-and-Toast. Indeed, whenever he finds me writing he insists that it is to you—and he is right most of the time. Crowder's status with regard to Miss —— is apparently unchanged. I do not think there is any understanding between them.'

"Often I have heard General Crowder and Dr. Gorgas laugh over their old cook's peculiar characteristics and odd ways. Molly's ambition and aim in life was to have a handsome silk gown. For years she had saved to attain this end. At last, having accumulated one hundred dollars, she confided to the two men her secret ambition, and asked them to send to New York for the handsomest black-silk gown that could be had for one hundred dollars. Gowns were cheaper in the early 'eighties than in this extravagant age, and the young lieutenants were aghast. They protested, but in vain. Molly was determined to have the gown. Unskilled in such matters, they consulted Mrs. Happersett, and measurements having been taken, the gown was ordered from B. Altman & Company, New York. When it arrived it was really a work of art. Molly was enchanted and was the envy of all her friends when on Sundays and holidays she wore the gown in all its elegance—but minus shoes and stockings. Lieutenant Crowder and Dr. Gorgas, in admiration and consternation at the picture Molly presented, assured her with all truthfulness that she was wonderful to behold.

"After we had been at Fort Clark for some months, Dr. Gorgas came up from Brown to spend several days. We took horseback rides, and I played for him 'La Golondrina,' 'La Paloma,' and 'Siempre.' He enjoyed this as far as it went. There was no engagement, but after this visit letters were more frequent.

"'I am conscious,' he wrote, 'of many disadvantages under which I labour in winning the place I wish in your esteem, particularly that of being entirely separated from you. Words are poor means of expression or of winning regard. I think if I could be thrown with you from day to day, and have you appreciate how dear you have become to me, it would be something in my favour. But this is my misfortune, and I have to appeal to you not to let it work to my disadvantage. I am very glad of this opportunity of speaking on the subject nearest my heart. Our relations have not been such that I felt at liberty to obtrude my feelings upon you in writing unless your letters gave me some opportunity. Any change in them, you must be aware, is entirely in your hands. If I have trespassed in this matter, please pardon me. The greatest object I have just now is to stand well with you. . . .

"'Duro has improved immensely in personal appearance lately. He is a handsome, intelligent looking animal, and a first-rate retriever, and has a good nose besides. He caught an uninjured quail on the parade the other day. I think of him because he has his paws on the arm of my chair, looking on as I write, and as he sympathizes thoroughly with his master in everything, I know he wishes to send you his best love.'

"In the fall of 1884, being near Dr. Gorgas's home at Tuscaloosa, Alabama, I accepted an invitation from his mother to visit her. When I did so, I was not aware that Dr. Gorgas was at Tuscaloosa, he having sudden orders to proceed from Fort Brown to Fort Randall, South Dakota, for station. The surprise, therefore, of seeing him when I got off the train was great. The pleasure it gave me, however, was not unmixed with embarrassment. I wondered if his family knew the exact state of affairs. Dr. Gorgas's sister and brother were with him, and we had a pleasant drive out to the University where his mother was living. The picture Mrs. Gorgas made as she came from the dear old portico to greet me with the gracious manner so peculiarly her own, made a lasting impression. She captured in one second the obdurate heart that had withstood for two years the siege of her handsome son. I then and there capitulated, and have always maintained that I fell in love with Mrs. Gorgas before I did with the Doctor, and that I owed my great happiness to her, for she aided in every way to bring about our engagement. That Mrs. Gorgas could so entirely forget self in her desire to further the happiness of her son in love with a young Northern girl who was almost an entire stranger to her, showed as perhaps nothing else the strength of her beautiful and unselfish character.

"The quaint old university home was full of young people. That evening there were dancing and singing, and the Doctor asked for the Spanish airs he so loved, 'La Golondrina,' 'La Paloma,' and 'Siempre.'

"Mrs. Gorgas was the librarian of the University of Alabama, beloved and honoured by the students and all who knew her. The Doctor and I walked over to the library with her the next morning, and I met there President Lewis of the University, Professor Parker, Dr. Eugene A. Smith, and other distinguished men. It was Mrs. Gorgas who suggested that the Doctor should take me for a walk to the river, through the beautiful piney woods, and it was on the banks of the old Black Warrior River, seated on a fallen tree in the shade formed by the dense growth of pines, that I, most happily for me, capitulated.

"It would be untrue to say that Yellow Jack was the best man at our wedding—but it would be perfectly true to say that in a sense he was an usher."

CHAPTER II

ANCESTRY AND YOUTH

I

ON BOTH his father's and his mother's side William Crawford Gorgas came of distinguished ancestry. His father was General Josiah Gorgas, a Pennsylvanian—Chief Ordnance officer of the Confederacy; his mother was Amelia Gayle, whose father for many years preceding the Civil War had been one of the most influential public men of the Southern States. North and South thus contributed of their best in forming the character and abilities of the child whose lifework was to have such a far-reaching influence upon the progress of the modern world.

The name Gorgas suggests a Spanish origin, and it is therefore not surprising that the family tradition traces the ancestral beginnings to Spain. However, it is only a tradition. By the time the Gorgases make their appearance in definite outline they have become completely Dutch. The migration of Spaniards to the Low Countries was common in the 15th and 16th centuries, and it is not unlikely that the remote progenitor of the American branch came to Holland in the armies of Alva or of one of his successors. By 1680, however, when the first Gorgas reached this country, the family had become unmistakably Dutch in language and Protestant in religion. This ancestor brought with him a Dutch Bible, one of the most valued possessions of the present generation. In the next two hundred years this Dutch or Spanish blood became pretty completely mingled with the other racial stocks that made up the American population of 1776. At the present time Germantown and the adjoining section of Pennsylvania shelter a large number of Gorgases and the burying grounds in the same neighbourhood are full of them. The Gorgas descendants intermarried with many of the leading Pennsylvania families. The Doctor's great-great-grandmother bore the engaging name of Psyche Rittenhouse, and his grandfather, Joseph Gorgas, married a lady who figures in the family annals as the "beautiful Sophia Atkinson." This latter couple became the parents of Josiah Gorgas, the father of William Crawford. For the first twelve years of their married life they lived prosperously at "Running Pump," a place on the Lancaster Pike, not far from Harrisburg. Misfortune, however, overtook them; Joseph was evidently more accommodating than businesslike, for his habit of endorsing the notes of friends brought financial ruin to his family. The consequence was that the boyhood of Josiah Gorgas, born in 1818, was a rather difficult one. He has given a glimpse of these early days in his journal. "In 1824," he wrote, "I was a little boy running about the streets of a village in the interior of Pennsylvania, called Myerstown, in Lebanon County. In 1834 I was the youngest apprentice in a printing office in Lyons, New York; probably I was distributing the *Carriers' Address*, for it was the duty of the youngest to carry about the papers of the village subscribers."

However, the boy had a soul above that of a printer's devil; he had industry, force of character, and intellectual tastes; he was the type that instinctively seeks education. He also had an enthusiasm for armies and war; he loved the out-of-doors and was fond of the rough pioneer life that a temporary residence in early Ohio brought him; the most vivid picture of Josiah, preserved in the family papers, shows him continuously on horseback, exploring the wild forest, then full of marauding Indians, sometimes in company with his niece, Cordelia Chapman. The young man satisfied his two ambitions—scholarship and a military career—by obtaining an appointment to West Point; graduating in 1841, sixth in his class, he immediately began to specialize in ordnance. He gave such promise in this work that the Government sent him to Europe to study the armament of the great military nations, and, on his return, placed him in charge of the arsenal at Watervliet. The outbreak of the Mexican War found Josiah Gorgas a first lieutenant; a packet of letters survives, written to his mother during the siege of Vera Cruz, which are chiefly interesting at the present time for their description of the ravages of yellow fever among the American troops. "Nearly all have been sick," he writes, "and they have died by the hundreds." Young Gorgas himself suffered from the prevailing malady, though only for a few days.

In 1853 Josiah Gorgas was assigned to the command of the arsenal at Mount Vernon, a few miles north of Mobile, Alabama. That year was famous in the history of yellow fever, for one of the worst epidemics on record was then ravaging the West Indies and the Gulf States and in particular Mobile. The present generation cannot understand the panic precipitated by such a visitation; the plague fell so suddenly and so mysteriously, it attacked all social classes so indiscriminately, its mortality was so high and the medical profession stood so helpless in the face of its onslaught, that any community in its path was simply made rigid with fear. The more prosperous classes had only one thought: that was to flee to some protected spot. Mount Vernon was located on high and dry land; for reasons which were mysterious enough at that time but which are clear enough now, it offered an excellent place of refuge. In the summer of 1853, the little town was crowded and, by the time Josiah Gorgas reached his new post, it had grown to several times its normal size. Gorgas was now thirty-five years old: his handsome figure, tall and erect, his splendid carriage, his ruddy face, his black hair and beard, his every fibre radiating health and energy—all made him a favourite in society and a man of rapidly increasing influence in the army. He was a bachelor, but a happy turn of fortune now changed his life course. His Mount Vernon headquarters stood next the house of the company surgeon Dr. Matthew Gayle. One afternoon Gorgas, sitting on his piazza, heard the low tones of a woman's voice coming from the neighbouring building. Its possessor was apparently reading, and the audience, it presently appeared, was composed of children. The voice now impressed Gorgas as the most arresting he had ever heard; he sat a long time spellbound, as its gentle cadences, of an almost unimagined delicacy and softness, yet clear and tinkling, completely filled the surrounding atmosphere. Men frequently fall in love, it is said, for apparently trifling causes—the curve of a head, the glance of an eye; Gorgas now fell in love with this voice. Several afternoons he sat there listening to it, for reading to the children was evidently a regularly appointed task. Inquiry disclosed that the owner was Miss Amelia Gayle, daughter of Governor John Gayle, of Alabama. The children were her two nieces, the daughters of her sister Sarah, then in Spain; she had taken them to her brother's house to escape the yellow-fever epidemic. Gorgas, always celebrated for rapidity in action, did not delay in making the young woman's acquaintance; and the voice, he soon discovered, appropriately expressed a sympathetic and gentle nature; especially did the tenderness with which she guarded her sister's children charm and impress this upholder of the old-fashioned domestic virtues. The courtship was a brief one, the wedding taking place in December, 1853.

The first child was William Crawford Gorgas, the subject of the present memoir. He was born October 3, 1854, in the old Gayle place at Toulminville, near Mobile. Everything associated with the birth of Gorgas was propitious. The splendid old house in which he first saw light, a fine Colonial mansion, sitting in a grove of oaks, and approached by a driveway lined with cedars, symbolized the finest traditions of the South. Fortunate as Gorgas was in his father, already rising to distinction in the army, the one human being who most influenced his growing mind was his mother. At the time of her marriage Amelia Gayle was twenty-six years old but her life had witnessed more stirring scenes and vivacious society than ordinarily came to the lot of a Southern girl of that period. Her father, John Gayle, had

Mrs. Amelia Gayle Gorgas, the mother of General Gorgas.

been governor of Alabama from 1831 to 1835, and afterward a member of Congress and a United States District Judge. He thus fulfilled all the requirements of a "statesman," as that word was understood in the South before the Civil War; and his erect and stalwart figure, his elegance, poise, and dignity properly embodied this very important character. Governor Gayle's wife had died, in her thirty-first year; his oldest daughter, Sarah, had married young; the general remarried after two years, but the stepmother was delicate in health, and so the duties of the household, in large part, had early fallen upon his second daughter Amelia. She had proved herself entirely competent for this rôle, and, as a girl of twenty, had earned credit as the hostess of her father's house in Washington. Slight in frame, graceful and quiet, a splendid dancer, a spirited horsewoman, she yet had a commanding presence—the kind that instinctively though unobtrusively becomes the centre of things on entering a room. From a technical standpoint Amelia perhaps was not beautiful, but her abundance of jet-black hair, her great deep-brown eyes and her extremely mobile features had a sympathetic and impelling quality that harmonized well with her delicate and musical voice. The essential element in her charm was that Amelia never ruffled any one; tact is the quality which all her intimates chiefly emphasize; her husband, her children, her friends, all insist upon the supreme degree to which she possessed this talent for putting everyone at ease, for guiding the thoughts and plans of others, for making her own will prevail. She was one of those women born to rule, but to rule through gentleness of manner and of intention. Her mind possessed the quality of boundless patience and persistence—persistence of the kind that never irritates and never causes pain, but, almost as unconsciously to itself as to others, pursues the appointed course. Amelia Gorgas possessed also the indispensable talent for entertaining. Perhaps the greatest secret of her charm was her vivacity in conversation, and her gift for kindly repartee; she had a shy sense of humour and an unlimited faculty for story-telling and reminiscence.

It would have been surprising had Amelia Gorgas not proved an excellent story-teller, for she had an extensive fund of experience on which to draw. Plantation life in Alabama in the 'thirties or 'forties; dancing parties and dinners at the Governor's house at Montgomery; life at Washington in the days when Webster, Clay, and Calhoun were the giants of the Senate; one who had been a part of such adventures and one who had such a tenacious memory and such humour must have always been a source of entertainment to her children. The early life of William Crawford was thus filled with anecdotes of this kind. His mother would tell of her father's early troubles, as Governor, with the Cherokee Indians: of their disputes over tribal lands; of the visit of Francis Scott Key in an attempt to settle these difficulties; of Mr. Key's dignified but somewhat abstracted bearing and of the poems exchanged between himself and her versifying mother—all of which are still preserved in the family archives. She had many poignant memories of that same mother, married at fifteen, and assuming, at that age, the duties of mistress of the Governor's house; of her death at thirty-one, of lockjaw; of the long agony while she waited, hour after hour, for the returning footsteps of her husband, absent on official business—finally, in despair, summoning her expiring energies sufficiently to write him a message of farewell. But probably the most vivacious anecdotes concerned Washington in the late 'forties, when her father represented his district in Congress. Here father and daughter lived for several years in the same house with John C. Calhoun. Calhoun was then nearing seventy, Amelia was twenty, yet the two became warm friends and inseparable companions. Every morning the grim white-haired statesman and the girl walked to the Capitol; Amelia even had the privilege of sitting on the floor of the Senate and listening to the debates, which were pretty exciting ones, for the slavery issue was assuming great proportions, and the rumblings that afterward ended in civil war were distinctly heard.

An especially treasured memory was the laying of the cornerstone of the Washington Monument in 1848; Robert C. Winthrop was the orator of the occasion, and Amelia Gayle and Mrs. Burt, the niece of Calhoun, were the only women on the platform. She could tell many stories of the White House in those days, where she was a frequent visitor, and she never wearied of relating how Calhoun, one evening when they passed this mansion, pointed his long bony finger at the structure and said, in his most acid tones:

"Amelia, if I had been willing to sacrifice principle, I could have occupied that house!"

But the anecdote in which she particularly delighted concerned Henry Clay. The Kentucky statesman's philandering tendencies were no secret; that he had a sentimental interest in the pretty niece of Mr. Calhoun was also well known. One day Amelia went to the door when Clay dropped in for a call. The passage was dark, Clay's eyesight was not keen, and Amelia was therefore somewhat astonished when the venerable statesman put his arm around her waist and kissed her. Greatly excited she ran into the drawing room, where Mr. Calhoun was reading his paper.

"Oh, I have been kissed by the great Mr. Clay!" she exclaimed.

Calhoun put down his paper and again wagged the menacing forefinger.

"Amelia," he said, "don't you put your trust in that old man!"

II

The marriage of this Southern girl and this Northern soldier proved to be a happy one. The two were different enough in temperament and tastes, and sympathetic enough in loyalties and enthusiasms, to create a quiet and elevating domestic atmosphere. The elder Gorgas had a literary bent, a taste that led him, at the beginning of his marriage, to keep a journal—a volume now preserved in the Library of Congress. This document has great historic value as a description of Richmond in war time, and as an inner portrayal of the workings of the Confederate Government; at the present moment, however, it has especial importance for its picture of the early Gorgas household. This picture is an altogether charming one. Fatherhood was a serious occupation for the elder Gorgas. The happiness of his wife and the creditable development of his children were the most important considerations in life. The impression these pages give is that of a man somewhat austere, possibly at moments rather stern, but affectionate, painstaking, and ambitious, of strong allegiances and deep-seated antagonisms. That he took the greatest interest in the questions that were then agitating the land is apparent. Foremost of all he was a vigorous Democrat; though Northern born and trained, he championed the extreme Southern view on the question of slavery; and there is no limit to his scorn for "Black Republicans," and for those who were seeking to impose their own conceptions on the Southern States. Perhaps because of his marriage the South in all its phases held the firmest hold on his heart. The diary begins with a somewhat disheartened picture of Gorgas and his family exiled in an uncongenial country; the Government had assigned him to the command of the arsenal at Augusta, Maine. Gorgas constantly contrasts bleak New England with his beloved Alabama and he sighs for the "frankness of Southern manners." "The merry jingle of the sleighbells is but a sorry compensation for the rustle of leaves, the voice of birds, and the odour of flowers" of the South.

He carries this same spirit into his comment on men and things. He refuses to attend the dinner of the Speaker of the House in Maine because "he is an arrant Black Republican—a species I detest." Both Gorgas and his wife look forward to a far more pleasant future than this. They find distasteful the roving life of an army officer and pray for the day when they can own a cotton plantation in the South. "I dislike to part with things, especially growing things, which I collect about me, and I constantly fancy how happy I could be with a spot of earth which I can call my own, which I could plant and improve; where the same things would constantly be about me; where I could live and die and where my children might live and die." "Amelia could be quite happy if she could see herself twelve or fifteen years hence the mistress of a hundred bales of cotton and forty or fifty ebony faces. I dare say she would spoil every darky about her for the use of everyone but herself."

Bleak the New England country may have been without, but the glimpses of the Gorgas family within which the diary gives are exceedingly genial. The elder Gorgas had the pleasant family habit of reading aloud and the first sight we attain of William Crawford is as a member of this group. The book is the recently published "Little Dorritt." "Willie" is three years old, but his father portrays him listening with the keenest attention. "Willie," he records, "is very bright, quite grave, and tolerably mischievous and troublesome." The child displays delight in the singing of a woman guest; a fact that is rather surprising, for the ability to distinguish one tune from another was not one of the accomplishments of his maturer years. Apparently Gorgas as a child was much like other boys. He loved swimming and boating and hunting, but the chief delight of his boyhood was a donkey on which he spent a good deal of his time. He was something of a tease; his four sisters, whose ages were not far removed from his own, still remember how he used to abstract their dolls, hang them in a tree, and exact all kinds of penalties before bringing them down. Evidently, however, these sisters bore no permanent grudge, for nothing delighted them more than to assist their somewhat belligerent brother in his tussles with his schoolmates. In his after life, Gorgas seemed preëminently peaceful and ingratiating; in his childhood and youth, however, a lively scrimmage was never distasteful. Like most Southern children, he possessed a piccaninny who was an inseparable companion, and there are some lively pictures of the fisticuffs in which the two boys frequently engaged. At school also Willie had his mighty combats. On one occasion he stood alone against his whole class, the weapons being slates; his sister Minnie ably seconded him, piling up the ammunition which the boy, sometimes with excellent judgment, hurled at the advancing foe. Possibly the father's stories of West Point had bred this love of combat in young Gorgas; at least war always fascinated him; he early determined on a military career; any man who could talk of battle, and any book that related the exploits of soldiers, held first place in his affections. His mother, who was extremely religious, was delighted to find that his favourite reading matter was the Bible. Again and again did she come upon the child, lying prone on the floor, immersed in the pages of the sacred volume. Her pleasure was somewhat dissipated when she learned that piety was not the predominant motive; what really held the child spellbound were the battles of the Israelites. To Gorgas as a boy the book had little sacred character: its real value was as military history. This zeal for fighting never left Gorgas. Amiable, kindly, and tactful as he afterward became, he never shrank from battle, though his talents of this sort usually expressed themselves in subdued and non-violent fashion. The high temper which Gorgas frequently manifested in his early years also disappeared as he grew older, or at least was invariably held in check; yet composed and easy-going as he always seemed to be and gentle and soothing as were his manners, those who came into conflict with him felt that beneath his quiet exterior there reigned an iron determination and a rigid persistence which never for a second swerved from its appointed course.

Despite his love of battle, and his not infrequent conflict with his fellows, Gorgas was an exceedingly lovable child. He was frank, cheery, smiling, good-natured. Mentally he was not a prodigy. Outdoors beckoned him more successfully than the schoolroom; baseball always stirred him to the depths, but he had difficulty with his reading and spelling. His first six years were not eventful; the family was constantly migrating from one military post to another; and Willie's everyday existence was that of the normal American boy, with its mild excitements and its trivial pleasures. However, a great change came over Gorgas and his family in his seventh year. The cause was the outbreak of civil war. Gorgas was present at its very beginning and was an eyewitness of its final agony. "I remember," says Miss Jessie Gorgas, "my mother telling me this: 'Willie and I were sitting in the open window at the armoury at Charleston, South Carolina, about nine o'clock, his little hand in mine, listening to the guns at Fort Sumter, the beginning of the Civil War. He seemed much impressed, and turning to me, said, "Mother, isn't it solemn?"'"

It was indeed a solemn and serious business for the Gorgas family. First of all it confronted Josiah Gorgas with a momentous decision. He was a Northerner and an officer in the Federal Army; his associations for many years with the officers and men had become an indispensable part of his life; yet his marriage into a Southern family, his many years' sojourn in the South, his love of Southern people and the Southern land, had virtually transformed him into a Southerner. Politically he was a Unionist, and the threatening break-up of the Nation had been a painful prospect for many years; yet Gorgas was an uncompromising Democrat, and he unquestioningly accepted the political principles of the South, including slavery itself. His situation was by no means a solitary one. Thousands of Southerners threw in their fortunes with the North and thousands of Northerners cast theirs with the South: just as Thomas, the Virginian, remained faithful to his Federal allegiance, so now Gorgas, the Pennsylvanian, decided to stake his future with the Confederacy. That the sympathies of his wife would go with her own region was inevitable, yet she scrupulously refrained from attempting to influence her husband. "Decide according to your own conscience," was her only admonition; wherever his duty called him, she added, she would go also. The decision meant a break with Gorgas's Northern relatives, yet it was a step which he never regretted, and, as the war increased in its intensity, he became even more and more Southern in his emotions and convictions, even developing a certain bitterness, which is manifest in his journal, toward the Northern enemy.

To the Confederacy, Josiah Gorgas proved a great acquisition. He brought it skill and devotion where they were most needed, for he probably knew more at that time about munitions than any other man in either army. Jefferson Davis at once commissioned him a brigadier, and made him Chief of Ordnance in the Confederate forces. He was stationed for a brief period with the Government at Montgomery, but when Richmond became the capital he established his headquarters in the arsenal in that town. Here he laboured zealously for the Southern cause from 1861 to 1865. His administrative ability, his skill at producing armament, and his general wisdom in council made Gorgas one of the leading men in the Confederacy. He really became the Kitchener of the Southern cause. Much as Kitchener startled England in 1914 by declaring that the war would last at least three years, so Gorgas discomfited those Southerners who foresaw an easy victory by declaring that the conflict was to be a long and a difficult one. Gorgas knew the North, its resources and its determination; he knew as well the natural poverty of the South in all the materials that make possible successful warfare. He also completely understood the nature of the task that confronted him. It was to create an ordnance department and to equip the Southern armies out of almost nothing. That he succeeded in doing this has long been regarded by military experts as one of the most astonishing achievements of the Civil War. Both Grant, in his "Memoirs," and Jefferson Davis, in his "Rise and Fall of the Confederate Government," bear tribute to the effectiveness of his work. The historian long since decided that Gorgas's success in keeping the Southern Army supplied with munitions prolonged the war for at least a year.

III

And so it happened that William Crawford Gorgas spent his most susceptible period amid the exciting atmosphere of Richmond in the Civil War. He was seven years old when the conflict began and eleven when it closed; for any boy the experience would have been stimulating, but for one born with a zest for the military life, no more congenial early environment could have been desired. Jefferson Davis, Albert Sidney Johnston, Robert E. Lee, Stonewall Jackson, as well as the cabinet officers and guiding statesmen of the Confederacy, were the familiar figures with whom he was thrown into everyday association. Their plans, their achievements, their failures and their hopes formed the regular topics of conversation in the Gorgas home and the little Gorgas constantly haunted the Richmond arsenal and was frequently his father's self-imposed companion in his daily task. Nor was there anything philosophic about his allegiance to the Confederacy; his enthusiasm was purely emotional and sometimes pathetically expressed. There were hard times in Richmond; food and clothes were scanty; bread riots were not unknown; and Confederate soldiers constantly moved through the streets ragged and unshod. These latter unfortunates especially appealed to the sympathy of Willie Gorgas. One whole winter he insisted on going barefoot; despite the protests of his family he stuck sturdily to his resolution; only in some such tangible way, he believed, could he make himself a part of his bedraggled heroes and express his sympathy with their sufferings. Moreover, he felt that such an act of self-abnegation made him a part of the army in which he was too young to play a more active rôle. He found another satisfaction, of a more practical kind, in helping to feed returned prisoners in the public parks, and he assisted his mother in her daily rounds of the hospitals.

One inspiring day came when the father took Willie to view the body of Stonewall Jackson, lying in state in the capitol. Incidentally, the boy attended school at Richmond, at a Mrs. Munford's, but the scholastic impulse gained little headway amid the stirring history which was being made about him. Far more vivid was his recollection of the tragic days when the Confederacy was approaching its doom; and the final hour, when the Federals swarmed into Richmond on the heels of the retreating Confederate Army and Government, was the most painful memory of all. By this time Gorgas was eleven years old, but experiences such as he had lived have a maturing effect. His father, as part of the army, was ordered to leave with Davis and the rest of the cabinet. Summoning William he solemnly informed him that the safety of his mother and sisters rested in his hands. Precise instructions were given as to his plan of operations. All stores, especially military stores, were to be destroyed; the arsenal, containing great accumulations of munitions, was to be fired; as the Gorgas home stood near this dangerous building, it was evident that the family could not indefinitely occupy it with safety. When a certain building caught fire the boy was directed to lead his mother and sisters to the house of Thomas Bayne, his uncle. He enjoined him especially not to forget the family cow. Soon a considerable part of the city, including the arsenal, was ablaze; and the sight of the exulting Federal troops coming over the hill added to the excitement. The Gorgas family abandoned their home, and started up Cary Street to their appointed refuge; William led the procession, with his invaluable cow tied to a halter; his four little sisters followed, clinging to the skirts of the mother, who held the baby in her arms. The town was full of disorder; a mob of both blacks and whites, stimulated by liquor, was engaging in wholesale plunder, and the fire of a hundred buildings illuminated a scene of riot and horror. Suddenly a terrific explosion took place; the air was full of bursting projectiles; the arsenal had caught fire. Every member of the Gorgas family, except one, bore the shock with coolness; the one that gave evidence of excitement was the cow, which frantically cavorted right and left, pulling its youthful custodian in all directions. Willie, however, persistently held the rope; amid crackling flame and exploding shells, at the corner of Cary and Fifth streets, a fragment of shell hit the excited animal; she gave one spring into the air, hurling William head first against a cobblestone, and so dazing him that, when he regained his composure, the cow had completely vanished from the history of the Gorgas family. Willie keenly felt his disgrace; he had not fulfilled his father's injunction and he refused to be comforted.

"It's not so bad, Willie," said his mother. "Just think, that shell might have hit your baby brother instead of the cow."

"I thought at the time," Gorgas said afterward, recalling the incident, "that women had a greatly exaggerated idea of the value of babies."

For almost a year General Gorgas was separated from his family. He was present with Jefferson Davis when news came of Lee's surrender. "'We have just received, Gorgas,'" the latter quotes Davis as saying, "'the worst news that we could have. General Lee has surrendered his army.' He was standing when he spoke and then sat down and placed his hands upon his head for a moment. After further conversation he got up, buckled on his sword and pistol and dismissed us. He looked as he stood, thin, spare, erect, every inch a chief—he was sorrow-

© *Harris & Ewing.*

General Josiah Gorgas, Dr. Gorgas's father, a Pennsylvanian who became chief ordnance officer of the Confederacy.

ful but self-possessed, hopeless but self-restrained to the last." Meanwhile, the Gorgas family had found its way to Baltimore, Maryland. By the time the boat which took them reached Fort Monroe President Davis had been captured and was lodged there in chains; as young Gorgas passed the fort, he stood at salute in honour of his unfortunate chief. In mature life the Federal Government had no more loyal citizen than this same Southerner and none who rejoiced more sincerely at the result of the Civil War, but the description which he gave of himself in a public speech in Baltimore, in 1915, correctly portrays his sentiment at this time. "I first came to Baltimore," he said, "a ragged, barefoot little rebel, with empty pockets and an empty stomach. My father had gone south with the army. At the fall and destruction of Richmond my mother's house, with all that she had, was burned, leaving her stranded with six small children. She came to Baltimore, and was cared for by friends."

IV

Vanished now were Josiah Gorgas's hopes of a cotton plantation and fifty darkies; instead, at forty-seven, he found himself impoverished, his profession gone, with a wife and six children dependent upon him. His story for the next ten years represents an attempt to reconstruct his fortunes and give his children an appropriate start in life. He passed four unhappy years as the manager of a blast furnace at Brierfield, Alabama. No greater contrast from the existence he had previously led could be imagined. For four years General Gorgas had spent his exciting hours as one of the inner circle of a great revolutionary movement; now he found himself reduced to the prosaic business of making pig iron. Compared with his animated Richmond, Brierfield was a rough frontier community—a mere outpost of the country which was afterward to become the Alabama iron and steel district. Worse still, the manufacturing venture, in which Gorgas had invested all his savings, proved a failure; his experience represents the melancholy attempt of a soldier of fifty to establish himself in business life. "On the whole," he writes, "we are a very dilapidated set." A better outlook dawned, however, about 1870. The South found one method of providing for the popular and successful but somewhat distressed leaders of the Confederacy. The country at that time had a considerable number of colleges and universities struggling for existence; not infrequently these leaders were selected as presidents. The University of the South, at Sewanee, now presented such an opening to General Gorgas. It had been founded several years before the Civil War, but had never opened its doors. By 1869, however, its progenitors, the Bishops of the Episcopal

Church, South, believed that the time had become sufficiently propitious to make a beginning. A few crude wooden structures had been erected, a few students assembled, and General Gorgas was invited to become the head. He accepted and remained at Sewanee for ten years.

These years, which witnessed his growth from childhood into maturity, were happy ones for William Crawford Gorgas. By the time he left Sewanee, in 1876, he had developed into a stalwart and handsome young man of twenty-one, tall, slender, agile, extremely athletic, the saving grace of his baseball team, a swimmer who already had more than one saved life to his credit, a devotee of the rod and the gun, and an adroit horseman. As he grew into manhood many of his mother's physical and temperamental traits came to the surface. He had Amelia Gayle's black hair, her ruddy skin, her fine oval face, her thin and decisive mouth. His eyes, too, quiet and twinkling, radiated the mildness and the gentleness which had made his mother so popular and influential. He possessed also his mother's soft cadences; he invariably talked in subdued tones; he seldom showed excitement, yet the persistence and determination that afterward became his most conspicuous qualities were already familiar facts to his associates. In a certain sense, indeed, Gorgas's exterior, then and afterward, was misleading. The reserved force that slumbered in his depths was seldom apparent at a first meeting. Yet it was always there, and at Sewanee Gorgas had many times exhibited himself in this more forbidding light. His old associates still recall that this subdued talker was about the handiest man in the region with his fists; though he was never given to brawling, a few occasions when he had effectively used his natural protectors are still part of the traditions of Sewanee. The one most quoted tells of the day Gorgas was riding in a railway car alongside a Tennessee mountaineer. This gentleman having temporarily abandoned his seat, two ladies came in, to whom Gorgas surrendered the vacant space. The mountaineer, returning, demanded his place in violent and unseemly language, the result being that Gorgas, with one blow, sent him sprawling on the floor. There are other anecdotes of the same kind, all indicating that, although fundamentally serene and sunny, Gorgas was also not lacking in the more robust virtues. The man's affection was perhaps the quality that, above all others, gave the key to his character. Self-repressed as he was in most things, the love that joined mother and son was never concealed. Even when he had reached his fiftieth year his mother always addressed him in her letters as "my darling," and the sight of the two, sitting side by side, and holding hands, was a common one. For his father also Gorgas had a similar feeling. The one way in which the elder man could control the younger was through the affections. One episode, much quoted in the Gorgas family, illustrates this, as well as the young man's power of concentration and self-command. William's early days at Sewanee were not marked by great devotion to scholarship. His letters of this time betray a decided carelessness in spelling and other literary details; thus his "aunts" become "ants," his "appointments," become "ap-pintments," and one of his relatives is suffering from some strange malady catalogued as "newralagh"—possibly neuralgia. Such tendencies caused despair to the elder Gorgas, a precisian in this as in other matters. One day William chanced to overhear his father discussing his unfortunate case with his mother; the young man's disinclination to study and his low standing in his class were clearly disappointing to the ambitious parent. William had perhaps no great aptitude for books; but he had a conscience, and he at once began a close application to the college routine. The change was no sudden reformation; Gorgas kept at it for the rest of his course, the result being that he soon became one of the best students at Sewanee; the day even arrived when the delighted father could record in his diary that "Willie has turned scholar since nearly a year ago and is perhaps the first scholar here. The medal for scholarship from

Alabama has been awarded to him. It is a very beautiful gold medal. His mother and sisters are very proud of it and him, to say nothing of my feelings on the subject." It must be recorded, however, that the famous weakness in spelling was a fault that Gorgas never completely vanquished—and in this failure he was not alone among great men.

And at Sewanee Gorgas again manifested two traits that might at first seem antagonistic—a genuine feeling for religion and a zest for the military life. At times he seemed almost to combine the two. He was a ferocious performer on the baseball field; and like the ancient heroes, he not infrequently began the combat with a prayer for victory. He satisfied his more decorous religious instinct by joining the Episcopal Church; and simultaneously he began to cultivate again that yearning for death on the battlefield. A career in the army was the one ambition which his father discouraged. Gorgas could have had an excellent opening in the law, with relatives in New Orleans; he even spent a year, after graduating from Sewanee, studying this dismal subject; but then the panoply of war again wrought its unescapable fascination. The problem for the Gorgas family was now to get William an appointment to West Point. The task was a difficult one. By moving to New Orleans the young man had lost his residence in Tennessee, and residence in a district was one of the qualifications. Gorgas spent considerable time moving from one place to another, hoping to satisfy these requirements, but did not succeed. His father, who helped him to realize his ambition, though he had no enthusiasm for it, did what must have been for him a humiliating thing: he appealed to President Grant for a presidential appointment—and again without result, for these appointments had all been mortgaged years in advance. This campaign consumed so much time that Gorgas passed his twenty-first year, and thus became too old for admission to the military academy.

Apparently his yearnings for the American Army were not to be satisfied, and had Gorgas been an ordinary young man, without that determination and persistence which were his guiding qualities, he would have dropped the plan and found his future in a more humdrum existence. But he had set for his goal a military career, and even these discouragements did not change his resolution. Looking back now his West Point failure seems almost like a dispensation, for certainly Gorgas as a cavalry or an infantry officer could hardly have exercised the influence in the world that fate had marked out for him. There was one way, and only one way, in which Gorgas now could get into the army; that was by way of the medical corps. Yet the subject on which he had shown no interest as a young man was medicine.

Of the two professions he would unquestionably have chosen the law, distasteful as that was to him. But medicine at this crisis had one advantage that compensated for the mere anatomy, physiology, and pathology with which it was encumbered; it was an indispensable part of every military establishment. In order to get near the powder and shell Gorgas was willing to endure this otherwise valueless lumber. Again his father was aghast at the suggestion. Medicine as a great profession—yes, that would be splendid; but an army doctor! The general had become rather familiar with the type in his own military experiences, and the prospect of his son in such a position did not flatter his paternal pride. Yet, as usual, there was nothing to do in face of the boy's quiet insistence. He would be a military man, even though in no loftier light than that of a military doctor. The autumn of 1876 therefore found Gorgas enrolled in the Bellevue Medical College in New York City, living on the modest stipend which his father could send him.

Here Gorgas spent the years from 1876 to 1880. He was himself surprised to find what a fortunate choice of a career he had made. The profession which he would never have chosen, except as a stepping stone to the army, presently enthralled him. The dissecting room and the operating theatre now began to draw out his finest mental qualities. No longer was he a hard-working student as a method of giving his parents pleasure; he discovered a tremendous zest in study for its own sake. After some wandering Gorgas had at last found his occupation. Industry now became the ruling principle of his life. Medical standards of the late 'seventies were not as high as they are now; medical students could loiter through the course in a fashion that would at present bring immediate dismissal; many of "Billy" Gorgas's fellows of that day took their responsibilities with lightness and geniality; but this eager young Southerner bent himself to the serious business of work. Many times at night a crowd would gather in the corridors; beer and toddy, poker and social gossip engaged their interests almost as keenly as the mysterious human body; on such occasions, however, Gorgas would usually be found alone at one remote end of the room, his nose plunged deeply in a book. Afterward, at military posts, he became something of a poker player himself—though a modest one; his face, his friends said, was ideally moulded for that inscrutable sport; but he had no interest in such occupations during his student days. Other brief glimpses of him show that his religious instinct was still strong. Several of his classmates tell how this imperturbable young man interrupted their party long enough one night to read them several chapters of the book of Ruth; and they still recall that he would kneel and say his prayers without the slightest self-consciousness.

The life in the main was a hard one. The financial point was especially rasping. The first two years the General was able to send remittances, but for the rest of his course Gorgas had to finance himself, mostly with borrowed money. One time he contemplated dropping his work for a year, so that he could work and replenish the treasury; however, he bridged the crisis in other ways. He was too poor to go home for Christmas or summer vacations, and at times it is apparent that he actually went hungry. However, his rapidly accumulating scientific information came to his assistance; with a friend as straitened as himself he studied the requirements of the human body, and worked out the most economical dietary. The result was the regular morning shout, as the gay young men seated themselves in a low-priced restaurant on the East Side: "Buckwheat cakes and syrup for two!" Money troubles might press, but Gorgas was young and his life in New York City was almost a continuous delight. Studious as he was, the lighter sides of metropolitan existence appealed to him. Now began his efforts, lasting through a lifetime, to learn to dance—destined to remain an unfulfilled ambition; he spent many hours rowing on the Hudson; evidently religion did not make him soft, for he took a daily swim, even continuing this exercise through November, December, and January. "Andrew Jackson used to take his plunge every day of the year in the Tennessee River," he told his protesting friends, "and what Andrew Jackson did, I can do!" His letters make no attempt to conceal his fondness for pretty nurses. "On this ward," he writes his sister during his hospital days, "we have trained nurses, which makes it more attractive to the doctors, both because you are better served and because my head nurse is quite pretty." "We had our commencement at the Academy of Music," he writes on his graduation, "one of the handsomest theatres in the city. I got about the handsomest basket of flowers given: it could not have cost less than $15 and was given by one of my dear little nurses. I am afraid the little lady must have spent the savings from two months' salary, and, what is worse, I shall have to break myself one of these days returning it!"

It was apparently an impecunious but not an unromantic or an unprofitable existence. Gorgas roomed with another Southerner, John Bowen, of Paris, Kentucky, who was just about as poor as himself. As a means of saving money, the two young men divided the housework between themselves. Gorgas got up early every cold winter morning and made the fire, while Bowen did the family mending. One morning Gorgas gave this amateur seamstress his sadly worn trousers—they needed patching. The

Kentuckian made a beautiful job of it; but Gorgas's enthusiasm was somewhat dissipated when he discovered that Bowen had used his soft felt hat for material. Only one extravagance did these young men tolerate; Gorgas's enthusiasm for the theatre, constant throughout his life, now had its beginning. The top gallery in the old Union Square Theatre was the popular paradise of a Saturday night. Medical students in those days did not engage the front row in the balcony: they simply took it, even defying the two policemen who stood guard. They vented their approval of the stage transactions in primitive fashion. If the curtain did not rise promptly enough, whistlings and rumblings issued from the top gallery, and applause was more frequently manifested with the feet than the hands. "The Two Orphans," with Kate Claxton, was now the rage of the town. The poignant scene when the little girls, one blind, were huddled under the gaslight, with the paper snow of the old Union Square falling upon their devoted heads, especially stirred the emotions of the young medicos. When the villain seized the blind girl, Bowen, Gorgas's Kentucky roommate, leaped to his feet and yelled over the balcony, "Take your hand off that girl, you scoundrel, or I'll blow a hole through you"—putting his hand to his hip pocket. The house was in an uproar. Gorgas grabbed his friend and finally succeeded in forcing him to his seat.

Gorgas made an excellent record as a student; Dr. William H. Welch was then the presiding genius of Bellevue, and the Alabamian became one of his most appreciative pupils. Part of his last year he served on the staff of the insane asylum at Blackwell's Island. He received his degree in June, 1879. His father, recently made President of the University of Alabama, still protested against an army career. "I have no objection," he wrote, "to your passing the army examinations; nor would I object to a couple of years' service. But it would not be a life to look forward to as a permanent thing. It is not in the army that the sphere of a doctor is ennobling. I hope that something better will present itself before you graduate. Still I don't in the least object to preparation for the army examination. I think it confers a certain distinction to have passed it."

But Gorgas, or fate, knew better. He spent a brief time as interne at Bellevue Hospital, and, in June, 1880, he entered the medical department of the United States Army. By this circuitous route he had attained his goal.

V

The next two decades of Gorgas's life, from 1880 to 1900, were the everyday matter-of-fact career of an army doctor. He spent several years at various points in Texas—Fort Clark, Fort Duncan, and Fort

Brown; for three years, from 1885 to 1888, he performed his duties at Fort Randall, in North Dakota; the larger part of the next thirteen was passed at Fort Barrancas, Pensacola Bay, Florida. One might at first think that experiences in out-of-the-way places like these furnished a sufficient justification for his father's opposition to the career of army doctor. What were the possibilities of personal and professional development? Certainly the great doings of the medical world seemed far removed. Yet those twenty years marked one of the greatest eras in medical science. They witnessed the emergence of Pasteur, of Koch, and of Lister, or at least the general acceptance and the practical application of their tremendous discoveries. When Gorgas left Bellevue, the germ theory of disease was still the subject of debate among scientific men and of ridicule among the laity; by 1900, however, it had taken its place alongside the Copernican and Newtonian discoveries as one of the immutable facts of the material universe. An entirely new and unsuspected world had been uncovered beneath the microscope. The secret of contagious disease, which had baffled experimenters and theologians for thousands of years, now stood as plainly revealed as sunlight. Surgery, thanks to the work of Lister, had been robbed of most of its terrors. Great progress had been made in checking many of the most destructive plagues that had for ages assailed mankind. Many diseases —diphtheria, hydrophobia, typhoid, tetanus—which had previously made life a horror for the physician, had lost most of their terrors. When Gorgas, armed with his academic degree, betook himself to these distant and desolate army posts, the science of medicine was still in the dark ages. When he emerged as a commanding figure, about 1900, medicine had developed into a mighty force, destined to become more powerful than armies or navies or statecraft, in directing the course of the world.

A wise Latin aphorism defines an orator as a "good man, skilled at speaking"; and in medicine, too, character is as important as are knowledge and skill. And during these twenty years Gorgas's mental portrait had become more definitely drawn, though the outlines preserved the same strong characteristics as in his earlier days. As years went on his two predominant qualities more and more asserted themselves. These were a sunny and radiant exterior, a pliability and mobility of temperament that enabled him to adjust himself harmoniously to any person and to any surroundings; and, concealed in his depths, unsleeping determination and persistence. For the most part, however, the old associates of the man recall only his amiability and his lovableness. It is a quiet and genial and modest Gorgas that figures most conspicuously in their recollections. No environment could be more serviceable in developing a man's self-sacrifice and humanity than that in which Gorgas now found himself. There was no fortune and little fame in the career of an army doctor forty years ago. On this point old General Josiah Gorgas was right. The Government started Gorgas as a first lieutenant, with a first lieutenant's pay—$1,500 a year, and certain items known as "commutation." Such was the material reward. For living quarters Uncle Sam provided a modest but entirely comfortable house, usually located in one of those army posts built in the old days for the purpose of holding the Indians in check. In his Texas days this was a fort on the shores of the dirty and sluggish Rio Grande; and in his Dakota days it was a fort on a bluff overlooking the Missouri River, seventy-five miles from a railroad, surrounded by the never-ending prairie, with no neighbours except a few red men and half-breeds. The things that are not always accurately called "civilization"—cities, towns, diversified society, theatres, clubs, libraries, and the like—formed no part of this existence. Even many of its comforts did not exist. A small group of officers and their wives and children made up the little community. Cultivated and entertaining as this social world might frequently be, it was still an exceedingly restricted one. Life was a constant routine of going to the same dinners,

William Crawford Gorgas, as a student at the University of the South, Sewanee, Tennessee, from which he received his A. B. degree in 1875.

listening to the same stories, laughing at the same jokes; whist and euchre parties—it was before the advent of bridge—now and then afforded relaxation; the inevitable quarrels of such a small society added a little spice, and a faint whiff of scandal came as an occasional godsend. Thus those indispensables of modern existence known as "contacts" were necessarily few.

This kind of existence, however, did not pall upon Gorgas. Small as his world might be, distant as it usually was from the interests and excitements of American life, it was for him still a world, still made up of the things which he always found most entertaining and worth while—men and women and children—and therefore an unceasing fountain of delight. First and foremost he had achieved his ambition; he was a member of the United States Army. The West Point graduate still remained in Gorgas's eyes about the finest product of the American system. His companions noticed that, in the conversational hours, Gorgas had a way of twisting the talk to West Point and to great military heroes of this and other nations. Yet for the rougher side of army existence—it was a period of heavy drinking and gambling—Gorgas had little enthusiasm. His one manifestation of a more frivolous kind was the persistence with which he pursued his dancing lessons. His old comrades use this as an illustration of his determination of character. Nature never intended Gorgas to shine in the ballroom; the most assiduous attentions of his friends did not succeed in teaching him much more than the elementary steps; yet, year after year, he kept industriously at work. Major Bridgman, a master at the art, still loves to tell of the hours he spent at this praiseworthy task; the two men would retire to the mess room, the major's soft whistling serving as orchestra; an evening or two afterward the Doctor would triumphantly take a partner in full public view. At more robust diversions, however, Gorgas improved his skill. Hunting, fishing, and riding claimed a considerable part of such time as he could give to pleasure. He continued also his exercises in boxing—a sport at which he never lost his cunning.

An army doctor in those days was more than an army doctor: his activities usually extended far beyond his post, for in the frontier community men of science were scarce, and any one possessing medical skill was compelled, for humanitarian reasons alone, to respond to the calls of the native population. Such work as this, usually of an arduous kind, brought little money reward. The army surgeon was a kind of missionary; he was expected to hold himself in momentary readiness at the call of the poverty-stricken population within the circle of a hundred miles. The Government permitted him to charge for such services, but very few could pay. Such a practice also demanded talents of a comprehensive nature. An infant ill with diphtheria; a woman in childbirth; a frontiersman suffering from a gangrened leg—there was practically no branch of medicine to which Gorgas was not called to lay his ready hand. One day he was pulling teeth, the next performing a tracheotomy—perhaps in the hastily assembled hospital of a lumberman's cabin. Even the Indians of the plains quickly learned to love this unselfish "medicine man" and unhesitatingly abandoned the exorcisms of their own miracle workers for the pills of civilization. The doctor must hold himself ready at all hours and in all weathers. His wife passed many an anxious all-night's winter vigil, waiting for his return from some distant excursion on the prairie. The recollection of several terrifying blizzards is especially keen. These storms sometimes swept down most unexpectedly. A call would come from a half-breed's cabin perhaps thirty miles away; the thermometer registered thirty below zero; the sleigh would be made ready; and the doctor, clad in buffalo robes and ear-muffs, would disappear into the void. Then, an hour or two afterward, a blizzard might start in all its fury; darkness came on and daylight sometimes dawned before the snow-covered figure again appeared. On two separate occasions Gorgas nearly lost his life in such a Dakota blizzard, but he himself always took these experiences cheerily enough. "Oh, for a few hours on the muddy Rio Grande!" he once exclaimed, returning from such a freezing experience; and this was the closest to anything resembling a complaint. Yet in these Southern posts the heat and the scorching sand of the desert were almost as distressful.

Life like this was more than an education in medicine; it was a training in those fine virtues of sympathy and patience so essential to the practitioner. And Gorgas took his work rather hard on the emotional side. He was one of those physicians who walk the floor nights over their cases. To his wife the Doctor's face and eyes were the certain signposts of favourable or unfavourable progress. He also had the habit of whistling softly when things were not going well. One story, told by Major Bridgman, should be recorded. Gorgas had attended the Major's wife on the birth of her first baby. He took the keenest interest in the child, to whom he stood as god-father, and he was especially precise in laying down rules for its care. On one point in particular did he sternly lecture the young mother. The baby, he insisted, should be left alone when it cried. No greater mistake could be made than to take it up! The conscientious Mrs. Bridgman obeyed instructions, severe as was the tax upon her sympathies. Whenever the baby cried, and it did so frequently, she refrained from showing the usual maternal weakness. One afternoon the child, placed in its carriage on the verandah, began to wail in most pitiful fashion. The mother sat for a time in the adjoining room with her teeth set, but the crying became so heartrending that she was just about to break the doctor's injunction, when suddenly the hubbub ceased. Alarmed, Mrs. Bridgman ran out to the verandah. There was Dr. Gorgas walking up and down with the baby in his arms. He had happened to be passing the house, and, forgetting his own instructions, had done his best to comfort his little patient. All his rules for the scientific upbringing of children vanished when his own daughter, Aileen, was born—in September, 1889, at Tuscaloosa—and Gorgas at once became an object of jeering to all the mothers and fathers whom he had attempted to pilot through similar crises. Aileen so closely resembled her father—in particular she had his dark eyes—that she was known in the post as "Little Doctor."

It was significant of the simplicity of the man that Gorgas, throughout his entire military career, was always known, in army quarters and in the surrounding country, as "Doctor." Though it was the fascination of military life that had taken him into the army he never made any point of his military rank. He successively rose in the grades; became first lieutenant, captain, major, colonel, brigadier, finally major-general. In face of all these promotions, however, his title in the army always remained the same. He never became anything but just "Doctor Gorgas." He loved to hear himself called thus simply, and his friends and patients for some reason preferred this title above all the resplendent handles to his name.

The frontier existence was not devoid of humour; it provided Gorgas with a stock of stories that added sauce to his conversation in later years. Perhaps his experience with his coloured laundress, Henrietta, was the choicest of the collection. One week she did not make her usual appearance; instead an excited messenger brought word that Henrietta had met with an accident; would the doctor come at once? He discovered that both legs had been crushed by a train, and that a double amputation was necessary four inches above the knees. Henrietta's chances for recovery were slim, but after weeks of unremitting care and attention on Gorgas's part her life was saved. She was restored to health, alas, minus both legs! It was necessary for her to earn her living: in such condition what could she do? Finally Gorgas, who had charged nothing for his professional services, made her a present of a pair of artificial legs; and, in time, Henrietta could not only go about comfortably, but was able to do the Gorgas washing. The Gorgas bill for the first week was larger than it had ever been before. When Gorgas remonstrated with Henrietta, she proudly drew herself up and replied:

"Suttenly it's more! 'Tain't everybody whut can git washing done by a pusson what has two wooden legs!"

All this time Gorgas was keeping in close touch with the great developments of the medical world. His fondness for reading and study increased as he grew older. "Oh, if I could only break my leg, what a fine time I could have!" he once exclaimed, meaning that his enforced convalescence would give him leisure for his favourite studies. Despite the constant demands upon his energies, however, Gorgas did find time for much reading. His methods in this, as in everything, were original. He always had three books going at the same time—one scientific, one of general literature, and one a light modern novel or detective story. On the table he had a watch face up. He would read the books in turn, giving twenty minutes at a time to each; he found a reward in this method which would perhaps astonish the psychologist, for he asserted that it enabled him to remember what he had read. The Government generously supplied him with medical journals and medical books; that he kept well abreast of the times is evident from the fact that he was one of the first of American surgeons to practise aseptic surgery. And all this time he was coming into constant contact with that disease which was to furnish him his great life work. There is something almost fatalistic, indeed, in the way that yellow fever dogged his whole life. How it led to his marriage has already been described, but the story goes back further. Had it not been for yellow fever Gorgas would probably never have been born at all, for, as already told, it was the terrible epidemic of 1853 that sent Amelia Gayle, his mother, to Mount Vernon, and lodged her in the house next the one in which Josiah Gorgas was living—a happy accident that brought about their meeting and marriage. The physician who attended Gorgas's mother at his birth was Dr. Josiah Nott, of Mobile, a yellow-fever expert, who, despite his eminence, was at that time a much ridiculed man; he nourished a certain fantastic notion that this disease was conveyed by the bite of insects, and he had even in this connection pointed an accusing finger at the mosquito! Dr. Nott had recently presented this idea in an elaborate paper in the New Orleans *Medical and Surgical Journal.* The most astonishing item of all was his explanation of the commonly observed fact that the night-time was especially dangerous in an infected region. The reason, Dr. Nott intimated, was that the mosquito was especially active in the night-time. Human prescience, unfortified by knowledge, has seldom scaled higher flights than this.

Gorgas was a medical student at Bellevue when the great yellow-fever epidemic started in Memphis in 1877—still a horrifying memory to the older generation. In company with half-a-dozen Bellevue students he left for the plague-ridden city, to offer his medical services. The authorities met this group of pilgrims on the outskirts of the town, thanked them most movingly for their generosity, but refused to admit them. Gorgas and his friends were not immune, and there was every chance that, as soon as they were exposed, there would be several more casualties. The Doctor's experience at Fort Brown, already described, removed this disability. After that the Government usually summoned him wherever yellow fever appeared. This is the reason he was twice sent to Fort Barrancas, in Florida, and his skill in opposing the disease at this place gave him much reputation in army circles. One scene from this Florida experience vividly portrays the fear that yellow fever excited thirty years ago as well as the grotesque ignorance that prevailed concerning it. The yellow-fever doctor in those days had more than merely medical duties to perform; not infrequently he was undertaker, grave-digger, even clergyman; so great was the fear of contagion that funerals were held at midnight, and even the family kept at a distance. One night at Barrancas, Dr. McCulloch, one of the army physicians, and Mr. Richard Gorgas, the Doctor's brother, were awakened from troubled slumbers by Gorgas, who asked them for a prayer book. Soon afterward, from the direction of the hospital, they could hear the measured tread of pall-bearers—hospital attendants—as they passed on their way to the cemetery in the woods. The two men witnessed the scene from the back porch. In the light of the swinging lanterns that aided a cloud-obscured moon, the cheap, black-covered coffin on the attendants' shoulders was dimly visible. Gorgas afterward described the horrible details in which he took part—laboriously digging the grave in the wet, heavy soil; wrapping the corpse in its simple white shroud; filling the unoccupied spaces of the improvised coffin with quicklime; the difficult interment and the filling up of the grave, and the reading of the burial service by the light of the lantern.

In these years Gorgas had much time to meditate on that great mystery—the cause of the disease. The suddenness of its appearance, the strange pranks of infection it played—now assailing a person who had apparently never been exposed, now leaving untouched another who had almost daily associated with it—offered a constant puzzle to his inquiring mind. But Gorgas got no nearer the secret than dozens of other specialists. One episode, illustrating his own ignorance on this subject, he never wearied of telling. The incident is especially pointed, for it took place on the eve of the wonderful day when the secret was to be uncovered. Gorgas—now a major—had charge of the yellow-fever camp at Siboney during the Spanish War. One of his patients was Dr. Victor Vaughn, afterward President of the American Medical Association. "It was largely through Dr. Gorgas's skill in the management of yellow fever," writes Dr. Vaughn, "that the death rate in our army in Cuba was so low. The sight of his kindly face was a stimulant that did much to tone up the muscles exhausted by the exercise imposed upon the body by *el vómito negro*. His kindly words to his patients served as a better tonic than any name in the pharmacopæia."

On the advice of Dr. Gorgas and Dr. Vaughn, the commanding officer of Siboney burned the whole little town, with all the medical and quartermaster's supplies. In the existing state of medical knowledge —this was in 1898—such a comprehensive procedure was necessary as a safeguard against the spread of yellow fever! Gorgas and Dr. Vaughn were thrown much together in after years, for consultation on medical matters affecting the army. After one decision Gorgas turned to his associate and remarked, with a twinkle in his eye:

"This is your judgment, and it is mine, Vaughn. But remember that your judgment and mine have at times been at fault. Do you recollect that I recommended the burning of the village at Siboney in 1898, in order to stamp out yellow fever? I have often wondered how many infected mosquitoes were destroyed in that conflagration!"

CHAPTER III

YELLOW FEVER MEETS ITS MASTER

I

IN 1898 Gorgas returned to Havana, and, after a few months, became chief sanitary officer. The title sounds unromantic and unmilitary, yet the conquest of Cuba had really been placed in his hands. To all outward showing the American Army had reduced the island to terms; Spain had surrendered and withdrawn her troops; yet she had left behind an antagonist more formidable than soldiers or warships. Several times before armies had successfully invaded the West Indies; all, however, had met an inglorious or disastrous end. In 1762 an expedition of Englishmen and colonial Americans seized Cuba; after occupying it for a few months, they had abandoned it in humiliation. In 1800 a French army, the pick of Napoleon's troops, had landed in Haiti; in less than a year this army had vanished from the earth, leaving the rebellious Haitians triumphantly in possession of their soil. Armed soldiers had not vanquished these Anglo-Saxons and these Frenchmen. An enemy even more ferocious and persistent had accomplished their destruction. It worked silently and inexorably, striking at human life from an ambush that mere men could never penetrate. This enemy was the disease known for more than two centuries as yellow fever—the same enemy that had dogged Gorgas's pathway all his life. The man who could conquer yellow fever would be the real conqueror of Cuba.

And such a conquest would mean more than the elimination of the disease from this devoted island. It would mean saving a considerable part of the tropics from a scourge that had made them almost uninhabitable for untold ages. It would mean also the safeguarding of a large part of the American coast from the same destructive pestilence. Concerning the origin of this disease historians are not now agreed. Until recent times yellow fever had been regarded as having come into existence on American soil, and the early experiences of Cortez and the Mexicans have generally been accepted as the first European contact with the disease. The scientific world is no longer unanimous on this point. There are certain signs indicating that Africa may have been the original birthplace of yellow fever and that the first carriers to America were African Negroes who came to this continent with the Spanish Conquistadores. Whatever the beginnings, however, and the point is certainly obscure, it is unquestionably the fact that America was the means of introducing it to Europe and to white men generally. Spain paid a heavy penalty for the abominations which she inflicted upon the early American natives, for her soldiers carried the *fiebre amarilla* home to their native cities, where fearful epidemics became for two centuries periodical features of their existence. Almost the most destructive outbreaks recorded, indeed, are those which assailed the leading cities of Spain. The most appalling aspect of yellow fever was its high mortality. In Barcelona in 1821 more than 90 per cent. of the afflicted gave up their lives. In the island of St. Lucia, in 1664, an army of about 1,500 soldiers lost all but 89 men.

Though visitations to other parts of Europe are recorded—even Swansea, in Wales, having had its experience—the main headquarters of the disease, since the discovery of America, had been the West Indies and the coast of the Gulf of Mexico. For nearly three centuries it had lurked, a perpetual menace, in all these towns, but Vera Cruz and Havana had always been its favourite hiding places. There is a particular appropriateness in using these terms in describing yellow fever. Its chief peculiarity was that it was least harmful to the communities in which it was most common. For a century and a half Havana had not passed a single year without its deaths from this disease. Yet the fact remains that practically no natives of the city itself paid the penalty. It was a malady that constantly smouldered; it was, in medical terms, "endemic"; yet the gay Havanese went about their daily tasks and pleasures, despising an enemy that apparently entertained no hostility to themselves. Deaths were constantly taking place; terrible epidemics were periodically bursting forth; but the sufferers were Cubans who came from the interior or—most numerous of all—strangers from other lands. Havana was one of the safest cities in the world, so far as the acclimatized population was concerned, but it was a merciless death trap for the unwary visitor. The explanation is found in that medical phenomenon known as "immunity." Yellow fever is one of those diseases which almost never assail the same person a second time. Even a slight attack, so slight as to be hardly noticeable—perhaps merely a passing indisposition—protects the sufferer from a second visitation. The truth is that practically all the natives of an "endemic" centre, such as Havana, have had yellow fever in this extremely light form as children and are therefore protected against it for the rest of their lives. In ordinary times, therefore, the mortality remains low simply because there is no material on which the disease can feed. So far as yellow fever is concerned, Havana might be compared to a city destroyed by fire—a fire that has ceased to burn because it has destroyed all combustible material and contains only a few smouldering ashes. If one applies fresh fuel to these ashes, the fire will burst into flames anew. "It's only the foreigners that get yellow fever," was almost a popular proverb in every community where the disease was definitely settled. Facts apparently substantiated this statement. The cities that have acquired peculiar odium as centres of yellow fever are those through which a constant procession of strangers is taking place. Vera Cruz and Havana were usually full of outsiders. A foreign army provided ideal material for this disease; the Americans who invaded Vera Cruz in 1846 died like flies; the Spanish Army which attempted to subdue the Cuban insurrection in the 'nineties found the Yellow Jack a more redoubtable foe than the poorly equipped *insurrectos*, while the American Army before Santiago lost many lives from this disease. Had Spain not surrendered, indeed, it is almost certain that the United States would have been obliged to withdraw its troops.

Though yellow fever, like an exhausted conflagration, lay constantly in wait for fresh supplies of fuel, it had another quality that was more diabolical still. It was as persistent as it was malicious and it would not be denied its prey. If the strangers on which it fed were not forthcoming, the yellow-fever germ would seek them out. For two centuries the coast cities of the United States had served as its most promising hunting grounds. New Orleans, Mobile, Charleston, Baltimore, Philadelphia, New York, New Haven, Nantucket Island, Boston, and other places had many times satiated this voracious appetite. In none of these cities was yellow fever "endemic"; the disease could exist perpetually only in countries which were warm all the year round, for the frosts of autumn and winter immediately destroyed the cause; in most American cities, therefore, the yellow fever came as a summer plague, falling upon them with ferocity and disappearing almost as unexpectedly as it had appeared. The mortality from such invasions was always high. In 1793 a yellow-fever epidemic killed 4,000 men, women, and children in Philadelphia, or one tenth of the entire population. This was one of the worst visitations in American history, though no more destructive than the one that terrified the Mississippi Valley in 1878, reaching its most alarming phase perhaps in Memphis. Probably the Philadelphia epidemic of a century before owes its fame chiefly to the vividness with which it has been described. The famous Dr. Benjamin Rush and Matthew Carey have left accounts which have a strong resemblance to Defoe's description of the great London plague. Reading their graphic pages, indeed, one might fancy himself in the English capital in 1664–65. The same terror, the same panic in face of an unknown and impalpable enemy, the same manifestation of the worst passions of human nature, as well as of the best, mark the Philadelphia story of 1793 as they do the London visitation of the preceding century. The disease appeared just as suddenly, and it started, as did the Plague of 1665, on the waterfront.

At that time Philadelphia was enjoying a period of unusual prosperity; it was the nation's capital, though Congress had adjourned several months before and President Washington, as was his custom, had retired for the summer to Mount Vernon. That luxury and even that dissipation which usually accompany prosperity were manifest on every hand, and the pious naturally saw in the arrival of Yellow Jack a divine punishment for the city's sins. A community must have sinned grievously to have merited such a vengeance. There was scarcely a home that was not afflicted; the rich quarters as well as the poor abounded in the disease, the clean as well as the filthy, and all ages and colours rendered their tribute. In a few days the city was in a state of the wildest disorder. As usual, all fled who could get away; for weeks there was a continuous procession of carts, coaches, wagons, and "chairs," transporting families and furniture in all directions; in the towns to which the refugees went they were most unwelcome visitors, and in many cases they were turned back at the gates. All phases of business and community life came suddenly to an end; banks closed, factories shut their doors, leaving thousands without employment, newspapers stopped publication, and churches ceased their functions for want of congregations. Sick persons sometimes fell dead in the streets, their corpses lying for weeks without burial. Almost the only occupations were the absurd attempts to check the disease. There was an idea that the "purification" of the atmosphere would bring relief; to accomplish this bonfires were lighted at every street corner, and cannon were constantly booming. All those who ventured out carried sponges at their mouths, or smelling bottles of vinegar or camphor; not only men, but women, were constantly smoking cigars, for tobacco was regarded as a preventive; while others spent most of their time chewing garlic. A tarred rope was also believed to have protective virtues, and nearly everybody who stepped outdoors carried such a talisman. But personal safety, so it was believed, consisted chiefly in avoiding all human kind. All social intercourse came to an end. One man meeting another on the street would immediately cross to the other side. Friends ceased to be friends and even the closest ties of relationship were ignored. The most distinguished citizens were buried unceremoniously, with no human attendant except the Negro who drove the death cart. The appearance of anything that resembled such a funeral was a signal for the population to flee in all directions. In many cases husbands abandoned their sick wives and wives their sick husbands; instances were not unknown in which parents fled from their children and children left their parents to die in neglect. The afflicted were sometimes left to perish miserably without medicine, or a drink of water, and even women in childbirth frequently received no care. There were, of course, plenty of cases of heroism to balance these instances of inhumanity. Stephen Girard, the eccentric millionaire, especially distinguished himself by his devotion to the sick poor; but the abandonment of the city by the prosperous and the terror before an invisible foe that seized the remaining population, left Philadelphia largely at the mercy of the disease. The situation continued until the appearance of frost, when the plague vanished as mysteriously as it had arrived, and the town again adjusted itself to normal conditions. One writer records, as an evidence of the state of the popular frenzy that had ruled all summer, the delight with which the populace looked upon a conventional funeral proceeding in leisure and dignity through the streets. It had for so many months been the custom to hustle off unattended corpses at midnight, or to leave them unburied in vacant lots, that even this sombre manifestation of normal existence was a cause for general rejoicing.

Probably the public terror inspired by yellow fever was caused chiefly by the fact that it behaved so mysteriously. It was unlike any other known disease and the most grotesque explanations were given of its cause. It was disseminated by "noxious gases," by "swamp miasma," by fermentation, by dry particles of dust, by the explosion of subtle poisons in the air, by putrefying vegetable matter. Certain learned gentlemen maintained that it was caused by the Gulf Stream, while others insisted that eating apples conveyed the infection. The medical faculty almost came to blows over the question of contagion. So great a man as Dr. Benjamin Rush declared that yellow fever was not contagious—that it was not communicated by the sick to the well, and he found the explanation of the Philadelphia epidemic in decaying coffee on the docks. This dispute over contagion was not so absurd as it now seems to our enlightened eyes, for certainly yellow fever behaved in most perplexing fashion. People who constantly associated with the disease did not necessarily contract it while thousands who had never come near a patient dropped in their tracks. Hundreds who fled the city subsequently became ill, while just as many who remained in town successfully weathered the storm. Men and women could sleep with yellow-fever patients, wash their clothes, even wear them, and yet never "catch" the disease. Many brave souls in the Philadelphia epidemic who rescued corpses from the fields and carried them in their arms to burial places—thus deliberately, as they thought, courting death—came through unscathed. Meanwhile, many a more craven soul, who had locked himself in a room at the first sign of distress, who had never touched or spoken to a human being, and had had his food pushed through a crack in the door, had quickly fallen a victim. It is not surprising that Dr. Rush raved against the idea of contagion; yet his writings and those of other early commentators contain one detail which signified nothing to him, but which seems to the present generation almost a grimace of the comic spirit. Dr. Rush notes that "moschetoes" were very plentiful about Philadelphia in 1793, and Noah Webster, describing the New York visitation of 1795, says that "musquetoes were never before known by the oldest inhabitants to have been so numerous." The accounts of practically all epidemics since have contained the same comment.

This Philadelphia epidemic took place more than a century ago, but the scenes portrayed by Rush could be duplicated in more recent times. There was not a year in the 19th Century when this plague did not claim its victims in many American cities. The Gulf places, especially New Orleans, were probably the greatest sufferers, yet one of the worst epidemics recorded is that in Memphis in 1878, when this one city had 17,000 cases and more than 5,000 deaths, with most of the horrors that accompanied the Philadelphia experience of a century previously. In that same year there were more than 100,000 cases and 20,000 deaths in the United States. Outbreaks in the 'eighties and the 'nineties were constantly taking place.

II

Such was the monster whose destruction now became the chief duty of Gorgas. Many years had passed since the days of Dr. Rush and Noah Webster, but it cannot be said that the scientific men of 1898 knew much more about yellow fever than did their predecessors of the 18th Century. The germ theory had been demonstrated, it is true, and the fact that the disease, in some fashion, was transmitted from the sick to the well was generally accepted; but the specific organism had not been discovered and the mechanism of contagion was unknown. An Italian bacteriologist, Sanarelli, had indeed isolated a bacillus which he asserted was the guilty agent; but a group of Americans had brought international laughter upon him by showing that this was merely the long-familiar microbe of hog cholera. One conception of contagion, however, had gained general credence by the time Gorgas began his work. No one knew what organism was the infecting agent, but everybody knew how it was transmitted. The belief in *fomites* was practically universal. This is a Latin word meaning kindling wood or tinder. In yellow fever it was applied, in a figurative sense, to the garments of the patient, the bedclothes in which he slept, or, indeed, to any external substance with which his body had come into contact. To touch such things was believed to touch the tinder that spread the yellow-fever flame. The way to check its spread, therefore, was to seek out and destroy all such contaminated things, and this, as late as the year 1901, was almost the only way that the medical profession knew of guarding the public from the disease.

Gorgas, when he began his work in 1898, was as completely in the dark as were all other sanitarians. But at this time the yellow-fever situation in Havana was not discouraging. There were only a few deaths per month, not more than were taking place in most American cities from typhoid and scarlet fever. There was no mystery about this. The population of Havana at that time was composed chiefly of natives, and therefore of immunes. The city had been occupied for several years by the Spanish Army; hence very few strangers had come in. The Spanish Army itself had returned to Spain, and this evacuation had deprived yellow fever of much of that fresh material which is necessary for its sustenance. Consequently, the yellow-fever situation was far more favourable than it had been for many years.

Yet the general condition of the city was frightful. This, however, was nothing particularly new. Disease and filth had for so many generations been the condition of Havana that the natives had come to regard them as quite the normal state of existence. The city had one of the most beautiful harbours in the world and the location was an extremely healthful one, but the conditions of sanitation were most primitive; and Havana for generations had been a pest hole, dangerous not only to herself but to the entire American Hemisphere. This was the state of affairs in ordinary times. For five years preceding 1898, however, Havana had been the centre of especially atrocious military operations. In that period the last consideration had been the welfare or the health of its inhabitants. Such rudimentary measures of sanitation as had regulated the city in peace times had been ignored. The city which now came under Gorgas's jurisdiction was little better than a huge cesspool. Unspeakable odours assailed one everywhere; streets were filled with decaying vegetables, dead animals, miscellaneous sewage, and refuse of all kinds. The hospitals were so overcrowded—in some cases Spanish officers had converted them into barracks—that many sick could find no place of refuge and lay stricken in the streets. Children wandered homeless, the existing government being unable to provide for them, and everywhere beggars with livid sores pleaded pitifully for alms. Perhaps the sombreness and despair of the whole situation were most completely symbolized by the only scavengers upon which Havana was then depending for its cleansing—the flocks of black vultures, voracious and tireless, which were constantly hovering over the dishevelled and putrescent streets, entirely inadequate, however, to the task of ridding them of their excrescences. But one interesting fact stood out even ominously—though few could read its meaning. The yellow-fever rate was extremely low. The large number of deaths that were taking place were caused by dysentery, typhoid, and other zymotic diseases, while the disorder that had given Havana its most evil fame was taking very few lives. Seldom had the city been so free from its most persistent enemy.

Still the theory that this tropical scourge was caused by *fomites*—by contact, that is, with clothes, bedding, furniture, or other materials which had been associated with yellow-fever patients—was strongly held, especially by the surgical department of the American Army. Gorgas had been sent to Havana to stamp out this disease, or rather to prevent the outbreak which was generally anticipated, and his instructions directed him to place his chief reliance upon general sanitation. Gorgas at that time knew no more about the transmission of yellow fever than did his superiors. He had closely followed such progress as the laboratories had made in the study of the disease but this progress had not been extensive. At that time science had only one method of fighting it—the segregation of the sick, the quarantining of infected localities, and general cleanliness. Like most medical men of his time, Gorgas believed that yellow fever was a filth disease; the one sure way of protecting a city was therefore to make the city clean. There was something impressive in the fact that Philadelphia, Baltimore, and New York, in which epidemics were formerly not infrequent, now knew this tropical horror no more. What could explain its disappearance except the general improvement in public cleanliness which had taken place? The logic of the situation was clear. Make Havana as neat and clean as these great American cities and the plague would similarly vanish. As Gorgas surveyed the rotting city which had now come under his jurisdiction its most pressing need was apparent. "Let me give it a good scouring and a good bath," he said to himself, "and yellow fever and other diseases will disappear." He set to work at his congenial task with an energy and completeness that soon gave his name a unique fame.

In a few months American newspapers and magazines, which were watching the American experiment in Cuba with attention and even solicitude, discovered excellent "copy" in the sanitation of Havana. They began publishing contrasting photographs, showing the famous city in the pre-Gorgas and in the after-Gorgas era. The first displayed a Havana street, full of rubbish and dead cats, disfigured by puddles of stagnant water, with dirty gullies serving as open sewers, filled with household refuse and decaying vegetables. The companion piece displayed this same thoroughfare after its subjection to the American cleaning squad. Except for certain resemblances in the architecture, one would never have guessed that it was the same place. It had now become as orderly, as clean, and as civilized in its appearance as Fifth Avenue. All the tin cans, vegetable heaps, and other extraneous matter had been removed. These pictures really gave only a faint idea of the transformation that had taken place. Gorgas had not confined himself to a few conspicuous localities; he had penetrated the most hidden recesses of the town, had discovered sections of whose existence most Havanese were themselves unaware, and had subjected them to the minutest attentions of his scouring squad. How a man could do the things that Gorgas did and not start a new insurrection was a marvel; it was itself a tribute to that tact and geniality which were perhaps his most useful traits. He did not content himself with cleaning up the outside; he went into homes, into backyards, into factories, into business offices, everywhere enforcing his ideas of absolute cleanliness. Not a single building was overlooked. Bakeries, butcher shops, hotels, grocery stores, and cafés were all housecleaned in the most approved New England fashion. If alterations were necessary to make the change permanent, such alterations were ordered—and made; new plumbing was installed in wholesale fashion; stables were supplied with cement floors and new drainage was put in; the city's milk supply was inspected and censored; garbage was disposed of in the most approved manner; and the houses of the poor, probably for the first time in their history, came into contact with chlorinated lime. At the end of several months' scrubbing and burning and disinfection Havana emerged, something new in the history of the world: a tropical city as clean within and without as any of the proud centres of the temperate zone. It was a beautiful job that Gorgas and his associates had done and the American people loudly gloried in it.

Great as was the popular astonishment at such a performance, the sequel held one surprise more astounding still. If Gorgas had any inclination to be proud of his achievement, his pride was presently destined to have a fall. Seldom has such a superhuman task been so inadequately rewarded. For all this labour did not have the slightest effect in preventing the disease at which it was chiefly aimed. This elaborate cleansing was an excellent thing for the happiness and general well-being of Cuba; but it accomplished nothing so far as the yellow-fever germ was concerned. The general death rate of Havana greatly declined; such disorders as typhoid, dysentery, and the like all but disappeared. But the deaths from yellow fever began rapidly to increase; if the sanitation had had any influence at all, it had stimulated rather than destroyed the disease. Of course, this was not the case. The explanation was found in the fact that while Gorgas and his perspiring cohorts were working day and night, with their brooms and brushes and pails of smelly disinfectants, another phenomenon was taking place. The cessation of the Cuban war had stimulated immigration from Spain. This began in the latter part of 1899 and soon reached unprecedented proportions. In the year 1900 more than 25,000 immigrants arrived at Havana, practically all of them from the mother country. The likelihood of a long period of peace and quiet, the assurance of stability given by the American occupation, made Cuba one of the most attractive places of settlement for the hard-pressed population of the Spanish peninsula. Gorgas and his co-workers now promptly discovered why Havana had been practically free from yellow fever for two years. The disease had simply lacked the food upon which it must feed. It had stealthily lain there all this time, seemingly mocking at the heroic effort of the Americans to extirpate it, momentarily ready to spring at the prey as soon as it should appear. Its victims now arrived in the shape of these Spanish immigrants. All came from a country in which yellow fever had been unknown; all, that is, were non-immunes. As quickly as they landed upon Cuban soil the disease therefore assailed them; their debarkation in Havana was like shavings applied to a faintly flickering flame. And the result was just as instantaneous. Americans in the United States who had taken pride in the newspaper accounts of sanitation in Cuba experienced a sudden shock, for the leading item from the Pearl of the Antilles was now the new epidemic of yellow fever. General Fitzhugh Lee declared, in a newspaper interview, that the outbreak was the worst the island had ever known. The Associated Press asserted that there was not a block in Havana that did not have from one to seventeen cases. All these reports were exaggerations, but the situation was an exceedingly desperate one.

Naturally Gorgas was a disappointed man. His energetic and conscientious campaign had apparently accomplished nothing. Havana, the "spotless town" of the Caribbean, was just as intensely ridden with yellow fever as was Havana, the "pesthole." The Havanese, whose homes he had invaded with his

The Reed Board, which in 1900–1901, solved the century-old problem of the cause of yellow fever. Dr. Walter Reed (left, top,) Dr. Aristides Agramonte, Dr. Jesse W. Lazear (who lost his life as a result of the experiments), and Dr. James Carroll.

sanitary squads and whose furniture he had sometimes put in the streets for a cleansing, took a good-natured and slightly malicious joy in the course of events. They had made much fun of the sanitary operations while under way and the new epidemic apparently justified all their jibes. They called Gorgas's attention to a mysterious and particularly aggravating detail: the parts of the city that were cleanest and housed the cleanest population were the ones in which yellow fever raged with the greatest virulence. The poorer quarters did not suffer nearly so severely. It was a puzzling truth which was a mystery at the time, but which is no mystery now. The fact was, of course, that Americans and other non-immunes lived in large numbers in the better districts, and so furnished the disease its favourite material, while the native population, practically all immune, occupied the less cleanly sections. Apparently yellow fever, like death itself, loved a shining mark. It attacked cleanliness and ignored filth; it wiped out men and women who were most fastidious in their personal habits, and passed by those who gave little attention to the graces of civilized life. It assailed the palaces of the rich and ignored the cabins of the poor. It behaved like a grinning spectre, making mockery of all the lessons of sanitary science, all the time concealing the simple secret that would have made everything clear. Gorgas was as calm as ever; he was not the man to lose his head or get discouraged; but these baffling facts, this enemy that worked so silently and so inexorably, caused him endless anxiety. Leonard Wood, the new Governor-General, was also much alarmed, and the two men spent many busy hours devising new ways of combating the ancient enemy. The only resource, however, was more sanitation and more scrubbing. Again the squads searched out every back street, every blind alley, every hut, every cabin; the severest quarantine measures were applied to all incoming ships; yellow-fever patients were isolated in a secluded hospital at Las Animas, which Gorgas personally supervised; all in vain: the only response was a steady increase in the disease. Gorgas and General Wood maintained their composure, but a good part of the community was frantic.

The excitement was increased by a number of deaths that took place in high quarters. Nothing advertises a plague so much as a few important victims. A great domestic tragedy also gave the disaster a greater notoriety than the deaths of hundreds of obscure persons could have done. In the early autumn three prominent officers on the staff of General William Ludlow, the military governor of the city, died. The officers lived in the Palacio del Segundo Cabo. The chief commissary of the army, the first to come down with the fever, was promptly taken to Las Animas Hospital. His wife arrived two days before his death, in response to a cable sent to her in Cincinnati. When she realized that death was approaching, her grief was pathetic. To the horror of those who witnessed the scene, Mrs. P——, crazed with sorrow, threw herself upon her husband, thus covering herself with *vomito negro*, the gruesome accompaniment of death from yellow fever. Clasping her husband in her arms, she begged him to ask God to take her, too, and soon. Conscious to the very end, he prayed for this. It must be remembered that yellow fever was then believed to be infectious, contracted by contact with *fomites*, and it was evident that Mrs. P—— hoped to take it in this way. With difficulty she was persuaded to go to her room. Becoming more calm she talked about the funeral service, asking her friends to attend, and then requested that she be left alone. Soon after one o'clock a messenger brought word to Gorgas that Mrs. P—— had shot herself. "The next day husband and wife were buried in the little military cemetery at Camp Columbia, where the American troops were cantoned. They were laid to rest in the presence of a large concourse, military and civil. This tragedy profoundly affected the military community."[1]

Captain Page, a member of the commanding gen-

[1]"Sanitation in Panama." By William C. Gorgas.

eral's staff, had a chill while attending the service. He developed a severe case of yellow fever and died within the week. Mr. Cochrane, the American superintendent of the San José Asylum, died after having been a month in Havana. Mr. Patterson died at Las Animas Hospital; Major Cartwright died at Camp Columbia.

"They press Wood, and Wood punches me," wrote Gorgas at this time. "He left the other day for a two weeks' cruise about the island. Just as he was leaving, he sent for me and gave me authority to spend as much as fifty thousand dollars and to go ahead and increase my cleaning and fumigating. This I am doing."

But the renewed effort accomplished little in checking the disease.

III

There was one man in Havana who had watched the sanitary measures of the Americans with a somewhat skeptical interest. The reason was that this physician himself had a theory of the disease far removed from the principles upon which Gorgas was working. In the mind of Dr. Carlos J. Finlay the whole proceeding was absurd, so far as its effect upon yellow fever was concerned; the fact was that for many years Dr. Finlay had entertained no doubt as to the cause of the disease. That cause was fixed, conclusively determined; Dr. Finlay was as certain of it as he was of the movement of the planets. Gorgas and this amiable Cuban doctor were frequently meeting, and on such occasions Gorgas was constantly shown the error of his ways. How to rid Havana of yellow fever? Dr. Finlay perhaps could not accomplish such a task as that; but he definitely knew what caused the disease. For more than twenty years he had been preaching his favourite doctrine to Cubans, but all that he had so far gained by his insistence was the reputation of being a harmless crank.

But Dr. Finlay was one of those enthusiasts who care little for the ridicule of the crowd. For many years he had been one of the best-known and most charming characters in Havana. Though a full-fledged Cuban in thought and feeling, there was not a drop of Spanish blood in his veins. The son of a Scotch father and a French mother, it is perhaps not surprising that he combined, in his own person, a keen mentality, a tireless persistence, and the utmost geniality and graciousness of manner. He was, indeed, the perfect type of the "beloved physician." Certain American qualities, particularly a sense of humour, were perhaps the result of his American training, for he had obtained his medical degree at the Jefferson College of Philadelphia. His behaviour during the Spanish War had especially endeared him to Americans; though sixty-five years old, he came to Washington the day the United States declared war and offered his services to the American Army; he insisted on going to the front and took part in the campaign before Santiago. Thus Dr. Finlay was a well-rounded citizen and physician; he was a scholar, too, in other fields, with a fine taste in old Latin manuscripts, and something of an authority in heraldic and historic studies. But it was his amiability of character that had for so long endeared him to the people of Havana. His kindly face, adorned with side whiskers, and surmounted by a large crop of gray hair, his genial eyes gleaming through his gold-rimmed spectacles, his mild and rather hesitating speech—for he suffered from an impediment which had resulted from an early attack of cholera—were the appropriate outward signs of a nature whose leading traits were affection, devotion to the poor, and a steady, never-sleeping enthusiasm for his profession.

In 1881 Dr. Finlay read a paper before a medical congress in Washington, D. C., in which he asserted that yellow fever was transmitted by the *Stegomyia* mosquito. No more startling theory had ever been presented to scientific men. Since that time the mosquito and the liberation of Cuba from Spain had been the two chief interests of Finlay's existence. How had the man ever conceived such an astonishing idea? Mainly by the use of that talent for logic and reasoning which Finlay had perhaps inherited from his Scotch ancestry. There are about eight hundred varieties of mosquitoes, but Finlay had picked out the Stegomyia as the guilty agent. He had reached this conclusion by studying the peculiarities of yellow fever and the habits of this particular insect. Between the two he had detected certain suggestive coincidences. This mosquito lived only below a certain elevation; yellow fever prevailed within the same limits. The temperatures best suited to the existence of the mosquito were likewise the ones where the disease throve most successfully. The literature of yellow fever also disclosed to Dr. Finlay the important truth that mosquitoes were always abundant where an epidemic of yellow fever prevailed. These observations produced a conviction in his mind that all the laughter and arguments of his friends could not shake. He would discuss his favourite topic with any chance acquaintance, and at length; he never for a moment tired of it. At the slightest encouragement he would bring out his records and his mosquitoes—for he was so wedded to the hypothesis that he always kept a small menagerie of the stegomyia in his office, and always had a large supply of dry eggs on hand. Breeding mosquitoes, indeed, was his favourite occupation.

Yet Finlay's life is perhaps the saddest tragedy

in the history of modern medicine. It is a tragedy because Finlay had hit upon one of the greatest discoveries of the age but had never succeeded in demonstrating its truth. In fact, his own experiments had succeeded only in discrediting his favourite theory. A mere assertion, especially one so strange and unprecedented as the mosquito transmission of yellow fever, carries little authority; the discoverer must demonstrate it by experiments. The proved production of a single case of yellow fever by the bite of a mosquito would immediately have lifted Finlay to the peak of fame. In twenty years, however, he never succeeded in doing this. He made many experiments—more than one hundred—but did not bring forth one case that could stand the scientific test. Finlay applied innumerable mosquitoes which had bitten yellow-fever patients to healthy persons. No case of yellow fever ever resulted; the unfortunate fact in Finlay's history therefore is that he had himself discredited the mosquito idea. There is almost something grotesque in this thought that the one man who had done most to discredit the idea of mosquito infection was the one who had first, in unmistakable fashion, pointed the accusing finger at this troublesome insect. His work, as Gorgas afterward said, remains a splendid example of medical clairvoyance, a beautiful manifestation of the scientific imagination. That Finlay should have made this announcement as far back as 1881 was especially remarkable, for little was known then about the association of insects with disease. It is true that, in 1880, Sir Patrick Manson had discovered that the worm which caused *filariasis* was introduced into the blood by a mosquito, but this disease was practically unknown in Europe or the United States, and the discovery, which really marked a great milestone in medical science, did not create much interest. In 1889 came a piece of work which still remains one of the most wonderful contributions to modern science. This was the discovery by the two Americans, Dr. Theobald Smith and Dr. H. L. Kilborne, that the terrible plague of cattle known as Texas fever is transmitted by a tick. In 1897 Ronald Ross brilliantly demonstrated that the *Anopheles* mosquito was the infecting agent in malaria. Naturally these sensational developments aroused a new interest in Finlay's theory, which now assumed an almost convincing plausibility. But there was the work of Finlay himself to discourage additional experiments! As will be subsequently described, Finlay failed because he had not observed two facts of the utmost consequence; and it was the genius of American investigators that brought these facts to light and made the whole thing clear.

Dr. Finlay was one of the first friends Gorgas made in Havana. The two men served together on the yellow-fever commission, and for two or three years they therefore met almost daily; like the rest, Gorgas heard constantly of the stegomyia and, like the rest, Gorgas did not believe. Dr. Finlay, with all his zeal, lacked one desirable quality: he did not have the gift of convincing presentation; his words came haltingly and confusedly. "A most lovable man in character and personality," writes Gorgas; "no one could be thrown with Dr. Finlay daily as I was for several years without becoming warmly attached to him and forming the highest estimate of his scientific honesty and straightforwardness. Being familiar with yellow fever both historically and clinically, I was constantly bringing to his notice instances in the past which could not be accounted for on the mosquito theory. Dr. Finlay with the greatest ingenuity was able to explain how the mosquito theory could be turned so as to meet just such contentions. I remained unconvinced."

IV

But the yellow-fever situation was daily becoming more and more desperate. So serious was it that the Surgeon-General now appointed a commission to visit Cuba and investigate the cause of the disease. When this commission was appointed it aroused no particular interest. Hundreds of similar medical commissions had been created in the past, had completed their work, published bulky reports which few people read, and presently had faded into forgetfulness. There was nothing to indicate that this new yellow-fever commission would not have a similar history. No one could have guessed, in June, 1900, that its six months' labours would make it immortal and that it would result in a series of experiments which, for exactness and definiteness, would at once take their place as perhaps the most complete in medical history. The men on this commission were then little known outside of army circles, but their names now stand high in science. Walter Reed, James Carroll, Jesse W. Lazear, and Aristides Agramonte—these were the men who were to solve this, one of the most baffling mysteries of four centuries, with that inescapable finality which sometimes makes science as much a thing of beauty as art itself. The leader of the little group, and the genius that directed the joint operations, was Walter Reed. Up to that time his career had closely resembled that of Gorgas. Like Gorgas, Reed was a Southerner—a Virginian; like Gorgas, he had studied medicine at Bellevue in New York; his nature had the religious strain and the cheerful outlook on life that were leading traits in Gorgas. That same rough experience in frontier life—doctoring soldiers, cowboys, and Indians—which had done so much to strengthen Gorgas's character had likewise left their indelible impress on

Reed. Reed, however, had gone in more for abstract science than had his Alabama friend. Johns Hopkins medical school, which opened in 1893, had attracted Reed as one of its earliest students; here, under the tutelage of William H. Welch, he had gone deeply into bacteriology, and demonstrated a keenness of observation and a thoroughness of method which, in the judgment of his instructors, marked him out for great things. Reed's subsequent work in the army added to this reputation; it is therefore not surprising that, in 1900, Surgeon-General Sternberg should have selected him as the head of the scientific commission for the study of yellow fever. Temperamentally he was splendidly fitted for the job. Warm-spirited, gay, witty, full of enthusiasm and fun, he entered upon the work with the eagerness of a boy taking up a new game.

Already one discovery had been made which at that time had attracted little attention, but which, in itself, laid the foundations of Reed's work. A year before another Virginian, Dr. Henry R. Carter, of the Public Health Service, made an elaborate statistical study of the spread of yellow fever in houses. When Carter sent his paper containing the results of his study to an American medical journal, it was returned by the editor as "too long"; yet this rejected manuscript represented one of the most important scientific works which had been done up to that time on yellow fever, and in itself furnished the starting point for Reed's investigations. Even to-day Carter's work is not so well known to the layman as that of Reed and Gorgas, yet Gorgas himself said that "it places Carter in the class of the great original workers of our time." The observation which Carter made seems simple and obvious enough to-day; yet the fact remains that it had evaded all previous investigators and it was the failure to observe this truth that had caused all of Finlay's experiments to end so disastrously. Carter had served many years as a quarantine officer, and yellow fever had thus become one of the commonplace facts in his daily existence. For many years he had observed that when a man developed yellow fever on board ship none of his shipmates became ill, even those who lived in the crowded forecastle with him, until a time considerably in excess of the period of incubation of the disease in man; this led him to believe that yellow fever could not be contracted from the environment of a sick man for a considerable time after he became sick in that environment. But it was not until 1898, while in charge of a yellow-fever epidemic in Orwood and Taylor, Mississippi, that Carter obtained sufficient data to feel that its publication would become convincing to others. Here the disease affected mainly isolated farmhouses, and the conditions were thus ideal for study. A close watch upon particular houses yielded convincing results. Here is a farmhouse, for illustration, in which a patient falls ill of yellow fever. Men and women come and go carelessly, inquiring friends and relatives visit the family, and individual members even associate rather freely with the patient. Carter kept precise records of all these visitors; a certain number contracted yellow fever and a certain number escaped, and when this record was tabulated, it presented results that were so uniform that they amounted to a natural law.

Those persons who visited the house within a period varying from ten days to two weeks after the patient's seizure never contracted the disease. It was the visitors who came after this period who became ill. The mere presence of the patient was not essential to the transmission of infection; after his removal or death, the house was just as dangerous as before. What was the necessary conclusion from these facts? Evidently that the yellow-fever patient was not a menace to his environment when he first fell ill; for about ten or twelve days his family could associate with him and his friends could visit him without the slightest danger of contracting the disease. After that period, however, a majority fell ill. Perhaps more important still, it appeared that the sick man was not himself the immediate source of contamination, but his environment. Long after he had recovered or had been buried the house remained a persistent focus of infection. But even his abiding place was not a menace until ten days or two weeks after the onset of the disease. After that period had elapsed, whether the patient was still there or not, the house was likely to infect any one who entered it. The discovery of this period, when the sick man could not transmit the disease, followed by a period when he was exceedingly dangerous, should have opened the eyes of the scientific world, but the first men it greatly impressed were Reed and his associate Lazear.

There seems something like the working of an intelligent fate in the fact that the three men—Carter, Reed, and Gorgas—who seemed indispensable to solving the yellow-fever problem, were at work in Havana at the same time. Carter was there as Quarantine Officer, and naturally he presented his tables to his fellow Virginian. Reed gave them the most painstaking study.

"Are you sure your dates are accurate?" he asked Carter.

Carter had no doubt on that point.

"Then," said Reed, "it spells an insect host."

The facts that Ronald Ross's work on the mosquito transmission of malaria had recently been published unquestionably led Reed to this conclusion. Ross had shown that the malarial germ is not dangerous when first taken into the mosquito's body, but undergoes a change in its stomach that makes it infectious. The resemblance between this and Carter's discovery of "extrinsic incubation" in yellow fever is obvious.

It was one thing to form this conception but quite a different thing to demonstrate it. And the way proved almost as difficult for Reed as for Finlay. It was not until early July, 1900, that Reed, having learned of Carter's theory of "extrinsic incubation" turned to the Finlay theory of mosquito infection. Finlay himself furnished the mosquitoes, or rather the eggs, a plentiful supply of which he always kept on hand. But the early Reed experiments proved as unsatisfactory as Finlay's. The Finlay mosquitoes were fed on patients ill with yellow fever and then these same mosquitoes were allowed to suck the blood of men in normal health. Dr. Jesse W. Lazear and Dr. Carroll, both members of the Reed board, subjected themselves to these tests and came through without the slightest injury. The records now show clearly enough why these first experiments failed; Lazear and Carroll had indeed made precisely the same mistakes as Finlay. They had utterly ignored Carter's great discovery of "extrinsic incubation," and they ignored likewise another fact of equal importance which the Reed board subsequently brought to light.

A little discouraged by these results, Carroll and

Joseph L. LePrince, sanitarian, one of Dr. Gorgas's most effective lieutenants at Havana and Panama.

Lazear, in the next month, became somewhat careless with their infected mosquitoes. On September 16th, Gorgas was asked to visit his friend Dr. Carroll who was suffering from what seemed a "slight indisposition." Gorgas was shocked at the physician's appearance; he was lying in a state of prostration, his face flushed with a high fever, his eyes bloodshot, his restless body tossing on the bed. Dr. Carroll grew steadily worse, and in a few hours was in a condition of delirium. It did not take Gorgas long to diagnose the disease: it was the malady that had long since become such a familiar part of his own life. In his lucid moments Carroll explained that he had subjected his arm to the bite of an infected mosquito. The hardy experimenter had a severe attack, but, after several days' struggle, he was on the road to recovery.

While Carroll was still lying between life and death, Gorgas received a summons to another member of the Reed commission. This was Jesse W. Lazear, who, a month previously, had let the mosquitoes feed upon him with so little result. Gorgas saw at a glance that his friend was now mortally ill with yellow fever. Before he sank into his final delirium, Lazear told Gorgas his story. A few days previously he had been experimenting with infected mosquitoes at Las Animas Hospital. While he was applying one of the insects to the arm of a soldier, another mosquito, flying about the room, lighted upon Lazear's own hand. The physician resisted the impulse to brush it off and permitted it to suck its fill. It was, he added, unquestionably a Stegomyia. After telling so much, Lazear could talk no more; he became wildly delirious, and soon sank into the throes of one of the most terrible cases of yellow fever that Gorgas had ever seen. In a few days came the black vomit, and on September 25th, a little more than a week after the mosquito had injected its poisonous dart, Lazear died.

Naturally, two such events, the narrow escape of Carroll and the actual martyrdom of Lazear, produced the most sobering effect; Lazear, young, brilliant, dashing, was one of the best-loved men in Havana; tragic as his fate had been, however, it pointed its inevitable lesson and inspired a new determination in his fellow scientists. Reed, who had been absent in Washington on official duty when Lazear died, now returned to Havana. Up to that time the mosquito experiments had been more or less casual and haphazard; but these happenings and Reed's return gave them a scientific direction. The story of those next few months has been frequently told. It is the story of Reed and not the story of Gorgas. Gorgas naturally watched the progress of events with the utmost interest, but he himself had no share in this phase of the yellow-fever work. Yet the ensuing events were as dramatic as any of the old Union Square melodramas which he used to attend in his Bellevue Hospital days. In specially constructed quarters, named Camp Lazear in honour of their fallen associate, Reed and his associates wrenched from Nature secret after secret in the propagation of this disease. When they had finished their three months' work, the processes that control yellow fever stood as plainly revealed as the light of day. An especially heroic aspect of their work is that their experiments were conducted exclusively upon human beings. At that time it was believed that animals did not have the disease and could not acquire it, so that American soldiers, brave and cheerful volunteers, performed the part usually assigned to guinea pigs and rabbits in the laboratory. Reed placed his subject in a small room completely enclosed with wire netting fine enough to keep out all mosquitoes. Then he let loose in this room Stegomyias that had recently bitten patients ill with yellow fever. Most of the men so exposed presently fell ill with the disease—though happily all recovered. Adjoining this room, and separated from it only by a wall of wire mosquito netting, was another, in which non-immunes were placed. Their living conditions were precisely the same as those of their neighbours, with one exception: no infected mosquitoes were introduced. Not one of these men subsequently showed any signs of illness. A simple experiment disposed of the theory that the conveying agents were *fomites*—infected clothing, bedding, and the like. A number of extremely obliging soldiers for twenty days and nights occupied a room filled with the clothing of yellow-fever patients; they slept upon beds covered with black vomit and other physical accompaniments of the disease; the experience was a severe one, but its scientific value was great, for not one of these men came down with the infection. The *fomites* theory, which had controlled quarantine practice for more than a generation, thus spontaneously went the way of other great medical delusions. The success of these experiments depended upon two details of critical importance. Reed discovered that a mosquito, in order to become infected, must bite the sick person sometime within the first three days of his illness. For the succeeding ten days or two weeks—this was Dr. Carter's discovery—the mosquito is itself harmless; after that period has elapsed, however, it is more dangerous to human life than the most ferocious beast of the jungle. In these two facts lie the whole secret of infection through mosquitoes; but cunning Nature had for ages as shrewdly concealed them as she had the secret of mosquito infection itself.

When Reed had finished his work, the truth about yellow fever was manifest, yet there were those who doubted, and among the doubters was Gorgas himself. About this Gorgas never made any secret, then or afterward. He never took Finlay's enthusiasms seriously, chiefly because Finlay had apparently disproved his own thesis. When the Reed board finally decided to investigate the mosquito scientifically, Gorgas had little expectation that it would succeed. His experience at the bedside of Carroll and Lazear did quicken his interest, but neither of these cases had real scientific value, for the possibility of infection from other sources than the mosquito had not been excluded. He made frequent trips to Camp Lazear while the experiments were under way and constantly discussed their meaning with Reed. Even when Reed had completed his work, Gorgas's position was still one of extreme caution. That the Stegomyia mosquito could transmit the disease was unassailably proved; but was this the only way in which it was conveyed? Was it even the ordinary way? That, Gorgas held, had not been demonstrated. His position was entirely logical and scientific. Some contagious diseases are transmitted in more than one way; the common house fly conveys typhoid, but that is only one way in which it is carried. It might be the same with yellow fever. In the next few months, however, it was clearly to be shown that the Stegomyia, and the Stegomyia only, was the infecting agent, and the man who was to make this clear for all time was Gorgas himself.

V

"If it is the mosquito," said Gorgas, when the Reed experiments were under way, "I am going to get rid of the mosquito."

Reed himself smiled at the idea.

"It can't be done," he said, and his opinion was the one that generally prevailed in Havana at that time.

The truth is that most scientists regarded Reed's indictment of the Stegomyia merely as a brilliant academic performance. They could not see how it greatly lessened the general yellow-fever peril. In fact, Reed seemed to have reduced the situation to one of utter despair. He had proved that the Stegomyia conveyed the disease—yes; then what was the way of controlling it? Obviously by destroying the Stegomyia. Never had man faced a more hopeless task! Mosquitoes existed by the uncountable billions. Havana and its environs was full of them. They filled every alleyway, every street, every house, every nook and cranny of the city. At times they settled over the community almost like a cloud. The Havanese themselves had become accustomed, practically reconciled, to the insects; strangers looked upon them as the bane of their existence. The Reed discovery therefore came almost like a sentence of death. Havana always had had yellow fever, and now it seemed certain that Havana would always have it. To run around the city attempting to banish the disease by killing these gnats—what occupation could seem more useless and more ludicrous? One might as well attempt to banish the air in which the mosquitoes passed their brief destructive lives. What Reed had apparently accomplished was to add a new horror to daily existence. The houses of Havana now became filled with countless enemies. Every mosquito might be the carrier of death. To have one land upon a hand or arm seemed almost like being stabbed in the dark. The suddenness with which this minute beast was transformed from a mere annoyance into a murderous brigand was frequently illustrated in ludicrous fashion. One day Gorgas was discussing the subject with about fifteen learned doctors. A glass jar, covered with a cloth, containing a collection of the guilty insects, stood on the table. Most of the doctors had come from foreign countries to investigate the startling discoveries of the Reed board. Nearly all were extremely skeptical; they sat there thoughtfully stroking their beards, giving learned reasons why the Reed hypothesis could not be accepted. Through some accident the covering of the glass jar suddenly came off and the imprisoned mosquitoes emerged into the general atmosphere. The gentlemen of science, almost as one man, made a leap for the door and disappeared through it with such precipitancy that the wire screen was destroyed in their exit. The nervousness that they displayed was the common emotion all over Havana, especially in the foreign quarters. Reed had done a great thing for science, but he had not added to the peace of the ordinary citizen.

To the inexperienced the problem might at first seem not to be a difficult one. A man fell ill when he was bitten by a mosquito which had previously bitten another human being suffering from the disease. The original source of infection was evidently not the mosquito but the man; more accurately expressed, there were two independent agencies of contamination, the human being and the insect. If these two parties to the spread of yellow fever could be kept separate, the contagion would apparently disappear. Most observers were persuaded that it was impossible to keep the insects away from the invalid—they were too numerous and persistent; but could not the sick persons be kept away from the mosquitoes? The way to stop the disease was therefore a very simple procedure. As soon as a mosquito victim fell ill, he should be isolated, inclosed in a screened room, so that the voracious Stegomyia would be prevented from reaching its quarry. If every case could be treated in this way, it was quite apparent that the plague would presently vanish from the face of the earth. The logic was faultless, but the practice was full of difficulties. The truth was that the afflicted patient was almost as hard to control as the mosquito itself. Even under the most rigidly enforced health rules, there were plenty of cases, especially of the mild kind, that were not reported. There were thousands of victims, especially children, who were afflicted in such light form that they never knew it. But the parasite freely circulates in their blood and, if transmitted into a more susceptible subject, could produce the disease in its most virulent form. If the Stegomyia were limited only to notorious victims, sick people who could be screened, it would be possible to control the infection at its source; unfortunately the creature was constantly inserting its proboscis into patients who had yellow fever so lightly that they never reached the jurisdiction of the medical profession or the health department. There was therefore only one satisfactory way of approaching the problem, and that was by declaring warfare on the mosquito itself.

"They say we can't do it?" remarked Gorgas in his quiet way. "Perhaps we can't, but we shall try."

One other plan was suggested as almost a despairing hope. The possibility of inoculating against the disease afforded a momentary gleam of light. This was Dr. Finlay's favourite idea and the one that had guided most of his mosquito experiments. In the old days, before the discovery of vaccination, it was customary in certain countries to inoculate against smallpox; to take men and women, when in an especially healthy condition, and give them the disease artificially, in the hope that a light case would afford protection against a severe attack. The idea was essentially the same as Pasteur's procedure of inoculation with attenuated virus; the only difference was that, in the old days, before the development of bacteriology, the modern technique was unknown, and there was no certainty that a moderate attack of the disease could be obtained. Only too frequently smallpox in its severest form was transmitted, and deaths from the inoculation were so common that the practice was abandoned. Among the Chinese, however, inoculation was common for centuries; in Turkey also it was constantly practised; Lady Mary Wortley-Montagu, in her letters, tells how she was herself successfully inoculated in Constantinople. And now the sanitary authorities of Havana believed that the only practical use that could be made of the Reed discovery was the possible immunization of the whole population, or at least of foreigners, by inoculation. Gorgas had little faith in this procedure and took no part in the work, which was under the charge of Dr. Juan Guiteras. Gorgas was, indeed, a somewhat amused spectator. At the particular time, when the experiments began, infected mosquitoes were scarce; in fact, Dr. Reed had only one to give his co-workers—a mosquito so venerable and precious that she was popularly known as "Her Ladyship." A more vicious beast than "Her Ladyship" probably never inhabited this earth; she had given many persons yellow fever, and for fifty-seven days she had carried the germ until her body was little more than an animated culture tube of the disease; yet few patients have been more tenderly cared for. Her home was a large glass jar on the table in the centre of a sunshiny room; an oil stove, especially brought from the United States, kept her apartment at just the desired temperature. But "Her Ladyship" soon began to behave in most discouraging fashion.

"One morning about daylight," writes Gorgas, "I got a message saying that 'Her Ladyship' was in most critical and desperate plight. At some time during the night she had caught her wing in a mesh of the mosquito netting, and had struggled to free herself for so long a time that when she was discovered by the attendant in the morning, she was almost dead. I rapidly dressed and hurried to the hospital. Similar messages had been sent to Dr. Ross and Dr. Guiteras. We found her condition even worse than had been represented. Two or three of the doctors on the staff of the hospital had been promptly called in, and the services of several of our trained nurses had been likewise obtained. Her wing had been gently liberated from the mesh of the netting, and 'Her Ladyship' laid upon a soft bed of cotton batting. The oil stove was started up, and the room brought to a very hot summer temperature, but it was all of no avail. She finally ceased to kick, about nine o'clock in the morning, and died with a larger attendance of doctors and nurses around her table than had ever been present around the deathbed of any mere human in the City of Havana.

"This account may seem somewhat exaggerated, but the scene still comes back to my mind's eye very vividly. How earnest and serious we all were! A half-dozen of the leading practitioners of Havana were sitting around the deathbed of this mosquito, looking and feeling exceedingly mournful and depressed, and it was a very heavy blow to the Health Department of Havana."

The death of "Her Ladyship" was not so serious as it seemed, for the physicians soon abandoned all thought of fighting yellow fever by inoculation. Seven persons were infected by mosquitoes and of these three had the disease in such virulent form that they died. The fact that one of the deaths was that of Miss Maas, a twenty-six-year-old American nurse who had volunteered for the experiment, cast a gloom over the whole proceeding. Inoculation was evidently too dangerous a method of fighting yellow fever, and was accordingly abandoned. It was now apparent that the only possible hope lay in the method that Gorgas had been advocating—the destruction of the mosquitoes. From this time forward Gorgas became the chief agency in fighting the disease, and the methods that he evolved were the methods by which this plague was overthrown, not only in Cuba, but in most other countries.

Not much at that time was known about the Stegomyia or of mosquitoes in general. The fact that the majority of the gnats which afflicted the city were not members of the Stegomyia family was even unknown. Yet presently it was discovered that this mosquito had a distinct individuality, and that it was as different in its habits and its tastes from the several hundred other varieties as a cat is from a tiger. This latter illustration is not so far fetched as it may seem, for the Stegomyia has one characteristic in common with the family cat that other mosquitoes do not share. It is just as fond of the human race and just as completely a domesticated animal. Its motions, indeed, are not so conciliatory and benevolent. It haunts the abiding places of human kind chiefly because of its insatiable appetite for human blood. Possibly the student of nature may see in this fondness for human beings the inscrutable workings of evolutionary law. Of the nearly eight hundred varieties of mosquito there is only one known to convey yellow fever, and there is surely something more than accident in the fact that this is the one that can live happily only when most closely associated with men. Possibly the time was when the Stegomyia was a wild animal, so to speak, living, like the rest of its family, in swamps and marshes and the unfrequented forest, but for centuries it has been a house dweller. That in appearance it was conspicuously different from its brethren had long been familiar to close observers. It is about the only known mosquito that can make any especial claim to physical beauty. Its body is marked by a series of silvery half moons, its legs are alternately black and white, and the four brilliant stripes on its thorax also distinguish it as the handsomest of its tribe. The general effect of this mingling of silver and black is one of grayness and, seen under a magnifying glass, the effect is striking, almost brilliant; even to the unassisted eye the gnat, in markings and size, is easily the aristocrat of mosquitoes. And it has other traits that set it aside as exceptional. Among insects it is an intellectual giant. This expression, of course, is purely figurative; probably Nature has endowed the Stegomyia with no heroic mental qualities; its action is mere instinct, or the result of chemical interactions; yet it behaves in a way that almost suggests the working of a keen intelligence. Few human beings assail an appointed task so directly and so persistently as the Stegomyia in fulfilling the task which Nature has allotted it.

Thus the fact is that although human beings, in the year 1901, knew little about the Stegomyia, the Stegomyia was very well informed about human beings. By associating with man for untold ages it has learned his habits and his vulnerabilities. It knows, for example, precisely where to sting. Other pests of the air unguardedly light upon easily accessible parts, but the yellow-fever mosquito almost invariably attacks under the wrist, where the skin is soft and tender and not easily protected, or on the ankles. It almost never strikes on the face or the top of the hand—these places are too readily slapped. So completely is this mosquito a product of civilization that almost everything connected with its life is artificial. It is almost as minutely careful about the raising of its young as are human beings themselves. In this, however, the Stegomyia is over-refined, for its meticulousness in its breeding habits is the thing that immensely simplified Gorgas's task of exterminating it. The circumstance that only half the Stegomyias were dangerous was also helpful. It is only the female that ever annoys beasts or men, and this is true of all gnats. The male is a quiet, unobtrusive, decently living insect that does not consume blood but finds its food among fruit juices and other casual scraps. Nor does the female mosquito—the only sex that bites—go seeking blood as food. It needs it merely as a stimulus to the act of laying its eggs; it cannot perform this function, indeed, without this incentive. It is only after it fills its stomach with human blood that the Stegomyia manifests the real delicacy of its nature. All mosquitoes lay their eggs in water, but all, except the yellow-fever mosquito, are extremely careless on this point. Any mud puddle, any dirty brook or brackish marsh, will suffice. But the Stegomyia will do so only in or near a house inhabited by a human being and only in water contained in some artificial object. Both these accessories must be present or the insect will decline to perform its normal functions. Moreover, it insists on having clean water; that which has freshly fallen into rain barrels it prefers above all others. But it will not use even such a perfect breeding place unless the water barrel is near an inhabited house. The experiment has been tried of putting barrels filled with water around an uninhabited dwelling; the mosquito will never use them for breeding purposes. As soon as a family moves in, however, the barrel is swarming with mosquito larvæ. If one digs holes around a house full of people and fills them with water the Stegomyia will not lay eggs in them. If one fills pans with water and places them in these same holes, the Stegomyia will lay eggs abundantly. That is, it must have an artificial container or it declines to perpetuate its kind. It will not lay eggs in an ordinary puddle of water, but it will lay in a puddle that has collected in a concrete bottom. It is devoted to the numerous utensils, holding water, that are assembled in the average house—flower pots, tin cans, vases, drip basins, water pitchers, and the infinite impedimenta of the kitchen. In Havana if any one filled a glass with drinking water and laid it aside a Stegomyia would frequently light upon the surface and deposit the beginnings of a numerous progeny. For three centuries the complacent Havanese had been daily drinking mosquito eggs and larvæ and washing in them, for the most part unconsciously. How numerous were the water-containing utensils in the average house no one, up to that time, had stopped to consider, but it was something that Gorgas quickly learned. For this peculiarity of the mosquito held the secret to the eradication of yellow fever.

VI

Soon after the death of Miss Maas had so sadly demonstrated the uselessness of inoculation Gorgas therefore began his warfare on the mosquito. His chief energies, however, were not directed to the extermination of the fully developed insects. In this, as in all things, he preferred the more thorough method of destroying the contagion at its source.

Practically all the artificial receptacles in Havana, as already described, contained a considerable assortment of mosquito larvæ. They were popularly known as "wigglers"; they were the little worm-like creatures, about a quarter of an inch long, which had recently emerged from the egg, and which, after a brief experience as aquatic animals, were destined to ascend as full-grown mosquitoes. A strange warfare was this in which Gorgas was now engaged, somewhat different from that which he had imagined in his vainglorious youth—that of pursuing to their death the thousands of little mosquito larvæ leading an apparently innocent life in the water containers of Havana. Nothing like it had ever been known in the history of military science.

Gorgas's office was a room in the Maestranza, the ancient gray limestone structure on the harbour front, formerly used for army and navy purposes, but now become the general headquarters of the American Sanitary Administration. From this vantage point he kept immediate contact with his small army of inspectors, who were scouring the city in search of their prey. Like a good general he had divided the capital into districts or sectors, and in a brief time he possessed a complete record of every house and every family in this city of nearly three hundred thousand people. The vastness of such an enterprise would have discouraged most men; and it is not strange that Gorgas and his mosquito-hunting companions became probably the greatest jokes that Havana had ever known. The card-catalogue system had not then been elaborated to its present perfection, but Gorgas devised one that was adequate. Each house and each family had its separate piece of white pasteboard. This showed the number of water barrels, tanks, jugs, or other containers in the family's possession. Gorgas even shrewdly noted the location of these receptacles, for he foresaw that the owners would remove or hide them on the approach of the official visitors. For the destruction of the larvæ kerosene proved the most useful ammunition. A film of this, laid on the top of the water, did not permeate the mass, and therefore did not destroy its usefulness for drinking and other purposes. But it exercised a sorry effect upon the wigglers. This little creature has one trait in common with a much larger fish, the whale; it must periodically come to the surface for air, else it will drown. The thin layer of petroleum prevented it from doing this; the little wiggler would strike the oiled surface with its breathing tube but would get no farther, and in the course of nature it expired. Every inspector was accompanied by two associates armed with pails of oil; as soon as they found a water barrel, a tank, or other receptable, they would pour a little fluid over the surface. That ended the career of these particular wigglers.

But the oil in time evaporates, and there were plenty of mosquitoes waiting to deposit more eggs. The inspectors therefore covered the top with planking, leaving a fair-sized hole through which the rain water could find its way; and this aperture they covered with wire netting of mesh so fine that the smallest mosquito could not get through. So long as the barrels and water tanks were kept in this condition their career as mosquito breeders was finished. Every house, and hotel, and bar room and other inhabited building was visited once a month and any one who disturbed these arrangements was subject to fine. It was more difficult to keep free of wigglers the containers within the house. The inspectors explained the danger, called upon the householders to keep their pans and pots free of standing water, and constantly inspected the premises to see that their instructions were regarded. The Havana Council passed a law fining any one ten dollars who permitted mosquitoes to breed on his premises. But the housewives would hide their earthenware jugs on the approach of the inspector, who would sometimes be compelled to search the whole building to find them. He had a complete record of every container in every structure, and, as each was produced he would check it on his card. "Where's that other pitcher?" he would ask, if one were missing, nor did he leave the place until it was forthcoming. Every building was minutely searched for the almost innumerable places in which water could gather: puddles were even found in stoves and furnaces—frequently swarming with mosquito larvæ.

"Your whole plan's a failure," a Havana physician declared one morning, coming into Gorgas's office.

"What makes you think so?"

The physician had emptied every possible water receptacle in his house. Yet the place was still full of mosquitoes. Gorgas immediately sent a trusted inspector to investigate. For a long time he was indeed baffled; where were the pests coming from? Finally a box of books was unpacked, and at the bottom was found a small paint pail half full of water. The determined Stegomyia, in its search for breeding water, had wormed its way through the cracks in the books and deposited its eggs, which, emerging from the wiggler stage, had, with similar persistence, climbed into the sunlight. The anecdote illustrates the magnitude of the task which Gorgas had assumed.

Yet the problem, at base, was not a physical but a human one. The thing necessary above all was to establish sympathetic relations with the Cuban people and to make them heartily coöperate with the sanitary officials. Ordinarily this might have been a difficult task. The native Havanese did not themselves suffer from yellow fever and therefore had no immediate personal interest in its destruction. Their interest in the antics of the Americans was at first humorous; they stood good-naturedly on the side lines laughing at the crazy Yankees who were chasing mosquitoes. The serious inconvenience to which they were put might easily have engendered hostility. To cherish the home is a Spanish trait, and the unceremonious visits of foreigners, demanding that they breed no wigglers (under penalty of fine), that they install new plumbing, that in some cases they reconstruct their houses, might easily have aroused their Latin wrath. But the fact that the whole proceeding was conducted with such tact saved the situation. And this tact was the expression of Gorgas's own nature. Possibly the circumstance that his name was Gorgas somewhat helped; certainly the Havanese detected Spanish qualities in his manner. Perhaps his mildness, his consideration, his gentleness, his willingness always to smooth the path to a difficult undertaking, were an inheritance from his remote Spanish ancestors; at any rate, the Cubans looked upon Gorgas as one of themselves. Again and again an outraged Cuban would enter Gorgas's office, cursing the Americans in a language not deficient in expletives, but a quarter of an hour afterward he would come out, all smiles. One day a huge Negress, her face a mirror of contentment, was seen emerging from the Chief Surgeon's room; only a few minutes before she had entered, a spectacle of black and animated fury.

"What are you so happy about?" someone asked. "At last there's justice in Havana," she replied, "and the King is in there!"

All that Gorgas had done was to talk to her for a few minutes. Certain repairs were necessary to her premises: it was a crime to ask a poor woman to spend so much money! But Gorgas, in a few words, explained why it was necessary; he told his astonished guest what mosquitoes were doing to Havana—this was the first the woman had ever heard of the real cause of yellow fever—and gave her a brief and gentle discourse on good citizenship. It was probably the first time the Negress had ever received such consideration from a public officer, and the proceeding at once transformed her into an enthusiastic crusader against the wiggler. The incident is typical. Gorgas had the power of commanding, inflicting fines, and imprisoning—the whole United States Government was at his back; but he practically never used it. Persuasion and education were always his method. His business, he used to say, was to make the people of Havana themselves demand his sanitary measures, and his whole campaign was inspired with the determination to create that kind of public sentiment.

That he succeeded there are abundant signs. Normally a sanitary chief is about the most unpopular of public men, but Gorgas has become a patron saint of Havana and one of its finest streets has been named for him. More complimentary still, the rules he laid down have been scrupulously observed by the municipality ever since his time.

Perhaps one reason for this public affection was the realization of Gorgas's intense devotion to his duties. His office was never closed; day and night, Sundays and holidays, it was always doing business. Nor did Gorgas himself observe the ten-hour day. He knew all his many inspectors intimately and kept track of their every movement. He had a unique way of checking their work. Day after day he was himself roaming the streets and alleys and tenement districts of Havana, investigating water barrels, poking among tin cans and gutter troughs, talking with housewives, delivering little impromptu lectures—everywhere making friends for the American Administration and arousing sympathetic interest in his anti-mosquito work. He became very well known, especially among the poorer districts, so that, whenever he rang a front-door bell, a beaming señora would greet him almost invariably with the same words: "*No hay moquitos aquí, señor.*" ("We have no mosquitoes here, sir.")

This was the process of killing the yellow-fever

Dr. Carlos J. Finlay, a physician of Cuba, famous for his identification of the stegomyia mosquito as the infecting agent in yellow fever.

insect at its beginning—of destroying its larvæ and depriving it of places in which to lay its eggs; but it was also Gorgas's duty, so far as it was possible, to control yellow-fever patients. And in this phase of his work he displayed the same kindliness and tact. Within the limitations already suggested, the physicians coöperated with Gorgas in reporting cases. Cubans, like most Latin peoples, have a horror of hospitals, and would have resented any effort of Gorgas to hustle sick members of the family to such an institution. When properly approached, however, they usually consented to the new method of isolation. This was to keep the patient in his home, completely screened; at the door of the house guards were stationed, prohibiting the entrance of all except authorized persons. Thus the mosquitoes in the house at the time of the infection, which were presumably responsible for the illness, could not get out and infect other victims, and the mosquitoes outside could not get in. At the end of the case the house was submitted to fumigation and careful collections made of all the dead mosquitoes.

The results of this work began to appear rather more rapidly than Gorgas and his co-workers had anticipated. The fact that the Stegomyia was a house mosquito enormously simplified his work. This fact was not known when the campaign began. At that time it was generally believed that this type of mosquito, like most others, was blown hither and yon by currents of air, and that the winds, carrying clouds of the pests from a distance, were likely to make ridiculous the Gorgas effort. It was supposed similarly that the Stegomyia had considerable wing capacity of its own and could fly long distances. It was therefore feared that great swarms would fly in from the outskirts to take the place of those destroyed. Both these expectations were groundless. The Stegomyia was exclusively a domestic pest, with an exceedingly narrow horizon of operations; it lived either in the house or in close proximity to it. Day by day, therefore, Gorgas's reports informed him that his favourite enemy was getting fewer. When the house of a yellow-fever patient had been fumigated and the dead mosquitoes counted, the corpses became less numerous in each succeeding case. The time came when only a dozen or a half dozen were recovered. This decrease in mosquitoes was accompanied by another decrease that was even more encouraging. Cases of yellow fever were diminishing at an even more rapid rate than dead mosquitoes. Those "curves," which the statisticians so love, brought out this relationship in the most emphatic fashion; any one who still nourished doubts as to the connection of mosquitoes and the disease had only to glance at one of these graphs; the evidence was conclusive. For the 140 years from

1762 to 1901 there had not been a day when yellow fever had not prevailed in Havana. Every year of that long period had had its record of deaths. For the ten years preceding the American occupation Yellow Jack had taken its toll of more than five hundred lives a year. In 1896 there had been 1,282 deaths; in 1900, the year preceding Gorgas's work, the deaths had been 310—and these represented merely the beginning of the outbreak which the Gorgas methods checked.

Gorgas began his work in March, 1901; the deaths subsequent to this were precisely five, and these took place in July and August of that year. In 1905, it is true, there was another outbreak, but it was promptly checked by the Gorgas methods. Since then eighteen years have passed, and not a single case of the disease has been reported in the city that for centuries had been its main headquarters. Dramatic as yellow fever has always been, there is nothing in its history so dramatic as its sudden cessation. It was like a sea that had been tossed with storms for a century and a half and then, seemingly without warning, became as quiet as a mill-pond. No wonder the whole scientific world was awed in the presence of this tremendous fact. It signified that the human mind had once more risen superior to Nature and had penetrated one of the secrets which she had cleverly hidden for ages. To

Gorgas especially the real solemnity of the achievement was especially impressive. To him the thing meant more than merely ridding a community of its most persistent scourge; it really opened a new outlook for man. From this date his life took on a new meaning—a definite meaning. What had been done in Cuba could be done in other disease-ridden countries; what had been accomplished with yellow fever could be accomplished with other similar plagues. At that time mighty areas of the earth's surface were inaccessible to man, chiefly because of contagious disease. Gorgas had demonstrated that this was not inevitable. The belief that men could not live prosperously and happily in the tropics was now shown to be a myth. The redemption of such territories, the abolition of the diseases that had barred them to civilization, now became Gorgas's life work. He was forty-eight years old, and, in prospect, he had added as much space to the earth's surface as Columbus himself.

Yet Gorgas never made any such claim as this. The destruction of mosquitoes was to occupy the rest of his life, but he never withheld the chief glory from the man to whom, he believed, it was due. From now on the guiding influence of his life was Walter Reed. The two men kept closely in touch with each other during the performance in Havana. Each at first had certain doubts to remove. Gorgas, when he began, was not certain that the mosquito was the only infective agent but his own success quickly demolished these doubts. Reed did not believe that yellow fever could be abolished by killing mosquitoes and their larvæ; but his skepticism also was just as rapidly removed. The letters that passed between the two men at this time display the confidence and enthusiasm they entertained for each other. "The news from Havana is simply delightful," writes Reed on July 29th. . . . "It shows that your acquaintance with the local conditions was much better than mine. That you have succeeded in throttling the epidemic appears beyond question and it is to your everlasting credit. A man of less discretion, enthusiasm, and energy would have made a fiasco of it. Whereas you, my dear Gorgas, availing yourself of the results of the work at Camp Lazear, have rid that pest hole, Havana, of her yellow plague. All honour to you, my dear boy!" "Really, my dear doctor," Reed wrote Gorgas in another letter, "when I think of the absence of yellow fever from Havana for a period of fifty days, I begin to feel like rejoicing that I was ever born!" And Gorgas was just as generous to Reed. "Certainly," he wrote Reed on August 26, 1901, "the work of proving the mosquito to be the transmitter of yellow fever is as important a piece of work as has been done since Jenner's time, and, as far as the United States is concerned, probably of more importance; and yours was the guiding hand in the whole matter. . . . I am very happy to serve in the more humble rôle of being the first to put your discovery to extensive, practical application."

Reed lived just long enough to witness the fruits and the possibilities of his great discovery; his labours in Havana had so weakened his frame that he died, from an operation for appendicitis, in 1902, in his fifty-first year. He had no sincerer mourner than Gorgas, who, for the rest of his life, never missed an opportunity to witness his debt to Reed. One day General M. Weaver was walking down Connecticut Avenue, Washington, with his little granddaughter. He met Gorgas, then at the height of his fame.

"Persis," said the general to the little girl, "this is General Gorgas, one of our great men."

"No, my child," said Gorgas, in his soft accents, "not a great man; merely one who is trying to follow in the footsteps of a great man—Walter Reed."

CHAPTER IV

THE BATTLE WITH THE JUNGLE

I

THE triumph of Havana came at a particularly fortunate time. It gave the answer to a riddle that had puzzled the world for several centuries. While Gorgas and his associates were industriously cleansing the Cuban capital, the mind of the American people had been much concerned with the Isthmus of Panama. The difficulties which for four hundred years had prevented the building of the Canal—difficulties diplomatic, engineering, financial, and political—had at last been cleared away. The genius of President Roosevelt had swept practically all of them aside. A special treaty with Great Britain had disposed of the British claim to be jointly associated with the United States in penetrating the Isthmus. The colossal failure of the French company had made it inevitable that the construction should be the work of American engineers. The creation of the Republic of Panama, its cession to the United States of a strip of land ten miles on each side of the proposed canal, had for ever removed the danger of diplomatic complications with South American states.

From the day when Balboa crossed the Isthmus and gazed on the Pacific, the linking of the two oceans had been one of the greatest dreams of civilization. The thing looked so simple! Two mighty seas separated by only forty miles of land! The practical consequences of success, its bearing upon commerce, upon warfare, upon the peaceful associations of many peoples, dazzled the imagination. Yet the greatest engineering brains of Europe—the same master minds that had built the Suez Canal—had spent more than twenty years in attempting to bring about "the marriage of the Atlantic and the Pacific," and had reaped only failure, shame, and death. Could America succeed where Europe had met only disaster? In 1901 it was apparent that America was at least prepared to challenge this great adventure. In the next two years the preparations were diligently pushed and by 1904 everything was ready to "make the dirt fly."

There was one man, however, who knew that American wealth, American engineering skill, and American energy would not in themselves accomplish this great programme. This was the quiet but far-seeing and determined army doctor who had recently done something at Havana that had a more important bearing upon the Canal than blue prints and bond issues. The Charges River and the Culebra Hill were formidable barriers to be overcome—yes; but a still greater one, in Gorgas's opinion, was the mosquito. The doctor's papers disclose the general failure at that time to grasp this great truth. We find his fellow Alabamian, Senator Morgan, the fanatical enemy of Panama and still more fanatical champion of Nicaragua, writing him about "miasmatic vapours" as breeders of tropical disease—a foretaste of the misunderstandings that proved such discouraging obstacles in the next few years. Gorgas, however, began to bring pressure to bear upon General Sternberg, Surgeon-General of the army, pointing out the importance of the new sanitation in building the Canal. "I invited General Sternberg's attention," wrote Gorgas afterward, "to the enormous loss of life that had been caused among the French working at Panama, due to tropical diseases; that by far the most important of the diseases were yellow fever and malaria; that if we could protect our labourers on the Canal as we had the people of Havana, we should be able to build the Canal without anything like such losses as had occurred to the French. I also invited his attention to the fact that while there was a considerable difference in the conditions and environment at Havana, still I believed that the methods worked out at Havana could be so modified as to be applied successfully at the Isthmus."

Gorgas called his chief's attention to the necessity of having some experienced sanitarian in charge of the work. "And I should like to be that man," he added.

Gorgas's fitness for this job, of course, was so apparent that his selection followed as a matter of course. He was summoned to Washington in 1902, his rank having been raised to colonel in recognition of his success at Havana. The next two years Gorgas spent familiarizing himself with the problems awaiting him on the Isthmus. A trip to Egypt, where he represented the army on an international medical congress, gave him the opportunity of studying the sanitary problems involved in constructing the Suez Canal, but this experience yielded few lessons of value. Digging a ditch through a hundred miles of level sand was, as De Lesseps discovered, quite a different undertaking from building a lock canal through tropical jungle and mountains; similarly the sanitation of Suez had presented no difficulties. The fellaheen who did the manual labour had not suffered from yellow fever or malaria, the two chief stumbling blocks to progress at Panama. Several months spent in Paris, mainly for the purpose of studying French experiences at Panama, proved hardly more fruitful. That the French had suffered frightfully from disease was a notorious fact, but the De Lesseps Company had carefully concealed all documentary evidence. The thing that had brought great odium upon the French company was the manner in which it had deceived its stockholders and the world; it had depended upon the money contributions of the French peasants for its working capital, and it had therefore painted its prospects in the rosiest light. A reading of the *Bulletin* in which the old Panama Company recorded its fictitious triumphs would never cause one to suspect that life at the Isthmus had been a constant and unavailing struggle against disease.

Soon after returning from Paris, however, Gorgas made a preliminary visit to Panama—this was in March, 1904—and he had been but a few hours on the Isthmus when the realities of his task were brought before him in painfully graphic fashion. The French, who were still in control, received him with great cordiality. One of his first invitations was for a dinner held in a rather ornate building which has always been known as the *Folie Dingler*. This was the house which had been built, in 1884, as the residence of Jules Dingler, the chief engineer of the French Panama Canal. The cost of this establishment, said to have been $150,000, has long been cited as an illustration of French extravagance. M. Dingler brought from France his wife, his son, his daughter, and the latter's fiancé. Before the house was finished all four had perished of yellow fever, and Dingler himself, returning to France a broken-hearted man, died there soon afterward. A few hours spent in the building associated with such memories naturally turned Gorgas's mind to the seriousness of the task in which he had engaged. It was a fitting beginning of his ten years' work.

For centuries, indeed, no single strip of land had borne such an evil fame as the Isthmus of Panama. In the olden days it had been the scene of unspeakable villainies: massacres, piracies, human slavery in its most brutal forms, rapacity, and ignorance had apparently selected this spot as their most cherished abode. In physical aspect Nature herself seemed to have set aside the Isthmus as the headquarters of the worst manifestations of the human spirit. The whole forty-mile stretch was one sweltering miasma of death and disease. "In all the world," wrote James Anthony Froude in 1885, "there is not perhaps now concentrated in any single spot so much swindling and villainy, so much foul disease, such a hideous dung heap of physical and moral abomination. The Isthmus is a damp, tropical jungle, intensely hot, swarming with mosquitoes, snakes, alligators, scorpions, and centipedes; the home, even as Nature made it, of yellow fever, typhus, and dysentery." At each end of this pestilential neck of land was a city: Colon on the Atlantic side and Panama on the Pacific. Though these places did not lack attractive and picturesque attributes, from a sanitary standpoint—without sewers or piped water, the living quarters of the masses being miserable thatched huts—they offered suitable termini for the dark and gloomy jungle that stretched between. This was little more than an apparently hopeless tangle of tropical vegetation, swamps whose bottoms the engineers had not discovered, black muddy soil, quicksands, intercepted now and then by a tall volcanic mountain or crossed by rivers that, at flood tide, sometimes rose twenty feet and more in a single night. This vegetation was an impenetrable mass of palm trees, banana plants, mangroves, creepers of all kinds, bamboo, cotton woods, and the whole was a never-ending panorama of animal life. Chattering monkeys, shrill parrots, and parrakeets, birds of the most variegated plumage filled the trees; wild turkeys, wild boars, and wild hogs swarmed the tall grass, and poisonous snakes, great lizards, tarantulas, and all manner of reptile and insect life covered the oozy ground. This terrible place was not lacking in beauty; all kinds of tropical flowers bloomed there eternally, and its orchids had led more than one venturesome collector to his doom. The intense thunder and lightning storms that frequently illuminated the darkness, the showers of rain that constantly swept down upon it—huge masses of water that for the time obliterated the landscape—also had their own element of grandeur. But the general impression was one of dank terror. Hardy indeed seem the engineers who could hope to introduce their steam shovels and dynamite drills into this mass of living and decaying vegetation. The stories left behind by the Americans who, soon after the California gold rush, had constructed the Panama railroad—their struggles with water and mud and with the jungle flora that grew almost as rapidly as it was cut down—offered little encouragement to their successors, who now projected an infinitely greater undertaking.

But the chief terror the Isthmus had always held was as the breeding place of all kinds of tropical disease, especially yellow fever and malaria. Its reputation as the stalking ground of death reached all quarters of the earth. Ship captains had the most explicit instructions for approaching Panama and ship passengers always displayed nervousness and fear as they sailed into the harbour of Colon. "There are two seasons at Panama"—this was the common saying: "first of all we have the wet season, lasting from about the 15th of April to the 15th of December, when people die of yellow fever in four or five days. Next we have the dry or healthful season, when people die of pernicious fever in from twenty-four to thirty-six hours." The records of all the consulates at Panama contain stories of the ravages of disease. "It is quite customary," one sardonic chronicler records, "for a new consul to send his predecessor home"—of course in a coffin. When De Lesseps first visited the place in 1881, he was met by a French resident, M. Le Blanc, who attempted to dissuade him from his enterprise. "If you try to build this canal," De Lesseps was told, "there will not be trees enough on the Isthmus to make crosses for the graves of your labourers." M. Bunau Varilla says that Frenchmen looked upon work at Panama in the same light as a call to military service—it was an adventure in which death was more likely than not to claim the volunteer. "Why, do you really wish to commit suicide?" his friends asked this hardy Frenchman when he accepted service on the canal. "To go there is to run to your death. For God's sake think again before you decide!" The actual experience showed that these forecasts were wisely made. "Death," he writes, "was constantly gathering its harvest about me." "Funeral trains," wrote a journalist in 1888, "are as much an institution as passenger or freight trains." This writer had chiefly in mind Monkey Hill, a burial place near Colon. "Since the advent of De Lesseps canal men on the 28th of February, 1881, thousands upon thousands have been buried there. During two seasons of epidemic it is said that the burials averaged from thirty to forty a day and that for weeks together." A not unusual sight during the French period was a ship riding at anchor in the harbour of Colon, with not a soul on board; every member of the crew had died of yellow fever. Bunau Varilla gives his recollection of twelve English sailors applying at the doctor's office for admission to the hospital at Ancon; eight days afterward every man was dead. He recalls also the terror with which the prospective employees left the ship at Colon. "They felt their hearts sink at the sight of the warm, low, and misty shores of the deadly Isthmus." He took the names of a particular group to see how long they would stand the strain. "Without exception they were dead within three months, if they had not fled from the Isthmus." Yellow fever assailed not only the labourers, but the highest officials of the Company; Bunau Varilla himself suffered a severe attack but recovered. He tells of two engineers, chiefs of division, who arrived in October, 1885. "In a few months the same hearse had carried them both to their resting place."

The story of Henri Bionne and his dinner has all the gruesomeness of one of Poe's tales. It is well told by M. Cermoise in his book, "Deux ans à Panama."

"The guests had assembled and were waiting to sit down when M. Bionne should arrive. Suddenly a lady present, who had been looking at the table with particular attention, cried out in great agitation: 'We are thirteen at table!'

"At this moment M. Bionne arrived. He heard her exclamation. 'Be assured, madam,' said he gaily, 'in such a case it is the last to arrive who pays for all,' and he sat down not in the least disturbed by this sinister portent.

"Never was there so gay, so lively a meal. M. Bionne was at his best, a delightful and witty conversationalist. He drank to our success on the Isthmus; we drank to his good luck, for in fifteen days he was to take the steamer and return to Europe.

"Fifteen days later he sailed from Colon. At the end of forty-eight hours he was taken with yellow fever and died in a few days. The body was thrown into the Gulf of Mexico. He had not long delayed the payment of his debt! . . .

"Blasert also left the camp. His wife wished to return to Europe with her children. He accompanied them to Colon, put them on board a steamer, and returned to Panama that same evening.

"What could have affected him? Was it the result of the sudden change from life in the open air to that in town? At all events, the day after his return he took to his bed with yellow fever.

"And he had crossed the Far West and believed himself invulnerable. Certainly his moral character was above reproach. Alas! Nothing, neither strict morality nor crossing the Far West, renders one invulnerable to yellow fever. Some days later the unfortunate man died like a new arrival from Europe.

"He had also taken part in M. Bionne's dinner. . . .

"After M. Bionne, Blasert; after Blasert, M. Blanchet continued the black series. He had just made an expedition on horseback into the interior of the Isthmus, during which he had endured great fatigue. On his return the yellow fever declared itself, he took to his bed, and died in three days."

What were the total losses from disease under the French company? As already said, these facts will never be known. Yet that they were in themselves sufficient to explain the French failure is apparent. A Canadian journalist, writing in 1888, declared that there were 654 deaths in the month of October, 1884. According to M. Bunau Varilla, "the isthmian Minotaur," as he called yellow fever, killed twenty out of every eighty employees. The only reason the mortality was not higher was that a considerable portion fled as soon as they realized the dangerous task they had engaged in; thus yellow fever weakened French efficiency in two ways—in men actually slain, and in the fact that it drove the employees from Panama and spread the deadly reputation of the place so widely that there was the greatest difficulty in obtaining recruits. Gorgas himself, from such data as he could obtain, figured that the French had lost about one-third of all their white employees—a total, in eight years, of 20,000 lives. Had the sickness rate of the French prevailed when the Americans were at work, we should have had about 13,000 men constantly in the hospital, and, had their death rate prevailed, we should have lost not far from 3,500 men a year. As we were ten years in building the Canal this would have meant the sacrifice of 35,000 lives. This is only another way of saying that the Canal could never have been constructed. The humane sentiments of the American people would never have tolerated such slaughter, even though foreign nations had permitted the activities of our agents in recruiting labourers. This, then, was the problem that the Americans were facing in 1904—a problem far more serious than the engineering difficulties, great as these were, and exclusively as they seemed to occupy the American mind at that time.

Yet it was not strange that this fact was so imperfectly grasped. A less experienced man than Gorgas would have thought, in 1904, that all these stories were the wildest imaginings. When Gorgas made his preliminary inspection, in March of this year, there were no signs of yellow fever. The Isthmus was as apparently free from its most persistent scourge as New York or Washington. But

Gorgas was not led astray by such deceptive appearances. The disease was simply behaving in its accustomed manner. The population of Panama at that time consisted almost exclusively of its own peoples; there were practically no strangers in the Zone. And yellow fever, as already explained, is a disease that feeds exclusively upon strangers; the adult native population is invariably immune. There are two reasons why this neck of land had been its favourite hunting ground for more than four centuries. The first is that the Isthmus is a tropical country; the temperature is thus continuously high; the Stegomyia mosquito can live in perfect health twelve months in the year and perform its normal function of harbouring the yellow-fever germ. Once yellow fever is introduced in such a hot climate it never disappears; it may lie dormant, practically unnoticed, only now and then seizing an unwary victim, but it continues to perpetuate its kind. In the method already described the native population ultimately becomes immune; it is only when unaccustomed strangers arrive that the disease breaks out in all its fury. Those places in tropical America in which visitors are most frequent are therefore the ones that suffer most. Thus the climate and the geography of Panama had for centuries made it the headquarters of the disease. As the narrowest piece of land between the Atlantic and the Pacific it had for four hundred years been the passageway most travelled by strangers. In the days of Spanish preëminence and prosperity, the treasure ships from the whole western coast of South America had poured into the city of Panama as into a funnel; at this point the cargoes were loaded on mules and carted across the Isthmus, whence they were transshipped to Spain. These caravans always yielded large sacrifices to yellow fever. In those days it was the expectation that a considerable proportion of the ship's crew would die on the voyage home. Subsequently the great epidemics took place whenever the Isthmus was crowded with strangers. Thousands of Americans, in the California gold rush, found their way to the western coast by way of the Isthmus of Panama; and thousands left their bones whitening in the jungle. The building of the Panama Railroad in 1855 witnessed a terrible struggle with disease, and the calamities that overwhelmed the Chinese workmen have long been a familiar story.

Thus the fact that there was no visible yellow fever in 1904 did not deceive Gorgas. The prairie fire that had vanquished the French had exhausted its human material, yet its sparks lay smouldering, waiting to spring at the first shipload of Americans. That American engineering genius could construct the canal there was no question. But would it ever really have the chance to do so? That depended upon Gorgas and his little band of eager sanitarians.

II

Yet there was nothing to suggest the Spanish conquerors in the modest little group that debarked from the *Aliança* one day in June, 1904. There were only a few—Gorgas, Mr. Joseph L. Le Prince, Dr. Carter, Dr. Ross, Dr. Louis Balch, Dr. Louis A. La Garde, Major James Turtle, and Miss Hibbard, head nurse. Even Gorgas was sombrely dressed in civilian clothes, and the others hardly embodied the spirit of adventure. The truth of the matter is that they were rather a forlorn group. No one had much interest in them. No one took them very seriously. No one had given them the slightest assistance or encouragement in their work. The American Medical Association had attempted to obtain for Gorgas an appointment on the Canal Commission, taking the stand that sanitation was the part of the work at that time most essential. The suggestion had not aroused the slightest response. Gorgas had not even been able to obtain the most necessary supplies; things so indispensable as wire screening and disinfectants had been denied him and subordinates—inspectors and the like—had been assigned in most meagre degree. On the way down Gorgas had done his best to fill his associates with a little cheerfulness and enthusiasm. "I take it for granted," he would say, "that we shall eliminate yellow fever." Whether Gorgas really felt the optimism he did his best to spread is not clear; what is apparent is that there was not much excuse for it. It is hardly an exaggeration to say that these five men, when they landed at Panama to engage in the mighty task of ridding this jungle of disease, had little more than their own hands and their own determined spirit to work with. The American Government had plunged into the task with the same jaunty and ignorant cheerfulness that had marked its French predecessors. It had failed just as completely as the French to recognize that disease was the most formidable obstacle in its path. A more shocking instance of the inability to profit from the mistakes of others is hardly recorded in history.

For the first few months events moved with the most discouraging slowness. During this critical period the entire sanitary squad consisted merely of the small group named. It was an army excellently officered, but practically without privates. Gorgas's repeated requests for men were answered, when they were answered at all, by the injunction: "Oh, get a few niggers." That the work of the Sanitary Department demanded, first of all, men of character and intelligence and industry, apparently did not impress the official mind. When Gorgas cabled to Washington for coöperation, the only reply received was a tart reminder that cabling was expensive and to use the mails in future. The situation became so desperate that in the autumn Gorgas returned to Washington to make a final attempt to arouse interest in high quarters. The future seemed so doubtful that his friends urged him not to return; it was absurd to suppose that anything could be accomplished in the face of all this ignorance and obstruction. How could a handful of scientific enthusiasts, with almost no official backing, without a sanitary force, and with little money to spend, ever hope to prepare the Panama wilderness for the operations of white men? Gorgas himself was tempted to drop the whole thing and return to his regular work in the army. That persistence which had always been his chief asset, however, still forced him to the task. After spending a few weeks in the United States, therefore, he sailed once more for Panama. This time his wife accompanied him, and her recollections of the cheerless first few days in the unaccustomed scene may be given in her own words:

"I was immune to yellow fever, but sanitary conditions on the Isthmus were so bad that women were discouraged from going down, and when we arrived I was, I think, the first woman of the American Canal Colony, with the exception of the nurses.

"We disembarked at water-drenched Colon. The

streets, unspeakably dirty and mud-filled, swarmed with naked children; the ugly frame houses rested on piles, under which greenish slimy water formed lagoons. Such dilapidation and desolation! The only redeeming feature was the beauty of the foliage. The graceful, feathery coconut palm, dotting the landscape, gave the Isthmus the name of the Land of the Coconut Palm. Crossing the Isthmus took two hours. The dense jungle foliage swept the sides of our car. The train was comfortable, the roadbed smooth, and the beauty of valley and mountain did much to lighten the depression caused by the squalor and ugliness of Colon.

"At the Panama station Robert, the *cochero*, met us with a comfortable victoria, and we were driven through a sea of mud reaching at times almost to the hub, on through the upper part of the town to the entrance of Ancon Hospital. Here the road was good, and the little pony struggled valiantly to take us up the long steep hill to the ward where Dr. Gorgas and Dr. Carter had quarters on the second floor. The grounds resembled a beautiful park; and the various wards, well built and artistically placed by the French here and there along the hillside, looked most peaceful. The Sisters of Charity added to the quiet restfulness of the scene. They wore the dark-blue gowns of the order of St. Vincent de Paul, topped by the becoming white headdress known as the cornet.

"When we arrived at Ward Eleven, Dr. Carter was on hand to greet us, with a number of boys to help with the valises. A flight of stairs led to the gallery of the second floor. Although it was only a little after five o'clock, the short twilight gave a sombre though refreshingly cool aspect. My spirits rose. On the right, facing the stairs, was the large living room, comfortably furnished by the Commission with wicker chairs and small tables—a room of many windows. Following the gallery to the right was a bedroom running across the back porch, divided by a partition extending halfway to the ceiling, more like a screen than a dividing wall. Two small rooms across the back porch were fitted up as bath and servants' rooms. There was no running water, and, as I found out afterward, water was exceedingly scarce, being delivered daily in small quantities.

"With the amount of water available we freshened up a bit and went downstairs to dinner at the mess, an appetizing meal served Spanish style in a room lighted by lamps and candles. This large room had been screened and so was free from insects. After dinner Dr. Carter, Dr. Ross, Dr. Perry, Dr. Herrick, and a few other friends, members of the hospital staff, sat with us for a while on the upper gallery of our quarters—the St. Charles, the old officers' ward, where so many young, enthusiastic Frenchmen had succumbed to yellow fever. More yellow-fever cases and deaths occurred in this ward than in any other building on the Isthmus during the time of the French occupation.

"There is an alluring something about a night in the tropics. Dr. Gorgas experienced a melancholy pleasure listening to the sighing of the royal palms in the gentle breeze, in imagination visioning through the haze of his cigar the ghosts that haunted the old building. The history of the region always exercised a powerful spell upon his mind. He fairly rejoiced in the tales of Morgan, Pizarro, Pedrarias, and other illustrious scoundrels who had left plentiful and gory memories in every nook and cranny of that coast. I have sometimes thought that the charm of these old stories fascinated him as much as did the specific pursuits which had drawn him to the place. Years afterward, when he came to write a book on the Sanitation of the Canal, the Doctor would frequently wander from his subject and devote page after page to rehearsing the deeds of the old Panama pirates. In a way he really admired these ferocious dare-devils, and he would relate their crimes with a genuine schoolboy zest. I still recall him, on this first night at Panama, telling of their battles and lootings and massacres. 'I should like to have lived in those days,' said this mildest of all men.

"It was a beautiful and starry evening. Beyond stretched the great Pacific, the dotted islands in the distance dimly seen in the misty moonlight, every place teeming with the history of departed glory and vast enterprise. It was not only the past that was full of depressing scenes. The old, inevitable tragedy of Panama was even then being enacted below us. Fifty yards down the hill were the yellow-fever wards, where three poor fellows, a French Catholic priest and two Italian boys, were getting ready for the great journey. For four hundred years this had been a commonplace in that infested area. Naturally the question came to us, as we sat there talking over the past, whether the efforts of our little band could change the Isthmus in this respect.

"Early hours were the rule during all the years of the construction, and by nine o'clock everyone had gone to bed. Dr. Gorgas tucked the mosquito bar carefully about me, and I had reason to be thankful for this attention during the night when I heard the strange creeping noises on the roof and on the floor. Rats, buzzards roosting on the roof, bats and other creatures held high carnival to the none-too-soft accompaniment of the chorus of omnivorous and defiant mosquitoes.

"We were ready for breakfast at six the next morning. This meal, served on the front porch upstairs, consisted of fruit—oranges and papaya—a strong coffee, and Spanish bread, which is always good. No butter was served. We were on a high point, with only the road separating our ward from the sheer descent to the valley below, a descent so steep that a retaining wall had been built as a protection. The road was bordered by a row of stately royal palms, planted by the French some fifteen years before. Beyond a stretch of green valley the hills and mountains were seen emerging from the heavy mist which often envelops them by night. The sun was rising from the Pacific, a strange phenomenon, and the rays gave a jewelled appearance to the dew-soaked plants and the leaves of the trees. While we sat there, Dr. Gorgas still telling me tales of old Panama and the buccaneers, I heard someone coming up the stairs behind us, and a moment later a soft voice said in musical Spanish:

"'*Buenos días, Señora.*'

"Turning quickly I saw for the first time the little Tranquilina, who came to offer her services as *criada*, or maid-of-all-work. Tranquilina! What memories tender and sweet the name recalls! Very small she was, and frail-looking, indeed quite lame, but so agile in her movements that the realization of her lameness only came to us later. Just back of her stood a tall, slender, black-gowned woman, the head and shoulders enveloped Spanish style in the black manta. She was Tranquilina's mother, and her name, she said, was Remigia.

"Tranquilina, I must confess, did not impress me

favourably in the light of a maid. She looked like a pretty tropic bird, with her thin white gown quite rounded out in the neck, made with elbow sleeves, a red ribbon about her waist, her very small feet, minus stockings, encased in red satin slippers without heels, Panama style. In her dark hair, simply dressed, was a single flower. The soft penetrating voice, the smallness of her figure, and the appeal of her dark eyes fascinated me. But I needed a good ordinary housemaid—someone who could work in that warm climate and keep the apartment in order. In broken Spanish I voiced my doubts of her ability to fill the position. Tranquilina and her mother both assured me that she could easily do the work. In the end it was agreed that she was to stay until I could find someone else. The next day Tranquilina came with her parrot and several parakeets, took possession of the apartment and us, and remained ten years—the entire time we lived on the Isthmus. She was an excellent cook and waitress, and had unusual executive ability.

"As the days passed the spell of the Isthmus gripped us. We felt ourselves living links in the long chain of events marking its history. We had our place in the vast throng which for centuries had passed across that pivotal strip. A responsive chord was struck with the realization that we, too, were making history, a vital phase of it, in the digging of the great waterway that was to change the map of the world. Whatever the trials and hardships to be endured, the mental and physical strain, one could but feel it a privilege to be a part of that mighty enterprise. To visualize the great waterway finished thrilled the imagination.

"The city of Panama lay tantalizingly near, but trips thither except of necessity were discouraged by the sanitary authorities. From our high point at Ancon the pastel shades of the Spanish tiled roofs were easily discernible; also the animation and movement of the streets. One heard the shrill cries of vendors and the tumult of the town—the whole arousing curiosity and inviting exploration of the narrow streets, the churches, cathedrals, and *casas de empeño*, where one might pick up quaint pieces of jewellery and odd-shaped old hand-beaten silver. However, the rainy season was on, the streets were almost impassable, and this lessened the hardship of submitting to the decrees of the authorities. I was content to confine walks and explorations to Ancon Hill, in company with Laura Carter, who came down with her mother and brother. On these walks we frequently met doctors hurrying to the different wards, members of our American nursing force, and occasionally one or two of the Catholic sisters, who had been asked by our Government to remain to assist in the nursing."

CHAPTER V

YELLOW FEVER DESCENDS ON PANAMA

I

THE difficulties in these early days were caused chiefly by the fact that the work of Walter Reed and Gorgas at Havana had apparently made little impression upon the official mind. By the time the Panama work began any doubt that may have prevailed in scientific circles had completely disappeared. Laboratory workers and sanitarians in several parts of the world had repeated the experiments and found them flawless. Oswaldo Cruz had applied the Gorgas methods in Rio de Janeiro, with the result that yellow fever for the first time in centuries had disappeared from that city—never to return. A scientific congress held in Paris in 1903 had thoroughly canvassed Reed's work, and had officially recorded its verdict that the mosquito transmission of the disease was a scientifically determined fact. Yet this truth, indispensable as it was to the building of the Canal, had not penetrated the one group that should have been the first to grasp it—the commission entrusted with the work. The head of that commission was

John G. Walker, an Admiral of the American Navy. Admiral Walker's very appearance—his erect figure, his be-whiskered face, his air of command—fairly suggested the past generation to which he belonged. As an engineer and as an expert on canals Admiral Walker had gained a certain eminence; as the negotiator of the purchase of the French company he had performed a great public service. As an actual canal digger, however, his labours were not especially to the point. The Admiral's usefulness was limited by certain mental prepossessions. He had studied long the history of the French company, and, honest man that he was, he had been horrified by the tale of graft and deceit which it disclosed. He was convinced that this dishonesty in itself explained the failure of the French enterprise. The fear that something like French wastefulness and peculation would stain the American achievement haunted him day and night. So insistent was this apprehension that it really determined his whole policy.

"When this thing is finished," he would say, "I intend that those fellows on the hill shall not find that a single dollar has been misspent."

Economy, rather than construction, therefore became his byword. Any suggestion for a departmental appropriation he would suspiciously scrutinize and his greatest joy was that of cutting these allowances down to the lowest point. "Requisitions" became the horror of his existence. When Admiral Walker was removed from office, his successor found a large receptacle full of unopened letters; these were "requisitions" for supplies and essential materials forwarded by the canal force. The Admiral had such an aversion to spending money, even when needed for indispensable work, that at times he would not even open communications. At other times he would thrust them into his pockets. A familiar sight in Washington—for Admiral Walker made the mistake of attempting to construct the Canal from the national capital, paying only one or two visits to the Isthmus—was that of the chairman of the Panama Commission, with his overcoat and other garments bulging with documents pertaining to this great task—papers which, there was good reason to suppose, were frequently lost, thrown loosely into various corners of his office, and only on rare occasions opened and acted on.

This was discouraging enough, but there were even worse irritations. Admiral Walker had taken pains to become acquainted with Reed's work and the part played by the Stegomyia mosquito in transmitting yellow fever. As a result he had reached a definite conviction: this was that the whole idea was the veriest balderdash. And in his gruff and uncompromising naval way he did not hesitate to air his views. Admiral Walker was not famous for a keen sense of humour, but the idea that there was anything dangerous in the bite of a mosquito stirred him to uncontrollable mirth. To spend good American dollars on a group of insane enthusiasts who spent all their time chasing mosquitoes through the Panama jungle seemed to him an extreme form of official folly. The French in their wildest moments had never done anything so bad as that! On his trip to Washington in the early fall of 1904, Gorgas spent a considerable part of his time haunting Admiral Walker's office. He would talk for hours explaining the part played by mosquitoes in yellow fever and in malaria, and tell over and over again the story of Havana and Rio de Janeiro. His visits were long pleadings for sulphur, pyrethrum powder, wire screening, crude oil, inspectors—all the things and persons needed in fighting the disease. But his expostulations and his prayers had no effect. The Admiral flatly informed Gorgas that he was wrong. Everybody knew, he asserted, what caused yellow fever—and it was not the mosquito. It was filth. The thing to do in Panama and Colon and other towns was to clean things. These ports were reeking with unspeakable smells; get rid of them, declared the Admiral, and there would be no more disease. Clean the streets, remove the dead cats, whitewash the houses, and yellow fever would vanish as if by magic. Admiral Walker even proposed to draw up a set of regulations for doing this; let Gorgas limit his activities to following these rules! In vain did the Doctor tell how he had scoured and scrubbed Havana and made it almost the cleanest city on the continent—only to have yellow fever break out more furiously than ever. A dead horse festering in the streets of Colon was not so dangerous to human life, he declared, as a single Stegomyia mosquito! At this Admiral Walker would give an uproarious laugh, and stick Gorgas's requisition into his already well-filled pigeonhole.

Gorgas had no better success with General George W. Davis, the first Governor of the Canal Zone. Again he had to deal with an engineer of high standing—the man who had finished the Washington Monument—but likewise a man who had the outlook of another generation. General Davis's attitude toward Gorgas, however, was not severe or intolerant; it was kindly, benevolent, the pose of an older man who wished to keep an enthusiast out of trouble. "What's that got to do with digging the Canal?" he would ask, when Gorgas began talking in his favourite strain. "A dollar spent on sanitation is like throwing it into the bay," was another one of his aphorisms. Like most of the Commission, General Davis regarded the mosquito notion as beyond the pale. "I'm your friend, Gorgas," he would say pityingly, "and I'm trying to set you right. On the mosquito you are simply wild. All who agree with you are wild. Get the idea out of your head. Yellow fever, as we all know, is caused by filth."

Though these men had no fear of the mosquito they did have the most wholesome fear of the malady itself. That is the reason why the members of the Commission spent most of their time in Washington. They did make one or two trips to the Isthmus, it is true, but on these occasions they always took what they regarded as adequate safeguards against infection. Gorgas's sense of humour occasionally had a sardonic aspect, and these efforts to avoid contamination always aroused a certain amusement. The commissioners, for example, spent as little time as possible on dry land; they pitched their living quarters on a boat in Colon harbour—apparently forgetting that ships have always been favourite breeding places for yellow fever. In the morning, after a good night's sleep, they would come ashore, get gingerly on a train, and be whisked rapidly through the jungle to Panama; their business transacted, they would be hurried back to Colon and to shipboard—Gorgas and the members of his squad always amused spectators of these precautions. In the matter of supplies for the Sanitary Department the Commission was niggardly enough, but in one form of supply they were liberality itself. They recognized the pressing need of coffins: one of the most distinguished members brought down his own—it was well to be prepared in all things, especially for a contingency which was regarded as extremely likely in that climate. One of the sights that frequently greeted prospective employees, as they landed at Colon, was a pile of coffins on the dock. In this official forehandedness Gorgas and his associates also discerned a certain grim humour. The Doctor never tired of telling the story of how Major La Garde, one of his most faithful co-workers, amused himself at the expense of one of the commissioners—one, it happened, who seemed especially concerned about his own skin. The Major was superintending the job of unloading a cargo of coffins which had just arrived. A heap of matter-of-fact pine cases, evidently intended for victims of unimportant official and social rank, stood at one end of the dock. All by themselves, however, in exclusive grandeur, were six metallic coffins, in every way fit to hold the remains of gentlemen of more exalted breed.

This particularly pompous commissioner passed the dock as this ominous freight was being unloaded. He glanced at the six expensive containers, and looked enquiringly at Major La Garde. The Panama Commission comprised seven men, but it so happened that only six of them were visiting the Isthmus on that particular trip.

"Major," he asked, "why do you have six caskets of so much better quality than the ordinary coffin?"

Major La Garde received the inquiry with the utmost seriousness.

"Mr. Burr didn't come down, you know," he answered.

And he continued industriously unloading the emergency freight, while the commissioner went pensively on his way.

"I think he took to his bed at once," said Gorgas, telling this story.

But Charles E. Magoon, the second Governor of the Zone, had a liking for a laugh, even when it was turned against himself, and he had his own particular anecdote which he frequently related with relish. Unlike the Commission, Governor Magoon spent all his time on the Isthmus. He also had a common experience—that of the preliminary chill, fancied and real, that precedes the onset of yellow fever. One day, feeling this cold sensation creeping down his spine, he went over to consult this same Major La Garde. The latter—who was, of course, a physician—took his pulse and temperature and was sincerely apprehensive. He insisted that General Magoon should go to bed. Evening was approaching and the sun was sinking in the west. Panama was full of stories of men who, like Governor Magoon, had experienced this chill, had gone to bed, and then had never seen daylight again. The Governor was of a sentimental turn, he believed his last hour had come, but, before wrapping his burial draperies about him, he thought he would take his last look at the sun, the trees, the blue ocean, and everything else that made life so dear to him. So he went to the window and glanced out. The only thing his eyes lighted on was a hearse standing silently in front of his house. Convinced that Major La Garde expected his case to be rapid and fatal—one of the kind that end in a few hours—and that he had, with characteristic foresight, prepared for the inevitable, Governor Magoon gave a groan and went to bed. But he woke up the next morning well and refreshed and angrily made his way to the Major for an explanation. The fact was that the morgue stood opposite the Governor's house and this hearse had been stationed in front of it for a poor workman who had just died.

II

Thus yellow fever so completely filled the atmosphere in those early days that it provided even the humour of existence. But life, after all, was not particularly amusing. All the time an impending horror hung over Gorgas's head. He knew what fate lay immediately ahead of Panama. As soon as the first working forces stepped ashore Gorgas's apprehensions increased threefold. The steam-shovel men and their overseers could not dig the canal from swivel chairs in Washington—and they were a miscellaneous lot. All nationalities and all colours—and all shades of colour—were represented. "Tropical tramps" they were sometimes called; adventurers, filibusters—Americans, Europeans, Asiatics, Negroes from the Spanish and French West Indies, Jamaicans, Gallegos from Spain, Latins from every South American country. They were a daredevil crowd, and the consciousness of the horrors that threatened had the effect of encouraging, rather than of discouraging, their natural tendencies to riotous behaviour. Every railroad tie in the Panama line, they had been told, marked the death of a Chinaman who had lost his life building it—a grotesque legend which still survives. The engineering and the office forces were for the most part American—fine and upstanding young men who had been led to the Isthmus, not by love of profit, but by the scent of adventure and the impulse of high duty, and a desire to play their part in the greatest physical undertaking of the ages. As each ship dumped its human cargo at Colon, Gorgas renewed his efforts with a stupid officialdom. His position at that time was an exceedingly uncomfortable one. He knew that yellow fever was coming—that with the arrival of this great body of non-immunes it was inevitable—but he was almost powerless to prevent it. He could not stop it with his own bare hands—and this was almost all that had been left him. Outwardly his air was serene and optimistic; to most he gave no signs of the anxiety that was consuming him.

"It will come out all right," he would say. "We've got to work and show them." To his intimates, however, he would occasionally unburden himself. "If we could only convince them. If they only knew!" he would sometimes exclaim, almost in despair. To those who knew him well, there was one unmistakable sign when Gorgas was worried: he would go about his work softly whistling. And to his wife and to his closest friends this low whistle now became a familiar sound. That all the blame for the outbreak of disease would be charged to his negligence he well knew, but this was not the consideration that burdened all his waking hours. Inevitably would Gorgas compare his experience in Panama with that in Cuba. In Havana General Wood, the Governor, entered heartily into Gorgas's plans; being himself a physician, as well as a supreme administrator, he quickly grasped the significance of the Reed experiments, and put back of Gorgas all the wealth and influence of the American Government. But there was no Wood in charge of affairs at Panama! The presiding genius was "the old man of the sea," as, in his letters to his friends, Gorgas sometimes called Admiral Walker.

One illustration of his difficulties will suffice. The American executive forces had their headquarters in the Administration building of the French company in the City of Panama. There were more than three hundred non-immunes, for the most part young Americans. Gorgas's first glance into this building convinced him that it was one of the most dangerous spots on the Isthmus. Yet his superiors opened their eyes with wonder when he pointed out the danger spots. Gorgas's apparent indifference to the smells and filth of Panama and Colon was still a cause of constant irritation. The Doctor was not opposed to cleaning up these places; he simply knew that there was more pressing work to be done. In the Administration building he now pointed an accusing finger at certain water-holding receptacles—utensils in which the brushes used for copying letters were kept moist. There, he said—much to the astonishment of the clerks as well as Governor Davis—was the enemy! Their astonishment was not unlike that of the President of Panama, Señor Amador, when his attention was called to a large flower vase, full of water, in the reception room of the Presidential palace. Nothing was so dangerous to human life, this visionary American proclaimed, as a glass of clear clean water left around where the Stegomyia could deposit its eggs; all the smells of a thousand years were not so menacing as that! This was the trouble now with the Administration building. Mosquitoes were slyly creeping in through cracks in the doors and holes in the rotten screens, all searching for these pools of water without which they could not perpetuate their kind, and finding them in these little glass receptacles. The one pressing need was that the building be completely screened. Mr. Le Prince, the Chief Sanitary Inspector, made it his particular duty to get this done. The responsible official was a young American architect, who was more interested in constructing living quarters for the labourers than in protecting the windows and doors of this building. Day after day Mr. Le Prince would press the matter upon him, only to be rebuffed. This architect, like most American officials, regarded the Sanitary Department as fairly insane on the matter of mosquitoes.

"Oh, Le Prince," he would say, "you're off in the upper story."

"Supposing we have twenty deaths here," said Mr. Le Prince, "who will be responsible?"

"I'll stand the responsibility," the architect gaily replied.

A month after this conversation this scornful young gentleman was dead. Yellow fever had broken out in his own office and he was the first victim. An infected mosquito had found its way through one of those windows that he had refused to screen—with the usual result.

It was in November that the blow fell. There

had been one or two cases of the disease in the preceding months, but no large outbreak. Several members of an Italian opera troupe playing in Panama fell ill, and two died. From now on cases began breaking out in Panama, Colon, and the villages along the line—a few this week, and a few more next, until, by the early part of the year, everyone knew that a fair-sized epidemic was under way. And the scenes that had accompanied epidemics for hundreds of years were also enacted. The rush to get away soon assumed the proportions of a panic. The canal force, labourers, engineers, office men, seemed to be possessed of one single view—to start for home. "Oh, let's get out of this hell hole" was the almost universal sentiment. Men arriving on one day would take their departure the next—frequently in the same boat. When twenty-two cases broke out in the Administration building, and when several American officials died at Ancon Hospital, the desire to get away became almost a frenzy.

One of the most regrettable incidents in the history of the Canal now followed. In March Mr. John F. Wallace, the chief engineer, intimated to Mr. Taft, then Secretary of War, his intention of resigning, Just why Mr. Wallace wished to leave has never been explained. That he lived in dread of yellow fever was no secret. That he even believed that he had had a touch of the disease was also well known. He was one of the officials who had taken the precaution of bringing his coffin with him. Under these circumstances it is perhaps not strange that Washington officialdom should have put an unpleasant interpretation upon his expressed intention of retiring. Secretary Taft demanded his immediate resignation, and an immense amount of newspaper notoriety ensued. The effect upon the workers at the Isthmus was deplorable. It seemed to inspire the labouring and the executive forces with one ambition: a determination to scuttle. There was only one reason why they did not get away en masse, and that was the lack of shipping space to carry them. There was only one place to which they could flee and that was the jungle. Inevitably the nightmare that now arose in everybody's mind was the story of the French. That the old days of the De Lesseps Company had returned was the general fear and conviction. The shadow of Monkey Hill, where so many thousand brave French workmen lay sleeping, darkened the whole Isthmus. The alarm reached the United States and spread rapidly. Newspaper accounts, greatly exaggerating a situation sufficiently serious, were published in every state. The politicians and editors who had denounced the Panama route as an impossible one regarded the epidemic as a vindication. Senator Morgan of Alabama, who had recently written Gorgas that the Canal could never be built, found his gloomiest warnings approaching realization. In fact, these prophets of evil were not so far astray. The situation was indeed a critical one. At that moment the American adventure was tottering on precisely the same brink that had destroyed the French. The real meaning of this epidemic was that the United States could not build the Canal. That we could have got men to go to the Isthmus is not impossible, for Americans are venturesome and will dare any peril, but it is certain that their final destination would have been the gruesome cemeteries of Panama. The fate of the whole performance in the early part of 1905 lay in the hands of one man. Could Gorgas destroy yellow fever?

He started to work with his usual energy. Gorgas had learned much since his Havana experience. He had fought the fever in Havana in two ways. He had diligently screened every patient reported ill and he had made warfare upon the infecting mosquito. Which method had proved the more successful? On that point Gorgas now entertained no doubt. The mosquito itself—there was the foe! The Havana experience had taught Gorgas and his associates that any attempt to isolate yellow-fever patients and protect them from mosquitoes was not only difficult, but impossible. Less than one eighth of the cases, he estimated, were called to the attention of the physician or the sanitary authorities. The only practical method of campaign, therefore, was what Gorgas called a "flank attack"—the warfare on the insect. But even this attempt at extermination was subtle and indirect. Never had mankind witnessed such a strange method of procedure. Never had a sanitary force before directed its hostile efforts on so apparently harmless an enemy as clean, clear standing water. Probably most of the uninitiated, even those of the medical profession, would have regarded sweet water—so the Panamans called it—as beneficial to public health rather than a terrible public menace. Marshy water, dirty water, stagnant water, might be a public evil—yes; but how could one so accuse the fresh and invigorating rain that had just fallen from the heavens?

A century ago, Philadelphia, New York, Boston, and other Northern cities were subject to violent visitations from this disease. Yellow fever had vanished from such places, however, decades before Gorgas had shown the way to its extermination; some strange unknown means of banishing the disease had evidently been found. What was the explanation? Probably most observers would say that improved sanitation had accomplished this miracle. Not at all. A change in the system of water supply was solely responsible. In the old yellow-fever days, Philadelphia and New York had drawn their water supply chiefly from rainwater, cisterns and wells. But the simple process of putting pipes underground, drawing water from a remote region, and introducing taps in houses, had deprived the yellow-fever mosquito of its indispensable breeding places. Panama and Colon, the two cities with which Gorgas now had to deal, derived their water supply in a way that made them ideal nesting places of the mosquitoes. Neither city at that time had a foot of piped water. Both drew this essential substance from the free and open air of heaven. Rain was not an infrequent gift in this region. It fell constantly upon the roofs of Panama and Colon; thence it found its way into eave troughs, and thence into tin pipes and great barrels. Whenever the Panaman housewife needed water, she dipped it out of these latter receptacles and carried it indoors. Inside the house it stood freely exposed in a multitude of utensils. Water pitchers, jars, tinajas were constantly standing in all conceivable places; all water for drinking, washing, cooking, and other purposes, was thus kept constantly on hand, its surface exposed to the open daylight. Such surfaces offered a paradise to the yellow-fever mosquito. The female of this species, looking for the one inevitable place for the rearing of her young, would light upon one of these hospitable watery areas, deposit her eggs, and then fly away contented. The tin gutters in the roof also developed their uses for the same great biological end.

In the clear, rational mind of Gorgas, the elimination of these receptacles meant the elimination of yellow fever. Only in this way could the yellow-fever mosquito be destroyed in sufficient quantities to prevent the spread of the disease. The little epidemic on the cruiser *Boston* pointed the lesson. The officers on this ship gave a little party on New Year's Eve, 1904–05. They did not know it at the time, but the guests included a "walking case" of yellow fever—a man hardly ill enough to be conscious of his illness but sufficiently afflicted to be a source of infection. About two weeks afterward Dr. Carter was sent for in haste. Six officers and members of the crew were suspiciously ill; after an examination, Dr. Carter informed the captain that a yellow-fever epidemic had obtained good headway on his vessel. "One will die before morning," Dr. Carter said, "and two more will die soon unless they are moved at once to the hospital." This forecast proved true; one of the patients—ironically enough the ship doctor—gave up the ghost before daybreak, and three more cases of yellow fever had developed. Dr. Carter's investigation revealed plenty of mosquitoes, but whence had they come? A few can be brought on ship board accidentally, but the pests were apparently breeding in great numbers, and carrying the fever from the sick to the well. A detailed search revealed a dishpan of water standing outside the cook's headquarters.

The thing was so thick with mosquito larvæ that it was practically a purée. The way to end that particular epidemic was therefore plain. Dr. Carter simply emptied the dishpan over the ship's side and the next day fumigated the ship in order to kill all the insects on the wing. These precautions once taken, the disease abruptly came to an end. If Gorgas had needed an additional indication of the way to attack the enemy, he now certainly had it.

But an assault on the water barrels, cisterns, tinajas, and dishpans of the cities of Colon and Panama involved greater difficulties. The occupants of these premises were Latins. They had no fear of yellow fever themselves; it was a plague that assailed only gringos and other even less-desirable foreigners. The Panamans had their own routine of life, and the visits of American inspectors, telling them that they must never leave water exposed, at first were treated as a joke and in time were deeply resented. Fortunately Gorgas had authority on his side. Neither Panama nor Colon was a part of the Canal Zone, but the treaty with Panama had provided that Americans should have charge of sanitation in these cities. The officials, though as mystified as the rest at the queer antics of the sanitary squad, backed up Gorgas fairly well. A law was passed making it a misdemeanour, punishable with a fine of five dollars, to have mosquitoes in the larval stage on one's premises. A preliminary inspection disclosed that practically every home in Panama was subject to punishment under this fine. All were breeding Stegomyia in vast quantities. Gorgas divided each city into districts, placing an inspector in charge of each district. The record of every house was kept, as in Havana. Indeed, the story of the destruction of yellow fever in Havana and these cities in the Isthmus is much the same. The screening of rain barrels, the abolition of standing water containers, the cleaning up of eave troughs—the details are essentially identical; the behaviour of the people—their attempts to hide the evidences of their guilt—also duplicate the experience in the Cuban city. One new method, however, Gorgas introduced with telling effect. A new system of "trapping" mosquitoes and their eggs was perfected. Until the Havana days these determined insects had seemed to work with far more intelligence than their human foes. But now the mind of man began to pit itself against the mosquito brain, and to use guile as well as brute strength in its attack. As the containers disappeared from the houses and as the screened water barrels deprived the Stegomyia of their breeding grounds, they sought new vantage places for performing this indispensable work of reproduction. The large-leafed vegetation of the city afforded a refuge. Like most living things—animal and human—the Stegomyia, failing to attain ideal surroundings, will take the best that it can find. Clean fresh water in houses represents its first choice; driven from houses and eave troughs and water barrels, it will stoop to little hollowed-out places in the stones by the wayside. Such surfaces, filled with fresh rain water, were frequently found swarming with larvæ. They were even discovered in great quantities in the holy-water basins of the churches. The leaves of many trees form little cups, and these, collecting water, were eagerly availed of for breeding places. The calocasia, which grew in weedlike profusion around all the houses, was an especial favourite.

That the mosquitoes should select such secondary locations, after being driven from the house, suggested a new idea. Why not set traps for them? These "traps" were simple but extremely effective. Large basins of clean sweet water were placed in suitable locations. The mosquitoes, having no other receptacles, at once proceeded to light on the surface and deposit their eggs. The inspectors would periodically empty these basins, destroy the potential progeny, and fill them again. As fast as the parent mosquito started a family into being, the inspectors would just as promptly destroy it. This particular group of mosquitoes would therefore spend their evil existence in this kind of fruitless task and ultimately die leaving no descendents. The plan was successful, of course, only after all the breeding grounds—tin pans, water jars, pitchers, miscellaneous kitchen utensils, barrels, cisterns—had been rendered inaccessible. This reduced the enterprising insect to such unaccustomed watery nests as the axils of leaves, knot holes in trees, hollow places in stones, and the like—areas entirely unsuited to their aristocratic tastes. They eagerly accepted the much cleaner tin pans placed out for their particular benefit and thus involuntarily committed race suicide.

This new type of warfare was not without its humour and its romance. Breeding places were destroyed by oiling the surfaces of cisterns and other large containers, as in Havana. The oil used was crude, thick, sticky, and black. Late one hot afternoon one of the weary inspectors, after a hard day's work, emptied his remaining store of oil in the cistern on the roof of a hotel—the source of its water supply. That same afternoon an American navy captain, fresh from a long voyage, went to the bathroom to enjoy the infrequent luxury of a shower. He removed his clothing, soaped his Falstaffian body, and ecstatically pulled the chain. Instead of a cooling fall of fresh clear water, an avalanche of tar-like oil descended upon his rotundities of person. This was the first intimation this naval gentleman had ever had of the mosquito theory of yellow fever, and he was not an immediate convert. The slimy oil mingled with the soap and formed a kind of viscid paste; and the situation was not at once to be remedied, for there was no water on the premises and none available that night. The angry sea dog therefore was forced to spend ten or a dozen hours in this plight, and it took the combined efforts of a considerable part of the sanitary squad to fit him once more for his official duties. It is said that he spent the next week or two hunting for the guilty inspector. One day he was told to abandon the search; the poor fellow had caught yellow fever and died.

"I'm damn glad of it!" he bellowed.

Though the isolation of patients was not, in Gorgas's judgment, so useful as the destruction of mosquitoes, all reported cases were screened and kept free of mosquitoes. If the victims insisted, they were quarantined in their own homes—and most of the natives did insist. The French company, among its numerous excellent works, had built a beautiful hospital on Ancon Hill. The building, consisting of many pavilions, was complete and modern in every way and a credit to the profession. When the Americans took charge it needed only the installation of an efficient nursing staff to make the establishment complete. Splendid as this hospital was, it inspired a general sense of horror in Panama. The yellow-fever death rate in this building during the French period had been frightful. If patients did not have the disease when they entered they seemed in most cases to acquire it before they left. Men with broken legs would go to the place for treatment, and, long before recuperating from their injuries, come down with yellow fever. The average citizen of Panama had therefore come to look upon the hospital as a kind of morgue. "Oh, I prefer to die at home," he would say when the subject of removal was raised. This hospital splendidly illustrated the prevailing ignorance of the disease during the French period. It was little better than a culture tube for the very plague it was chiefly intended to combat. It was clean, well kept; but, as abundantly proved, cleanliness was no prevention of this disease. One single fact made it inevitable that Ancon Hospital should be a favourite breeding ground. The hospital, as most buildings in the Panama region, was much pestered by ants. To protect the patients, the Sisters of Charity who presided during the French régime had placed the legs of the beds in little stone basins filled with water. This made it certain that the ants could not crawl up the beds and annoy the sick. But they produced unforeseen difficulties. These little puddles of water made ideal breeding places for the Stegomyia! When the Americans took charge, they found these receptacles alive with mosquito larvæ. This was the reason why the Ancon Hospital was such a dangerous place. Its complete sanitation was a simple process. These stone jars were removed, the building screened, and it knew yellow fever no more!

Here the patients were treated and here all experiments and autopsies were performed. A corps of American trained nurses, brought from the United States, took the place of the French sisters who, although devoted and self-sacrificing, did not possess the technical knowledge necessary for this work. These American nurses, in charge of Miss Hibbard, struggled valiantly through those trying days of 1905 and 1906. They added not only to the efficiency of the department, but to its charm and even its romance. It is true that one of our more cynical doctors once said that "some were with the army in the Philippines, some were with Dr. Gorgas in Cuba, and some were with Washington at Valley Forge," yet the rapidity with which they were snapped up by the young doctors at the hospital was a matter of common comment. One case in particular is recalled. Miss —— unfortunately violated the rules to the extent of making short trips to the city of Panama while the epidemic was in full swing. Another case of yellow fever was the result—and an extremely severe one. "I had been away for a few days and when I got back," says Dr. Carter, telling this story, "I was rushed in a cab to the nurses' quarters at Anconcita. I found her tossing from one side of the bed to the other; neither morphia nor cocaine quieted her. Finally I said, 'Now, child, you have a fine constitution and you ought to get well. But if you don't lie still in that bed, you are going to die.' She insisted that she couldn't keep still, but suggested if Major —— (calling the name of one of the younger doctors on duty) would hold her hand she would try. I gave Major —— a call and stationed him at his post. She quieted down immediately and the major sat by her all night. The girl got well and it wasn't many years after that when I got cards to their wedding."

CHAPTER VI

ROOSEVELT AS DEUS EX MACHINA

I

IT WAS in this hospital at Ancon that the last dramatic scene was enacted. Here the bodies of all the yellow-fever patients were autopsied for the edification of science. In the early part of 1906 the dead grew fewer and fewer in number—for the work of Gorgas was getting the upper hand. One day in September, 1905, Gorgas entered the room while half-a-dozen white-clad figures were working hard over the cadaver of the last victim. Gorgas was in a cheerful mood that at first might have seemed a little out of keeping with the gruesome surroundings.

"Take a good look at this man, boys," he said to the young surgeons, "for it's the last case of yellow fever you will ever see. There will never be any more deaths from this cause in Panama."

This forecast was spoken eighteen years ago. Time has not behaved so inconsiderately with this prophecy as it has with so many others. It has more than justified it. Not only has there been no death; there has not been even a single case of the disease.

A campaign waged for less than six months wiped out a scourge that had afflicted this region for at least four hundred years. It had destroyed yellow fever in the one section of the world which was unquestionably its strongest fortress. By ignoring the silly advice of amateurs, even those officially in high place, contentedly letting the cities of Panama and Colon wallow in their filth, and by concentrating his sleepless energies upon one single aim—the destruction of the infecting mosquitoes—Gorgas had won what was unquestionably the greatest triumph in the history of preventive medicine. The cities should be swept and cleaned, of course—as they subsequently were—but even before that the little winged enemy of the human race must be eliminated. The real meaning of this performance was at that time imperfectly understood. This meaning was that the Panama Canal could be built. Everybody sees that now, though everybody did not see it then. Americans were not to be called upon to face the disasters that had rendered the French effort so profitless.

One would have thought that the official obstructions in Gorgas's way would have been removed. Strangely his accomplishment made little impression upon his superiors. The mere fact that yellow fever had broken out at all was regarded as an evidence of his incapacity. The discouragements with which this patient man had to contend during this epidemic are almost unbelievable. In the autumn of 1904, after the epidemic had got fairly under way, Mr. William H. Taft, then Secretary of War, and, as such, the official immediately responsible for the canal work, made a visit of inspection. Naturally the arrival of one so important produced a great stir. Up to that time few social activities had interfered with the somewhat drab routine of Panama; the dinners and receptions and balls that afterward became such a delightful part of life on the Isthmus merely began with this visit of the Secretary of War. The President of Panama and Señora Amador, all the bishops of the Catholic Church, and all the leading families of the region turned out to do him honour. Mr. Taft displayed the most charming sides of his nature; both he and his wife greatly enjoyed dancing with the Panamans and other guests, and Mr. Taft won their affection by the nature of his hearty laugh, his vigorous handshake, his always smiling face, and especially by the ease with which he pronounced the difficult Spanish names, and the tenacity with which he remembered them. Someone asked him how he performed this latter feat. He had cultivated the habit, he replied, of repeating carefully to himself the name of every person he met for the first time and trying to remember some distinctive thing about that person. In a few days, therefore, the Secretary seemed to have established the most friendly personal relations with most of the important men and women on the Isthmus. It was quite apparent that the reports made in the sanitary department had not impressed Mr. Taft favourably, and that the actual presence of yellow fever had not improved this impression. Gorgas especially wished to have a long talk with his superior, and finally an arrangement was made for a carriage drive into the country. The conversation was naturally pleasant and informal; but the Secretary's manner disclosed that a crisis had risen in the sanitary bureau.

There is not the slightest doubt that Mr. Taft returned to Washington firmly determined to make a change in the department. It is perhaps not surprising that Mr. Taft should have looked upon such a step as a pressing official duty, for the Panama Commission, to which he naturally looked for advice, had many times recorded its conviction that Gorgas was a failure and that his retention endangered the success of the Canal. What the consequences of such a change would have been it is impossible to say; fortunately, a new performer now entered upon the scene. This was Dr. Charles A. L. Reed, of Cincinnati, an eminent American surgeon who had already served as President of the American Medical Association and who, in 1906, was chairman of its Committee on Medical Legislation. In early February, 1906,

Dr. Reed arrived at the Isthmus. He had been commissioned by the American Medical Association, to investigate conditions quietly and report. A few Americans at Panama knew the purpose of his visit; from most, however, this was carefully concealed. Dr. Reed moved about the region in the capacity of a land agent; he remained about three weeks, his keen eyes searching every nook and cranny of the sanitary work. Almost immediately on his return, the newspapers, from the Atlantic to the Pacific, published the result of his investigations. Seldom has a scientific subject been treated in so slashing a manner, and seldom has a public body been subjected to such merciless analysis as the Walker Commission now received at Dr. Reed's hands. This eminent physician had been so outraged by the ignorance and prejudice of Admiral Walker and his associates that only the most outspoken language could convey his lesson. "One cannot but be impressed," he wrote, "with the anomalous condition by which a man of Colonel Gorgas's distinction, the foremost authority in the world in solving the peculiar problems that are connected with sanitation in the Isthmus, is made subordinate of a whole series of other subordinates who are confessedly ignorant of the very questions with which he is most familiar." Dr. Reed devoted his finest scorn to Carl E. Grunsky, the Commissioner who had been especially meddlesome with Gorgas.

Dr. Reed's report, indeed, has given Mr. Grunsky a certain immortality. The irate physician never once mentioned the Commission without adding, "more especially Mr. Grunsky," or "more particularly Mr. Grunsky," the result being that "Mr. Grunsky" soon became, in popular estimation, the chief artificer of all the inefficiency and ignorance which the report disclosed.

Dr. Reed laid emphasis on the shortcomings already set forth in these pages—the absurd assumption of knowledge on the part of the Commission; its persistence in ignoring the mosquito theory and the teaching of modern sanitary science; its cheese-paring policies; its devotion to red tape; its subordination of Gorgas and his work to practically every other consideration. "It is interesting," wrote Dr. Reed, "to enquire into the working of this wonderful mechanism. Thus, if Major La Garde, superintendent of Ancon Hospital, makes a requisition for supplies, he must make it in due form, take it for approval to the chief sanitary officer, then to the governor of the Zone, then to the chief disbursing officer; whence it goes to the Commission at Washington; then to Mr. Grunsky as committeeman; then back to the Commission; then, if allowed, bids are advertised for; awards are made; the requisition is filled under the supervision of a purchasing agent notoriously ignorant of the character and quality of medical and surgical supplies; the material is shipped to the Isthmus, consigned to the chief of the bureau of materials and supplies, who notifies the disbursing officer, who notifies Colonel Gorgas, who in turn notifies Major La Garde, who applies to the quartermaster—the boss of a corral—for transportation, and so much of the stuff as in the judgment of, first, the governor, next the chief disbursing officer, next the Commission, next, and more particularly, Mr. Grunsky, ought to be allowed to the superintendent of Ancon Hospital finally arrives or does not arrive at its destination. This is no fanciful picture; it is exemplified in practically every ordinary requisition that goes forward. And what is true of Ancon Hospital is true at Colon, at Culebra, at Miraflores, and at all points along the line that require supplies of this description."

In a few days the whole country was laughing over an illustration of this system given by Dr. Reed:

"An instance in point occurred a few days before my departure from Ancon: A woman in the insane department was delivered of a child; her condition was such that she could not nurse her offspring; the nurse applied to Major La Garde for a rubber nipple and a nursing bottle; he had none—the requisition of last September had not yet been filled; he made out a requisition, took it to Colonel Gorgas for indorsement, then to Mr. Tobey, chief of the bureau of materials and supplies, for another indorsement, then to a clerk to have it copied and engrossed; then a messenger was permitted to go to a drug store and buy a nursing bottle and nipple, which finally reached the infant two days after the necessity for their use had arisen. The articles ought to have cost not more than thirty cents, but counting the money value of the time of the nurse, of Major La Garde, of his clerical help, of Colonel Gorgas, of Mr. Tobey, of Mr. Tobey's clerks, of the messenger, the cost to the Government of the United States was in the neighbourhood of $6.75—all due to the penny-wise-and-pound foolish policy of the Commission, more especially of Mr. Grunsky."

Never has ridicule served a better public purpose than this pamphlet of Dr. Reed. Trifles have overthrown ministries and sometimes destroyed nations. The story of that nursing bottle had tremendous results upon the building of the Panama Canal. It was published in every newspaper in the United States, and commented upon, usually in hilarious and indignant fashion; it even found its way into foreign languages and travelled all over the world. In particular it made a deep impression upon the energetic gentleman then occupying the White House. The Reed report carried its inevitable lesson. The attempt to construct the greatest engineering work of all time, with a commission sitting in the Star

Building in Washington, issuing "requisitions" and interfering by cable with the earnest men who were engaged in the labour, could not possibly succeed. With one blow President Roosevelt applied the official axe, and all seven heads of the first Commission rolled into the basket. They no longer encumber the story of Panama.

To the unprejudiced observer this proceeding would have seemed to be a splendid vindication for Gorgas. Yet the strange obstruction that had so seriously interfered with his first year's work, and which, indeed, was to continue for his whole ten years at Panama, immediately became manifest once more. For this patient worker there was evidently to be no peace, and no coöperation from official sources. Perhaps the explanation is that Gorgas had to work always with engineers, with "practical men," who notoriously have little interest in "theories" and who, in their search for truth, do not go much further than the evidence of their own senses. To such minds the mosquito explanation of disease, at that stage of its development, made little appeal. The new Chairman of the Isthmian Commission, Theodore P. Shonts, and the new Governor of the Zone, Charles E. Magoon, were, above all, men of the "practical" turn. Personally they were quite unlike —Mr. Shonts aggressive, tactless, gruff, and domineering; Mr. Magoon polite, likable, and charming.

Mr. Shonts had been a railroad builder and manager in the West, Mr. Magoon a lawyer and government official. Unlike as they were in many things, they agreed on one, and that was that Gorgas was a failure. At that time of their appointment, in March, 1905, the yellow-fever epidemic had not been stamped out; indeed, May and June witnessed perhaps its most alarming manifestation. Naturally Gorgas was to blame, and the one way of stopping the disease was clearly to "reorganize" the Sanitary Department. Shonts was especially determined on this point. He knew little of engineering and nothing of medicine; he did not even have that popular acquaintance with the marvels of modern scientific progress that is the possession of the average layman. How ignorant he was, and how determined in his ignorance, soon became apparent. He had planned not only to supplant Gorgas, but he had fixed upon his successor. An old friend who was an osteopath seemed to him ideally fitted for the job. One day he made this suggestion to Mr. John F. Stevens, the new chief engineer—a man who admired Gorgas and loyally supported him in his work.

"But why do you want to make a change?" Mr. Stevens answered. "Gorgas is getting results. What does your friend know about sanitation?"

"Well, he has been in the South," Shonts replied, "and has seen yellow fever."

The whole thing seems now like a grotesque joke; the American Medical Association—probably the greatest single body of medical men in the world—had just taken the stand, after a thorough investigation, that Gorgas was making a conspicuous success against almost insuperable difficulties, and now the head of the Canal Commission proposed to displace him with an osteopath! Another perhaps even more dangerous candidate for Gorgas's shoes was an eminent physician, experienced in yellow fever, who was belligerent in his opposition to the mosquito idea and who, if placed in charge, intended to ignore the lessons of Havana in his fight against disease. Certainly the situation was no joke to Gorgas and his devoted band. One of the earliest acts of the new Commission was a recommendation to the Secretary of War that Gorgas, Carter, and all believers in mosquito transmission should be removed, and more "practical men" appointed in their place. Mr. Taft, Secretary of War, approved this recommendation and forwarded it to President Roosevelt.

At this time a delegation waited on President Roosevelt, asking the appointment of Dr. Hamilton Wright as Gorgas's successor. Dr. Wright had won his spurs in the sanitation of the Straits Settlement under Joseph Chamberlain. President Roosevelt wrote Dr. William H. Welch, Dean of Johns Hopkins Medical School, asking for advice as to this appointment. "I shall hold you responsible for every word you put in the letter," the President said characteristically.

Dr. Welch, in his reply, testified to Dr. Wright's fitness for the post, but added:

"Your statement that you will hold me responsible for every word in this letter obliges me to add that in my opinion neither Dr. Wright nor any one else is as well qualified to conduct this work as the present incumbent, Dr. Gorgas."

"Would to God," wrote the President in reply, "there were more men in America who had the moral courage to write honest letters of recommendation such as yours in reference to Dr. Wright!"

The situation had evidently reached a crisis. Had any other man been President at that time it is almost certain that Gorgas would have been displaced. Fortunately, however, Mr. Roosevelt had been President at the time of the Gorgas work in Havana. Mr. Roosevelt was a layman, but he had seen things with his own eyes, and he was not so disposed to dismiss the mosquito idea as was the newly appointed Commission. The situation, however, was a perplexing one, and, following his not infrequent custom, President Roosevelt went for advice to a close personal friend outside of official life. This was Dr. Alexander Lambert of New York City. The two men had been close friends and hunting companions for years. It was on a bear hunt in the Rockies, in 1905, that Dr. Lambert had attempted to persuade President Roosevelt to make Gorgas a member of the Panama Commission. On all occasions the physician had impressed upon the President the overwhelming importance of the sanitary work and many times he had described the vicissitudes of the French, and especially their tragic experiences with yellow fever. It was not strange, therefore, that Mr. Roosevelt summoned Dr. Lambert to help him decide the case of Gorgas.

It is not too much to say that this meeting, which took place one evening at Oyster Bay, decided the fate of the Panama Canal. It was at once apparent to Dr. Lambert, as he came into the room, that the President was greatly troubled. To disapprove an important recommendation of his new Commission, backed up by the Secretary of War, was naturally embarrassing; on the other hand, to dismiss a man of Gorgas's eminence in his field was to assume a heavy responsibility.

"I have sent for you," he began, "for a talk about your friend, Dr. Gorgas. As you know, I'm not satisfied."

"Why not?" asked Dr. Lambert. "What is the matter?"

"They tell me Gorgas spends all his time," the President answered, "oiling pools and trying to kill mosquitoes. Commissioner Shonts claims that he is not cleaning up Panama or Colon, that they smell as bad as ever, and recommends Colonel Gorgas's removal. The Secretary of War has gone over the matter and acquiesces in the recommendation."

It was, of course, the same old fallacy, so dear to the lay mind, appearing again—that "smells" and filth caused the disease. Dr. Lambert at once proceeded to show the President the folly of this misapprehension.

"What Shonts says is true," he said, "but removing smells and ordinary sanitation do not destroy mosquitoes. Neither do they have anything to do with the malaria and the yellow fever which the mosquitoes produce. We must exterminate those insects and eradicate these two diseases. We cannot build the Canal unless we do this. The decision is in your hands. It is for you to choose between the old and the new methods and the two ideas represented. You can back the old idea and clean out the smells and see your workmen die of malaria and yellow fever. Or you can first clean up your puddles and kill the mosquitoes, and after this is done, clean up the place by the ordinary sanitary methods. If you do this, you will have a healthy personnel with which to build your canal. The French failed because of the terrible death rate from yellow fever and malaria. My uncle, who was working with them, told me that he had seen 500 young engineers come from France and work in the swamps; not one of them, he said, lived to draw his first month's pay. Without exception they had been swept off by disease. Napoleon sold Louisiana to us because his army had been annihilated at Santo Domingo by yellow fever. You must choose between Shonts and Gorgas; you must choose between the old method and the new; you must choose between failure with mosquitoes and success without."

Dr. Lambert's words and manner were earnest and impressive. He still regards that evening as perhaps the most important in his life, for the success or failure of the Canal was hanging in the balance. And he put this phase of his argument in the strongest terms.

"I am sorry for you to-night, Mr. President," he went on. "You are facing one of the greatest decisions in your career. Upon what you decide depends whether or not you are going to get your canal. If you fall back upon the old methods of sanitation, you will fail, just as the French failed. If you back up Gorgas and his ideas and let him make his campaign against mosquitoes, then you get that canal. I can only give you my advice: you must decide for yourself. There is only one way of controlling yellow fever and malaria and that is the eradication of the mosquitoes. But it is your canal; you must do the choosing, and you must choose to-night whether you are going to build that canal."

President Roosevelt was manifestly impressed. He sat quiet during Dr. Lambert's appeal, and said nothing until he had finished. Then he looked thoughtfully at Dr. Lambert for a moment, and said:

"It is queer. I never appreciated before how essential it was. But I do now. By George, I'll back up Gorgas and we will see it through."

The President's next act was to summon Commissioner Shonts, who was then in Washington. After a few words the President shook his finger and said:

"Now I want you to get back of Gorgas!"

Mr. Shonts was not slow in acting on this instruction. From that moment his attitude toward Gorgas changed. For the rest of his term—which was not a long one—the Sanitary Department had the most cordial support of the Commissioner. Gorgas noticed the change in atmosphere, but it was not until several years afterward that he learned the reason. One day in 1912 he and Dr. Lambert were taking a little holiday on the top of Taboga Island, and in this appropriate spot, with the waters of the Pacific before them and the nearly completed Panama Canal in the rear, Dr. Lambert told him of this critical evening with President Roosevelt. "It seems," wrote Gorgas afterward about this episode, "that when Magoon had been here only about a month, the Commission joined in a recommendation that I be removed—that I had erratic ideas about mosquitoes, and did not take proper care of yellow-fever patients. Not one of these statements was true. When Stevens came down he reported to Shonts a month after that my department was the only one here which was organized on a consistent plan and which was doing good work. Magoon, of course, would not know whether the Department was well organized or not. He merely reflected the opinion of those around him, but it shows his mental attitude. It is interesting to speculate upon what might have been the result if the recommendation in regard to changing the sanitary officials had been carried into effect. At that time, in June, 1905, most of the physicians who had had experience with yellow fever had not been won over to the truth of the theory of its transmission by the mosquito. It was reported on the Isthmus that one of the most prominent and able of these physicians, who did not believe that the mosquito transmission of yellow fever had been proved, and who was now convinced that he himself had controlled yellow fever acting upon the filth theory of its causation, had been settled upon as my successor. Had this been the case, he would undoubtedly have stopped mosquito work and devoted his attention entirely to cleaning up. He would have been the more inclined to this course as it accorded with the beliefs and prejudices of the authorities on the Isthmus.

"This would probably have been kept up for two or three years, and there is no reason for believing that our condition on the Isthmus in 1908 would have been any better than was that of the French at the height of their work when they were having a death rate of 250 per thousand per year of their employees."

II

From this time forward Gorgas found a strong supporter in President Roosevelt. The meetings that subsequently took place between the two men were always satisfactory and delightful. In November, 1906, President Roosevelt paid the Isthmus an official visit. The occasion was a notable one both for Panama and for the United States. It was the first time an American President had ever left American territory during his term of office, and this fact in itself caused wide discussion. Naturally the excitement on the Isthmus was intense.

One of the picturesque figures at Panama was Captain George Shanton, a former Rough Rider, Chief of Police of Panama—an appointment he had received directly from President Roosevelt. Captain Shanton himself used to love to tell the story. He was on his ranch in the West when a telegram came from the President summoning him at once to

Washington. Naturally he was curious, and started east, and reaching Washington, hurried to the White House. The President was in a Cabinet meeting and Shanton was told to wait in an adjacent room. Becoming restless, he strolled about investigating the mysteries of the place. Suddenly the President entered through a door near which Shanton was standing, and without a word gave him a man's size right to the ribs. A typical Roosevelt smile followed. Shanton was so taken by surprise that although he was a man six feet four, he was unable to regain his breath, and, before he could greet the President, Mr. Roosevelt informed him that he wanted him to sail the following Tuesday for Panama as Chief of Police of the Canal Zone. "All arrangements have been made for your departure," he added, "and you are the man for the job."

"But, Mr. President," objected Shanton, "I don't see how I can go! I've located permanently in the West."

Mr. Roosevelt overruled his objections. There was no course but to accept, for his loyalty and his admiration for the President dated to Cuba. Having followed him there, he felt compelled to go anywhere that his Colonel ordered.

Shanton was a great success at Panama. He straightened out all local disturbances in a masterly way. Soon after his arrival news came that the

President proposed to inspect the Canal. There was much apprehension about the President's safety, both in the United States and on the Isthmus. The papers had discussed the point in detail, and a disturbance in Panama a short time before had given some cause for fear. Thus the responsibility of the world, according to Shanton, had suddenly settled upon his shoulders.

President Roosevelt arrived, accompanied by a numerous party, and guarded by the secret-service men. Thousands packed the streets near the railway station, despite a fearful tropic storm. The entire available police force of Panama and the Canal Zone was on the alert to protect the President. Shanton, astride a wonderful Kentucky thoroughbred, commanded the police and endeavoured to clear the streets. Enthusiasm ran wild, the crowds pressed and surged in every direction, and it seemed a hopeless task to maintain order. The President, surrounded and guarded by his little group of secret-service men, pushed his way through the crowd and entered his closed carriage, and the procession started for the Tivoli Hotel, making a brief journey through Panama territory to the Canal Zone. Amid the confusion and pouring rain Shanton on his horse followed the carriages closely to the hotel. But a surprise awaited both Shanton and the populace. The Chief of Police and the bodyguard were much astonished when they reached the hotel, for the President was nowhere to be found. Shanton's carefully worked out arrangements for his safety had apparently collapsed.

Spurring his black thoroughbred he hurried to the station, and then made for Ancon Hill, the residential section of the Americans on the Pacific side. Telephone calls were sent to every locality, but did not disclose Mr. Roosevelt's whereabouts. No one had seen the President after he had entered his carriage at the station.

The fact was that Mr. Roosevelt was alone with Gorgas. The two men were presently discovered at Ancon Hospital. On entering his carriage the President had asked Gorgas to drive with him, and told him that he wished to inspect Ancon Hospital at once. The two skipped out and in Gorgas's carriage were driven to the hospital. There the President made a complete first-hand investigation, going through numerous wards, meeting doctors, nurses, and patients. He expressed himself as well satisfied with conditions.

The President spent several hard-working days on the Isthmus, inspecting the work from early morning until late at night in the pouring rain. He told Congress that he chose the rainy season deliberately in order to see conditions at their worst. Gorgas accompanied the Presidential party on all the trips of inspection, ending the third day with an inspection of Colon Hospital. This visit turned out to be a memorable one for Gorgas and for the Department of Sanitation, and had far-reaching results. A lack of proper sanitary arrangements at one of the camps angered the President and brought forth a severe criticism, which at the time seemed out of proportion to the fault. The unsanitary condition was afterward proved to be due to the carelessness of one of the inspectors, who lied about the affair. Mr. Roosevelt's reprimand plunged Gorgas and the sanitary authorities in gloom.

When the Doctor met his wife at the depot in Colon that evening, on the way to bid good-bye to President Roosevelt, it was at once evident that something had gone wrong. The cheerfulness which seemed part of his nature was not apparent.

Nothing was said, however, until Doctor and Mrs. Curl's quarters at Colon Hospital were reached. And then Dr. Gorgas said little, just, "I have failed. President Roosevelt has criticized my work. No doubt I shall at once be relieved."

There was no bitterness, and no criticism of the President. What it meant to Dr. Gorgas and to the Sanitary Department to be openly criticized by the President of the United States in such a dramatic manner may be easily imagined. The affair seemed trifling, and the rebuke uncalled for in the light of the big things accomplished. The department had been under fire from the first, and the results already achieved—the elimination of yellow fever and the tremendous reduction in the sick rate—had come only after a hard battle; and now if the President were to withdraw his support and approval because one of the many camps on the Isthmus had been found to be in an unsanitary condition, owing to the carelessness of an inspector, who first denied and afterward admitted his fault, the end had come as far as Gorgas was concerned.

After the President's speech to the employees at the dock, which was enthusiastically received and applauded by the vast throng, he started for the steamer. Stopping suddenly, he said:

"Where is Dr. Gorgas? I want to see Dr. Gorgas!"

The Doctor and his wife were not far off. Greeting Dr. Gorgas cordially, the President asked them both to walk with him to the steamer. As they walked along, the vision of leaving the Isthmus with failure as a companion began to fade. They said good-bye to the President and Mrs. Roosevelt in a happier state of mind.

Dr. Gorgas bent down and whispered to his wife:

"I don't think we'll pack our trunks just yet!"

It was not until some months later, however, when the President's special message to Congress appeared, that Gorgas realized how pleased he really was with what had been accomplished by the Sanitary Department. Mr. Roosevelt announced that Gorgas was to be made a member of the Commission at once; and this was done.

In writing of the visit Dr. Gorgas said:

"President Roosevelt has come and gone. He reached here on Thursday and left Saturday night. He sent a wireless message directing that I should be of the party to come aboard Wednesday night to meet him, and when he left waited at the dock until I could be hunted up, so as to tell me good-bye. While here he issued an order reorganizing our departments. The governorship was done away with altogether. My department was made independent, and I report directly to the Commission, or rather to the chairman Mr. Shonts, who is really the man in control. The Commission was not changed, though Mr. Shonts asked to have me put on it. While this would have been an honour, it would not have added anything to the efficiency of my department. The department organization was all I asked, and is what I have been trying for for the last two years, so I am happy."

And later:

"President Roosevelt's message was indeed a corker. I had not expected anything of the kind. I do not think that an army medical officer ever had such recognition in a Presidential message. It probably marks the acme of my career. I have had greater recognition and success than I ever expected. The commissionership would not be of any value to me in connection with my work. For me it would be purely an honorary position, though of course I should like the honour. It might be an element of actual weakness, for as chief sanitary officer I have a pretty free hand in recommending. As a member of the Commission I should be bound by all the acts of the Commission. However, to be made a commissioner would add greatly to the dignity of my position both here and with the Surgeon-General's office."

From that visit the relations between President Roosevelt and Gorgas were always cordial. The support which Mr. Roosevelt had promised Dr. Lambert that night at Oyster Bay he never failed to give. Gorgas and Roosevelt seldom met, but their mutual respect and coöperation were important factors in finishing the Canal. One meeting, however, must not be forgotten, for it shows both men in an amiable light. One day in June, 1908, Gorgas, on leave, called by appointment on the President.

"Do you mind talking while I am being shaved?" asked Mr. Roosevelt.

The barber brought a folding chair, set it up and began work. The President talked about Panama as if he and his visitor were in entire accord. As Dr. Gorgas was leaving President Roosevelt said:

"I am delighted to see you, Colonel Gorgas. I am

sorry to have to send you away from Panama; but you are the only man available."

Gorgas's heart went down into his boots. He concluded that his enemies had triumphed at last. The President, noticing his expression, exclaimed:

"Haven't you heard of it? Well, upon my word, I've forgotten where it is, but I've ordered you somewhere!"

At this juncture Secretary Taft appeared and explained that Gorgas was to represent the United States at a scientific congress in Chile.

As Gorgas was leaving President Roosevelt said:

"I should like to continue this conversation, Dr. Gorgas, but I am busy now. Come and take dinner with me to-night."

"Thank you, Mr. President," said Gorgas. "I am sorry, but I have an engagement." Seeing Mr. Roosevelt's surprised look, he exclaimed: "But of course, Mr. President, I shall break my engagement with pleasure."

Much amused, President Roosevelt placed his hand on Gorgas's shoulder and said, laughing heartily:

"No, no, Dr. Gorgas, keep your engagement! I would not for the world interfere with your plans!"

Gorgas spoke of the incident to a friend, who, quite aghast, said:

"Don't you know that an invitation from the President is a command?"

CHAPTER VII

THE COMING OF COLONEL GOETHALS

I

A GREAT change took place in the administration of the Canal in 1908, when Mr. Stevens resigned as chief engineer. This resignation caused profound discouragement in Washington. A kind of fatality seemed to hang over this great enterprise. One after another of the men selected to perform the work had retired, and the frequent changes had created an unpleasant impression in the public mind. Both President Roosevelt and Mr. Taft, his Secretary of War, decided that some radical departure was necessary in order to give continuity and permanence to the organization. This is the reason that they created a new Canal Commission, composed chiefly of army officers. Men selected from the government services had at least one advantage over those taken from civil life. They could be depended on to stick to the job. And this was a quality very much needed in the acute stage which the Canal had reached. Gorgas himself became a member of this new commission. His associates were Major D. D. Gaillard, who soon became one of his closest friends, and whose fame as an engineer has become immortal through the construction of the Culebra Cut, since named the Gaillard Cut in his honour; Major William S. Sibert, whose creation of the Gatun Dam and Gatun Lake has similarly added new glory to American engineering; H. H. Rousseau, United States Navy; J. S. C. Blackburn and Jackson Smith. Lieutenant-Colonel George W. Goethals became chairman and chief engineer, and Joseph Bucklin Bishop, secretary.

Of all these new appointees, the name that stood out most conspicuously was that of the new chairman, George W. Goethals. At that time Colonel Goethals was not widely known, except in army circles, where, in his twenty years of active service, he had established his reputation as that of an able engineer and a masterful leader of men. His selection for this important post was largely the result of the personal impression he had made on Secretary Taft. Colonel Goethals had been Mr. Taft's guide in an inspection of fortifications; he had proved an amiable companion as well as a competent adviser in this branch of military science; when the time came to select a chief engineer for the Canal, therefore, Mr. Taft strongly urged his friend's qualifications upon President Roosevelt. In many ways the choice, as the event proved, was a fortunate one. It was based upon the assumption that the Canal needed a persistent driver; one who was possessed, above all, of administrative ability, a talent for handling large masses of men, and even a certain remorselessness of spirit in accomplishing his ends. All these qualities Colonel Goethals had in large degree. The son of Hollanders, born in Brooklyn in 1858, he had made his way in life exclusively by his own exertions. His name, in the original Dutch, was "Goet-hals," meaning "stiff neck," and his friends have always regarded this as a most happy description of the man who was destined to make it famous in two continents. At a first meeting—as Mr. Taft had found—Colonel Goethals was an impressive man. His figure was tall, vigorous, and erect; he walked with a decisive, determined stride; if his bearing indicated self-confidence at the same time it pictured force and sleepless industry. His round head, surmounted by crisp white hair; his oval face, red, somewhat weather-beaten, but handsome and finely chiselled; his white tufted moustache; his violet-blue eyes, clear and penetrating, at times kindly, reflective, and even sad—all these features suggested poise and determination; here was certainly a man who would suffer no equal in authority, and who would not himself avoid responsibility. In a few months this somewhat grim, self-sufficing and silent figure became one of the most familiar sights on the Isthmus. Clad usually in a spotless white suit, invariably smoking a cigarette, the impression conveyed to the onlooker, and perhaps intended to be conveyed, was that the Panama Canal, after its many vicissitudes, had at last found its master. About the whole personality of Goethals, as he flew about the Canal Zone in his little yellow railroad motor car, facetiously known as the "yellow peril," or stood in the centre of things, surveying the scene and issuing instructions, was an inevitable air of bossship.

This is no injustice to the chairman of the Canal Zone; a belief in one-man power was instinctive with him and constantly expressed. He stated the case earnestly to President Roosevelt.

"It's no use trying to do anything down there under present conditions," he said.

"What do you want?"

"Absolute authority. Give one man absolute power and make him responsible for everything. I am willing to try it."

The President, by executive order, gave Colonel Goethals the desired power, probably stretching the law in order to meet his wishes. Colonel Goethals thus found himself the unquestioned tsar of what was really a little principality. The Canal Zone, under military authority, constituted a miniature state with its own government, courts, schools, churches, and even police systems. It was this little province that Colonel Goethals ruled. And he vastly enjoyed the situation. The power he exercised was the relish and the sweetness of his life; it realized the highest aspiration of his boyhood. One beautiful moonlight night Goethals was walking on a little hill, overlooking the cut, with one of the best-known ladies of the Zone. His companion was much affected by the splendour of the tropical scene.

"Yes, it's a beautiful spot," the Colonel replied to her exclamations, "and I love it! But I love it for other reasons than its beauty or the things I get from it. Above all, I love it for the power."

He was silent for a moment and then went on:

"I remember once visiting a monastery of Jesuit Fathers. I saw the wretched cells they lived in, the little rude cots they slept in, the rough tables at which they had their meals. And then I remembered the vast power that the men who lived like that had once exercised. It was worth living simply in order to have that."

In his enthusiasm he raised his hand.

"That's the only thing in life worth having. Wealth—salaries—these are nothing. It's power. power, power!"

This little scene gives the key to Colonel Goethals's character and explains his life on the Zone. His passion for dominating everything and everybody he carried to extreme lengths. The most desirable gift of the executive is the ability to delegate authority, but this quality Colonel Goethals did not possess.

He was impatient of any associate or subordinate whom he could not control. He was utterly lacking in adaptability. He marked his appointed course and pursued it without the slightest deviation. He formed his opinions of men at a first glimpse, and practically never modified judgments of the kind. His conversation and his manners, like his acts, had no finesse and no spirit of accommodation. Though he had his genial moments, and though his nature did not lack its soft and even its sentimental side, he was consistently abrupt in conversation. On occasions this quality was an advantage, and it especially served a good purpose in dealing with the outrageous demands and threats of labourers—Colonel Goethals's handling of such crises being masterpieces of the kind; in other instances, however, it had a deplorable effect upon general efficiency. Perhaps in all this Colonel Goethals was a victim of his own lively intelligence; his blue eyes had the quality of piercing a man's very soul; and his mind was quick to seize the vitals of any question. Perhaps it was the fact that Colonel Goethals was not primarily an engineer, but an administrator—the executive head of the 40,000 human beings at work on the Canal—that caused him to look somewhat slightingly upon the efforts of his associates. His own published account of Panama says practically nothing about the Gatun Dam, the Gaillard Cut, the locks or other great feats of engineering, but is almost exclusively a description of administrative details. This book greatly pained the engineering force, indeed, because its only reference to their work was a statement that it "involved no new principles." In fact, the picture that the canal workers chiefly retain of Goethals is not that of the genius of blue prints and engineering details, but the hard driver of steam-shovel men, the energetic executive always demanding more and more "yardage," the queller of strikes and riots—above all, of the calm, unruffled judge, sitting in his office at Culebra every Sunday morning, listening, like a Venetian doge, to the complaints that every worker, even the humblest, was privileged to bring, acting himself as attorney, judge, and jury, dispensing primitive justice and solving petty quarrels; the patriarchal despot of the Zone.

It is at once apparent that Colonel Goethals was a man of very different stamp from Gorgas. One was as unyielding as a bar of iron, while the other was resilient to every human being; one was not particularly sympathetic or tolerant of any point of view except his own, while the other was open-minded. One controlled people by command, while the other accomplished his ends by persuasion, by good humour, and by a never-dying patience. One was a man of few words; the other, a man to whom human association was the greatest joy in life. It goes without saying that these two men would find little in common. It would indeed be absurd to gloss their relations. The conflict between Colonel Goethals and Gorgas constituted the chief topic of personal interest for the last seven years of the Canal and has been the subject of much comment since. Colonel Goethals made no secret of his contempt for the Sanitary Department, and Gorgas did not hesitate to say publicly that Colonel Goethals had been a constant impediment to his success. The reasons for this attitude are not at first apparent. Colonel Goethals was far from being an ignorant man; he appreciated the value of the mosquito theory and of sanitation as a factor in building the Canal. On the basis of actual accomplishment so sincere an admirer of efficiency as Colonel Goethals should have found especial delight in the work of the Sanitary Department. The serious problems had been solved before Colonel Goethals's appearance. "The real hard work was done within the first three years," Gorgas once said. Yellow fever had been stamped out; it had vanished from the Zone by the time Colonel Goethals arrived, never to reappear. Malaria was also well under control. These performances had given Gorgas great fame in all parts of the world. His name was in the mouths of scientists and sanitarians everywhere. Visitors were coming from all countries to inspect the Canal and his achievements were parts of current speech in every section of the United States. Gorgas was the man for whom every distinguished visitor to the Canal first asked. By the time Colonel Goethals arrived, indeed, Gorgas was the one man who had made a distinguished reputation as a result of the canal operation; his achievement was so startlingly dramatic, its relation to success on the Isthmus so apparent, that, in the popular mind, it was almost synonymous with Panama itself. Gorgas was the Canal and the Canal was Gorgas.

Despite this acknowledgment from the scientific men of two continents, Colonel Goethals soon fell into the habit of speaking slightingly of Gorgas and his department. His criticisms were freely expressed and became common talk everywhere on the Zone. He unquestionably resented the fact that the department was so much of an independent organization, that the business of keeping the Isthmus clean was not the duty of the engineering force. "Put him in the Sanitary Department," he would say, when asked how to dispose of an employee whose usefulness was not especially marked. "Sick him on the Sanitary Department; it hasn't much to do," he would direct when an unimportant and more or less inconvenient visitor came to Panama, claiming entertainment. That Colonel Goethals was sincerely determined on economy is the fact, and he was constantly accusing

Gorgas of extravagance. The Sanitary Department cost on the average $350,000 a year—in these days of billions certainly a small sum, and in view of the fact that sanitation was the basis of the whole Canal, a modest expenditure then. Colonel Goethals regarded this as wild extravagance. He could not understand, he said, why Gorgas needed so many men—men who were doing work, he declared, that could be distributed to other departments. Gorgas could argue for hours that this expense was a trifle, that the department was economically administered, but he made little impression.

"Do you know, Gorgas," Colonel Goethals said one day, "that every mosquito you kill costs the United States Government ten dollars?"

"But just think," answered Gorgas, "one of those ten-dollar mosquitoes might bite you, and what a loss that would be to the country!"

II

From the beginning of his Panama days Gorgas had been called upon to contend with a stupid and unfriendly officialdom; he had fondly expected that this kind of obstruction would end with the coming of the army commission; the fact remains that his last seven years in the Isthmus were, on the personal side, the most difficult of all. But Gorgas saw his duty clearly. His business was to keep down the death rate—to maintain the excellent conditions that prevailed in 1907, and with his usual singleness of purpose, and in face of all opposition, he doggedly set to work. To his friends he would insist that personal animosities were not important; their business was still to fight the mosquito. The yellow-fever problem had been solved, and he now concentrated upon a still more difficult one, that of malaria. Though it does not inspire the same panic as yellow fever, malaria is really the more dangerous. Yellow fever is an acute, fulminant disease; it strikes communities suddenly, sometimes wipes out large populations and, while it lasts, creates the wildest havoc. The mere fact, however, that it is a devastating epidemic in itself prevents it from being a grave menace to the progress of the world. Certain uninformed writers have accused it of crimes of which it is entirely guiltless. They have even asserted that it has wiped out civilizations, that it in itself has destroyed the most flourishing and cultured society of the western hemisphere, that of the ancient Mayas. Such an accusation rests on a flimsy basis. That yellow fever is not dangerous to established populations, but only to strangers, has already been made plain in these pages. In Havana it attacked freshly arrived troops and immigrants from over seas, but left the long-resident population unscathed; in Panama it passed by the Panamans, but ferociously assailed the new arrivals. The explanation is that in yellow fever the principle of immunity is always at work. Once a person has the disease, he almost never has it again. The accustomed population thus becomes immune, probably by having the disease in extremely mild form as children.

The thing that makes malaria such a dangerous plague is that this principle of immunity does not operate. A single attack does not protect the victim from a recurrence. Such a phenomenon as a population immune from malaria is therefore unknown. One can have malaria for an entire lifetime. Yellow fever strikes suddenly; in a week the patient is dead or on the road to recovery, but malaria is far more insidious. It does not so frequently kill, but it enervates the human system and makes the life of the sufferer little less than a walking death. That malaria has destroyed civilizations is probably a fact. Its prevalence on so extensive a scale in the Mediterranean is probably the chief reason why this part of the earth's surface has lost its preëminence as the leader in the world's progress. Many scholars believe that it was mainly responsible for the collapse of Greek civilization. Gibbon enumerates many causes for the fall of the Roman state, but says nothing about malaria, which was probably more of a destructive force than any of those he sets forth. The fact is that the human race cannot satisfactorily progress in places where this vampire is constantly exhausting its vitality. Yellow fever made the Isthmus of Panama a perpetual menace to strangers, but it was malaria that had for ages sapped the vitality of the native population and in itself made progress impossible.

Malaria is not only a far more dangerous disease than yellow fever, in its ultimate effects, but it is far more difficult to control. Sir Patrick Manson and Sir Ronald Ross had shown that the Anopheles mosquito was the infecting agent, just as Walter Reed and his associates had proved the criminality of the Stegomyia in yellow fever. The logical way to eliminate both diseases was by destroying the pests responsible for their spread. Gorgas had accomplished this, for all practical purposes, with the Stegomyia, but the warfare on the Anopheles was a very different affair. For it was not a house-bred and dainty beast, as was the Stegomyia. It was far more discursive and democratic in its habits. The Stegomyia breeds only in inhabited houses, and only in clean artificial containers—water barrels, pitchers, jars, glasses, and the like. The Anopheles breeds wherever water can be found. It does not insist on the presence of human beings; any dirty mud puddle, any pond or marsh will serve its purpose quite as well. The business of stamping out the yellow-fever mosquito is that of emptying water jars and protecting water barrels: the business of killing the Anopheles is that of draining swamps, filling in ponds, levelling roads, cutting grass, building concrete ditches, and performing other engineering feats. The Anopheles enters houses chiefly for the purpose of feeding on the blood of human beings, while the Stegomyia, for some unknown reason, prefers a human dwelling as a permanent abode. For the rest of the time the malarial mosquito is pursuing its course in the miscellaneous penetralia of nature. Making war on the yellow-fever insect is like making war on the family cat, while a campaign directed against the malarial parasite is like fighting all the beasts of the jungle. The Stegomyia is ready at hand, waiting to be killed, while the Anopheles must be sought in all the open places and the swamps of the forest.

Difficult as was the undertaking, however, and discouraging as were the circumstances under which he was forced to labour, Gorgas put himself to the task. He had had great success in eliminating malaria from Havana; for in two years he had reduced the disease to a point that meant its practical disappearance. In ten years, by the use of the Gorgas methods, the death rate from this infection had gone down from 564 to 44 a year. Thus Gorgas had every reason to hope for similar results at Panama. To get a fair idea of the proportions of the task, one has only to form a mental picture of the earth's surface in such a disturbed area as the Canal Zone, and visualize the innumerable places in which water could accumulate. Every such spot, large and small, became a breeding place for the malarial mosquito. First of all there were the natural water courses themselves—the rivers, lakes, brooks, ponds, swamps. The Stegomyia made little use of such localities, but the Anopheles found here its most desirable breeding grounds. Yet the malarial mosquito exercised certain discriminations; it did not deposit the eggs everywhere on surfaces of this sort; it hunted out the sheltered edges, protected by bordering grass and reeds, and here laid the beginnings of an enormous progeny. The canal work itself was constantly creating the most desirable places for the same great biological purpose. Every time a steam shovel made a deep hole, water would almost immediately collect, and the Anopheles would at once seek such a depression as a breeding ground. The bottom of the Canal was irregular and full of holes, large and small; here dirty water gathered, and here also malarial mosquitoes developed in great quantities. Puddles were every day forming in discarded machinery, and these likewise became favourite nesting places. Tracks in the mud made by wagon wheels usually filled with water, and thus became popular haunts of mosquito larvæ. Perhaps nothing caused more trouble than the footprints of horses and cattle.

These existed everywhere, in the roads and in pasture lands; they were sometimes five or six inches deep and provided a real paradise for mosquito breeding. Seepage outcrops on the hills acceptably served the same purpose. Indeed, there was hardly a square foot of the Canal that did not present one or more opportunities for the industrious Anopheles.

Perfection in malaria control would have meant the complete annihilation of all these accumulated masses of water, great and small. With unlimited funds and unlimited support the task could have been accomplished. Under the prevailing conditions, however, any such exhaustive proceeding was impossible. But the record made at Panama was an astonishing one. There was no necessity, of course, of banishing the malarial pest from the entire Canal Zone. This zone comprised about five hundred square miles, but most of this was uninhabited jungle, in which the presence of mosquitoes, even in great numbers, was no menace, because there were no human beings to infect or to become infected. Ingenious investigations disclosed that the average flight of the Anopheles was about two hundred yards; on occasions, indeed, it could fly farther, but, as a practical matter, two hundred yards was a satisfactory flight limit on which to base sanitary measures. That is to say, if a zone two hundred yards wide could be drawn around any inhabited area, and this zone kept free of the Anopheles mosquito, there was little likelihood of the transmission of malaria. This was the plan that underlay the anti-malaria campaign. All swamps within two hundred yards of villages or towns or inhabited houses were completely drained; not far from eight million feet of ditches were built for this purpose. This measure deprived the mosquitoes of their favourite breeding places. All underbrush within the same distance of inhabited areas was ruthlessly cut, and the grass, when it reached the height of one foot, was likewise removed. The elimination of such underbrush and grass, though it gave the landscape a somewhat barren appearance, was an especially successful method of eliminating the disease. The Anopheles is not a particularly virile mosquito; strong sunlight shrivels it up and kills it, and even a slight wind has a most destructive effect. For this reason it huddles for safety in underbrush and grass, and the removal of these protections has the most disastrous effects. Housewives were somewhat appalled at the remorselessness of the Sanitary Department in removing their beautiful flower beds; sanitation, however, was even more essential than decoration; these flower beds, like underbrush and grass, afforded protection to the Anopheles and brought malaria into the household—therefore they were inexorably removed.

Gorgas's forces were constantly in the field, levelling irregular ground and thus filling the watery depressions that furnished breeding places for the foe. It was, of course, impossible similarly to obliterate the ponds, lakes, and water courses. But the simple process of cutting the grass at the edges made them less dangerous, for it was these sheltered places that the female Anopheles selected for depositing her eggs. This, however, did not suffice. The actual extermination of mosquito larvæ became the necessary programme. In this occupation hundreds of patient workers were engaged. Kerosene and crude oil were constantly falling upon watery surfaces—substances almost instantaneously destructive to mosquito larvæ. Drip pans and other devices were kept twenty-four hours a day over streams, the oil so regulated that it was always dropping upon the surface. Oil carts, parading up and down the roads, sprinkling the deadly substance in roadside ditches, were a frequent sight. In all parts of the Zone, inspectors, hose in hand, were spraying suspicious areas. Especial ingenuity was displayed in making use of the mosquitoes' natural enemies, of which the jungle is full. Small fish have an insatiable appetite for the larvæ and pupæ, while spiders, small lizards, and ants find the adult creature a tempting morsel. Soon Gorgas was breeding these little animals in enormous quantities, for the express purpose of inciting them against the mosquitoes. Minnows and other small surface fish, introduced into a pond or water course, rapidly cleared it of mosquito larvæ. A force of human inspectors was every day at work, destroying mosquitoes in walls and other dark places where they are fond of taking rest; but a variety of insects was found far more effective. Noting the avidity with which spiders and ants hunted the Anopheles in these places, the sanitary squads reinforced them artificially, and horrible was the devastation that followed. A small lizard, common to the Isthmus, was especially propagated for this same purpose.

These measures, and many more, produced an astonishing decrease in malaria. Dr. Malcolm Watson, who afterward directed the eradication of malaria from the Federated Malay States, visited Panama, and, in a report to the Royal Colonial Institute, described Gorgas's malarial work as "the greatest sanitary achievement the world has seen." "I doubt if we shall ever see as great again," he adds. "It is perfect work and its organization is the only kind that would have succeeded under the circumstances." The statistics bear out these professional appraisements. The statistical "curves" show a steady decrease in the number of cases and deaths through a period of ten years. In 1906 the proportion of canal workers admitted each month to the malarial wards of the hospitals was more than 40 per cent. By 1913 this had dropped to less than ten per cent.

This, of course, contributed greatly to the efficiency of the canal force, yet the fact is that the anti-malarial work was not entirely successful. It was not so successful as was Gorgas's work with the same disease at Havana, where he had practically stamped it out. What was the explanation for this partial failure? Gorgas never hesitated to fix the responsibility. Colonel Goethals, as supreme dictator of the Canal, had the power to interfere seriously with his work and did so. From the first he showed a determination to abolish the Sanitary Department as an independent, or half-independent, organization, and to merge it with the general engineering force. It was Gorgas's quiet but persistent opposition to this destructive scheme that caused the difficulties between the two men. Gorgas insisted that sanitation was a science quite by itself; that only sanitary men could properly supervise the work; that medical men must have control even of such operations as constructing ditches and draining swamps, which Colonel Goethals declared were properly the duty of engineers. It was certainly an extraordinary situation: medical science in two continents was hailing Gorgas's accomplishments in stamping out disease in the Zone as one of the greatest of scientific achievements of all time, and yet Colonel Goethals was constantly interfering in a way that threatened disaster. Gorgas fought valiantly, in his own unaggressive way. But his best efforts and the best efforts of his associates did not prevent Colonel Goethals, in part at least, from carrying out his views. The most important of all the sanitary measures, the cutting of grass and the construction of drains, he insisted on transferring to the quartermaster's department. Gorgas was still nominally in control; the quartermaster's department was supposed to do this work under his instructions and in accordance with his plans; but the disintegration of his own separate force detracted greatly from his anti-malaria campaign. To it Gorgas attributed the failure completely to stamp out the disease.

He made this criticism in a public speech delivered in St. Louis in 1915. Colonel Goethals had recently delivered an address at Princeton University in which he spoke slightingly of the Sanitary Department at Panama, as well as of the engineering work. It was as a retort to these criticisms that Gorgas made his remarks at St. Louis. "I was much disappointed," he said, "that we did not get rid of malaria on the Isthmus of Panama as we did at Havana. I had fully expected to do so, and when we went to the Isthmus we put into effect the same anti-malarial measures that had been so successful at Havana. These measures were vigorously pushed for the first four years. At the end of our four years of work, May, 1908, all power on the Isthmus was concentrated in the hands of a single man, the chairman of the Commission. This officer thought it advisable to make certain radical changes in the methods of sanitation. These changes, ordered by the chairman, took execution of the anti-malarial work out of the hands of the sanitary authorities and placed them in the hands of men who had no special knowledge of anti-malarial work.

"I argued against these changes as forcibly as I could, but to no avail.

"Looking back over my fifteen years of experience in tropical sanitation, I believe that if I could have continued at Panama the same methods that I had used previous to 1908, the results would have been the same as at Havana, and the canal workers would have been as entirely free from malaria as were the citizens of Havana. And I feel equally convinced that if our chairman of 1908 had been able to put into effect in 1904 the methods he forced upon me in 1908, we could not have accomplished the sanitary success at Panama which we had accomplished prior to the year 1908."

The statement that inspired this criticism is found in the first chapter of General Goethals's book, "The Government of the Canal Zone":

"The construction of the Canal involved the solution of no real engineering problems—simply the application of known principles and methods which experience had shown would give satisfactory results, for the very magnitude of the work precluded trying anything new or experimental. The task was a formidable one, therefore, because of its size rather than because of the engineering difficulties that were overcome."

"So too," continues General Goethals, "in regard to sanitation. With Sir Ronald Ross's discovery of the cause of malaria which had led him to adopt means for its reduction and eradication in Egypt and India, and with Reed, Lazear, and Carroll proving the theory that yellow fever is transmitted by the mosquito, and *formulating rules* which freed Cuba from the ravages of that dread disease—there remained but the application of the methods followed elsewhere to secure similar results on the Isthmus with respect to these two diseases.

"The work in Panama developed nothing new."

It would be unjust to Gorgas's memory and scientific reputation not to correct certain misstatements in this paragraph. The implication that Gorgas merely adopted the methods for stamping out malaria used by Sir Ronald Ross in Egypt and India does not accord with the facts. Ross's eradication of malaria at Ismailia, Egypt—an exceedingly simple operation, as he himself says in his recent biography—was accomplished in six or seven days in September, 1902. This was a year after Gorgas had devised his own methods of fighting the disease in Havana. The statement about Walter Reed and his commission is similarly misleading. The relation of Gorgas's work to Reed's great discovery has already been set forth. All through his life Gorgas always took pride in describing himself as a mere follower of Reed. His own triumph was the practical application of Reed's discoveries. But the statement that Reed "formulated the rules which freed Cuba from the ravages" of yellow fever is entirely inaccurate. The formulation of these rules and their painstaking and successful administration were Gorgas's work. On this point the men closest in touch with the Havana experience may be quoted: "The world owes Gorgas a great deal," writes General Leonard Wood, who was Governor-General of Cuba at the time, "for it was he who put into practice in Havana, the hotbed of yellow fever, the system and methods which resulted in the control of the disease in that city. It was under his direction that the last great epidemic there was brought to a close during the summer months, a feat which was thought to be impossible.

"I know what he did and the value of his work, for he was a member of my staff at the time and worked in closest touch with me. Because of his work in Havana, I urged President Roosevelt to make him the Sanitary Member of the Panama Canal Commission. He applied the discovery of Reed and others through methods which he evolved in Havana, and it was upon the sanitary foundation which he laid in Panama that the Panama Canal was, in large measure, built. This can be said without in any way detracting from the great credit due the engineers for their part of the work.

"As the world grows older, a generous measure of credit for the construction of the Panama Canal will be justly given to William C. Gorgas."

On this same point writes Dr. Juan Guiteras, closely associated with the Havana work of 1901, and for many years Secretary of Health in the Republic of Cuba:

"I have looked up the publications of the Commission (the Reed Board) and find nowhere any writing of their formulating any set of regulations for the application of the new methods of fighting yellow fever in Havana. Nor was it to be expected that they would formulate anything of the kind. They were a scientific commission, dealing with facts made clear by experiment, and were not practical sanitarians, formulating methods of procedure."

Only one member of the Reed Commission is still living. That is Dr. Aristides Agramonte, of Havana, Cuba. In regard to General Goethals's statement he writes:

"The United States Army Board which demonstrated the real connection between mosquitoes and yellow fever did not at any time publish 'a set of rules' for undertaking the prophylaxis of the disease: as a natural consequence of the results obtained by the Board, Colonel Gorgas evolved the methods which were so effective.

(*Signed*)
AGRAMONTE.

Dr. Victor Clarence Vaughan, ex-President of the American Medical Association and Dean of the University of Michigan, who served as major and surgeon in Cuba, and who knows intimately the circumstances attending the fight against the Stegomyia mosquito, writes:

"To Gorgas belongs the credit of having originated and executed methods for the extermination of the Stegomyia. He carried this out so successfully in Havana that the city for the first time in several hundred years was free from disease."

CHAPTER VIII

THE MEANING OF THE CANAL

I

IT MUST not be assumed that troubles of this kind made miserable Gorgas's existence at Panama. The truth was quite in the opposite direction. He had his distressful hours, but his spirits were naturally cheerful, and there were few men better formed to enjoy to the full the lighter side of things on the Isthmus. His life there, indeed, was a very happy one. As soon as the early confusion passed, and the work of building the Canal settled down to a normal régime, there were plenty of distractions to compensate somewhat for official obstruction. In the early years, when the spectre of yellow fever enshrouded the Zone, existence was indeed full of seriousness and apprehension. Everyone was living in the presence of an invisible terror and the deaths and the funerals that were constantly taking place gave little chance for relaxation or gaiety. The Panama jungle was still, just as it had been during the French régime, a place of disease and tragedy. The conquest of yellow fever and the control obtained over malaria naturally produced a change of atmosphere. Panama, both in the cities and villages and in the Zone, now appeared in new and more beautiful colours. Cool and comfortable houses were built for the engineers, and their families and wives and children, who had hitherto been kept in the United States, began to settle on the Isthmus. The result was that, soon after 1905, a colony of charming and interesting men and women found themselves in intimate association; as the work went on, there was a ceaseless flow of distinguished visitors, and Panama, from the Atlantic to the Pacific, was, in its lighter hours, given up to festivities of all kinds. The social instinct in Gorgas was strong; he had a liking for interesting people; he had a strong taste for hunting, fishing, and miscellaneous sports, as well as for dinner parties and even more frivolous kinds of enjoyment. At Panama he took up again his singing and dancing, undiscouraged by his failures in early life to master these two arts. "One happy occasion," writes Dr. Darling, of the hospital staff at Colon, "often recurs to me of a party at the Gorgas home. It was Gorgas's niece, was it not, who cajoled him into singing 'In Zanzibar'? How we all enjoyed the delicious flavour of the song as rendered in the Colonel's tenor! And how he entered into the fun of the thing, and how he laughed!"

After Mr. Wallace had dramatically withdrawn from the Canal and Mr. Stevens had come as chief engineer, the Isthmian atmosphere became more tranquil, though yellow fever had not entirely disappeared. Mr. Stevens lived at Ancon, just within the hospital gate, in a bungalow near the one occupied by Dr. Lyster, Dr. Noland, and Dr. Summersgill. Mr. Stevens was an inspiration to the men; they held him in the greatest respect and admiration. He and Gorgas worked in the greatest harmony, and things became easier for the Sanitary Department. Conditions improved, and a wave of enthusiasm and energy enveloped the Isthmus and reached even the most humble employees.

Mr. Stevens decided to make Culebra his headquarters and built there a handsome frame house with spacious rooms and large screened porches. Most of the houses on the Zone were built on the same plan, though they differed in size and appointments. Mr. Burt and Mr. Wright designed the quarters to meet the requirements and suggestions of the Sanitary Department. When the new house was finished, Mrs. Stevens came down. Her arrival brought joy to all who knew her and immediately started a new social régime. The Stevens home on the Culebra Hills was often the scene of pleasant gatherings, representing the Zone and Panama. Bright, vivacious, and with a winning personality, Mrs. Stevens was *simpatica* to the Panamans as well as to the Americans. New homes were built for the engineers at Culebra and for many employees. Rooms were set aside for church services, and soon Culebra took on quite the air of a small town. Attractive quarters, designed for comfort in the tropics, were built along the line, a region comprising all the little towns and construction camps following the line of the Canal between Panama and Colon. These towns had pretty names, Corozal, Miraflores, Pedro Miguel, Paraíso, Culebra, Empire, Gorgona, Gatun, and on to Cristobal. Life was anything but monotonous. When other excitement failed, visitors came like Poultney Bigelow to write sensational newspaper articles—articles which were not useful in informing the public, but which served a good purpose in providing topics of conversation to this little colony of marooned Americans. Now and then there were tremendous and ominous slides in the cut, or animated discussions as to the kind of canal, sea-level or lock canal. Consulting engineers came down, congressional committees frequently surveyed the scene with a critical and deprecating eye—men who naturally received a cordial reception from canal officials, who understood the need of congressional appropriations. There were constant trips to Panama City and to Colon. The receptions held at the palace every Friday night by the President of the Republic and Madame Amador, both much beloved in Panama and the Zone, were attended by the canal officials and their families, members of the Cabinet, and the Panamans. Many of the Panamans spoke English quite well, and they showed a laudable desire to "speek" it; the attempts of the Americans to speak Spanish did not arouse a similar enthusiasm. Whenever these receptions were attended by the Governor the musicians stationed in front of the palace gave notice of his arrival by playing the "Star-Spangled Banner." Thereupon a silence fell upon the assembly. Every neck was craned to see his Excellency, dressed in the spotless white linen adopted by the Americans in that hot climate, pass down the long yellow room and kiss in courtly fashion the hand of Madame Amador. This was a pretty ceremony.

President Amador was himself an eminent doctor who had practised many years before he became President of the Republic. Despite this, he was decidedly pessimistic about the elimination of yellow fever. And Madame Amador would frequently say:

"You will never succeed in your efforts, Colonel Gorgas! We have always had yellow fever in Panama and always will have."

They made a wager. If yellow fever disappeared, Madame Amador was to give to Gorgas a dozen handkerchiefs embroidered by herself with his initials. It is immaterial what Dr. Gorgas's penalty was to be in case he lost, for in less than a year Madame Amador presented him with the handkerchiefs, beautifully embroidered as only a Spanish woman can embroider.

Sir Claude and Lady Mallett presided over the British Legation. Sir Claude had a fund of delightful stories, which included many interesting tales of the past, especially events which took place during the period of French construction. On the subject of the French and their sufferings, indeed, Sir Claude was the greatest living authority. He had served through the whole period and in reality had been a part of it. Lady Mallett, a bright and vivacious woman, was herself a native of Panama, a member of a distinguished Spanish family—the Obarrios—and her entertainments were perhaps the most delightful feature of life on the Isthmus. Of one of her dinners Gorgas particularly liked to tell: The honour guest was a distinguished Panaman statesman, very much in the limelight at the time. The table, with its foreign setting, was most attractive. Picturesquely coiffed maids in the national costume—the *pollera*—with heelless satin slippers, noiselessly served the different courses, most of them quite new to the Americans present. Course followed course. As the champagne circulated, conversation in both Spanish and English became more and more animated; both languages were sadly mangled, but there was no difficulty in conveying ideas. Then, for *postres* came the delectable coconut ice cream. The finger bowls, resting upon doilies of exquisite texture, were set aside in anticipation.

The guest of honour, entirely absorbed in Lady Mallett's gay conversation, helped himself to a generous portion of the cream, depositing it upon the centre of his doily, which he had absent-mindedly failed to remove. The doilies were greatly prized by Lady Mallett, who afterward confessed to a pang when she saw what had happened. But that was a mild chagrin; the real sensation came as she watched the precious doily slowly shrivel, its delicate texture not proof against the liquid cream. A faint hope still remained that the doily might be saved, when to her consternation Don——, twisting the wisp of doily about his fork, took the last mouthful of the coconut cream. Lady Mallett expected things to happen and with difficulty refrained from crying "Stop! Stop!" But without the quiver of an eyelash or a strained throat muscle, the coconut cream and fibrous doily disappeared. Twenty-three cobwebby doilies only remained to hand down to posterity.

Chief among the pleasures at Culebra, Camp Elliott, and other places along the line were perhaps the bimonthly dances at the Tivoli Hotel in Ancon. Taking the afternoon train, the ladies in their vari-coloured party gowns and the officers in immaculate white uniform gave the prosaic old railroad train a truly festive appearance. Parties were arranged for dinners at the Tivoli and afterward for the dancing in the ballroom until twelve o'clock. The dances were always held on Saturday night. Then came the slow progress of the homeward train, discharging at every station its load of tired but happy merry-makers. What tales the old back gallery of the Tivoli could tell, of whispered nothings between the dances, of lovers' disagreements or plighted troth; or just the prosy conversation of those of more mature years. For the Tivoli dances were alike for débutantes or grandmothers all over the Zone.

The sympathetic side of Gorgas came out perhaps most conspicuously in his work in the hospitals. Indeed, the hospitals of the Canal Zone played an important part in cementing a friendship between the United States and the republics of Latin America. As someone remarked, "they did more to foster good feeling and bring about American solidarity than did all the American congresses with their speeches and lavish hospitality." Regarding the Canal as a national enterprise, Gorgas carried the national idea into the organization of his department, selecting medical officers from the army, navy, and Public Health Service, as well as from civil life. The chief of the hospital division, Dr. John W. Ross, U. S. N., had been closely associated with Gorgas for many years at Fort Barrancas and in Havana. Their large experience in yellow fever and tropical diseases enabled them to foresee and prepare for the heavy demands that came. Under the management of Dr. Ross, the hospitals were quickly organized and abundantly equipped with the best of everything.

Ancon Hospital on the Pacific side, and Colon Hospital on the Caribbean on the northern end, which the French had built, were gradually repaired and used as base hospitals. Major Louis A. Lagarde, U. S. A., was appointed superintendent of Ancon Hospital, and Dr. Curl, U. S. N., of Colon Hospital. At all intervening sanitary districts small hospitals or dressing stations were maintained where the ill could be treated who could not be safely transported. Every day a hospital car filled with cots and screened against mosquitoes ran from Panama to Colon and back, picking up acute and suspicious cases to be cared for at the main hospital. There were thirty-six bed emergency hospitals along the line.

Young physicians and surgeons for the hospitals were secured from the United States; and the nursing corps, comprising at its maximum one hundred and thirty nurses, came from American training schools of the highest standing. Dr. Ross impressed on doctors, nurses, and all hospital employees that the comfort and happiness of the patient were always to have first consideration. This theory was carried out to such an extent that there was no more popular department of the canal government than the hospital service. The high-class medical skill and the treatment accorded the patients won the confidence not only of the canal employees, but of the Panamans.

At Ancon Hospital the pavilion system was used. When the yellow fever began, Gorgas took the fever wards himself at Ancon, and through all the worry, anxiety, and work of 1904 and 1905 he always found time to go through those two wards once or more a day. He took charge principally because only in this way could he keep in the closest touch with the yellow-fever situation, and secondly because he liked the work. Into his two wards all people suspected of yellow fever were sent; also any American having fever of any kind. In this way he treated many Americans, some three hundred a month. Besides the doctors and their families, and the nurses living at Anconcita, the young engineers and their families—some sixty in all—were brought up into the vacant French building at the hospital to avoid the disease. It was much like a big garrison there in 1904 and 1905. About forty took their meals at the mess. Mr. Fraga, one of three brothers who ran the café "El Suizo" in Havana, was the major domo. Gorgas presided at one long table, and Dr. Carter at another, the nurses having tables to themselves. The cooking was done at one central kitchen, a large concrete building with "Cuisine" inscribed over the

Dr. Henry R. Carter, whose studies in yellow fever laid the foundation for the work of the Reed Board.

door—a picturesque affair, fitted with great ovens, wonderful shining copper kettles, and other utensils. Over this cuisine presided in the early days a chef, who, to quote Dr. Carter, "knew more ways of spoiling fish than any man living."

On Sunday mornings visitors usually attended the services held before breakfast in the little room below the Gorgas quarters. "Dr. Gorgas invariably found time to be present at that little service on Sunday morning on Ancon Hill," the Reverend Britton King writes. "His quiet but cheery optimism gave out confidence to many, and the assurance that conditions would improve. I am proud to remember that for five years as visiting chaplain to Ancon Hospital Dr. Gorgas was my chief. During part of that period the duty devolved upon me of conducting divine service in the hospital chapel."

It was really Dr. John Ross who started the little church at Ancon. He was a great churchman, and his influence in any community tended for betterment. On Sunday morning Dr. Ross would round up all the young men and lead them meekly up Ancon Hill to the ten o'clock service. In the absence of a minister—a frequent occurrence at the time—the services were conducted by him, Dr. Carter, or Gorgas. Some of the prominent officials needed no urging to come to these services, but if there was any faltering, Dr. Ross did not hesitate to use persuasion.

Mr. and Mrs. Wallace, though they lived in town, were regular in their attendance, and the auditor, Mr. West, took an active part in the church services until his death from yellow fever. From the near-by wards Dr. Ross rounded up the convalescent patients, who came to the service in flapping straw slippers, a light bathrobe thrown over their pajamas.

Farther down the hill Father Quijano held services in the little Catholic church. To Dr. Ross it was immaterial which church was attended. His one object was to have people go to church, and in riding boots, white trousers, gauntlets, and big sombrero he made his round on his gaily caparisoned pony—gay after the Mexican fashion, with silver trappings—a greatly beloved figure, wherever stationed and particularly so on Ancon Hill during the few months his health permitted him to live in Panama. It was this affection that inspired such prompt acquiescence to his wishes. After he left the Isthmus it is to be feared that there was a fall from grace on the part of some. Church was not so regularly attended, and manhattans and martinis were consumed with more freedom.

In the days when things looked blue, and even those who had been in the fight before were irritable and dissatisfied, Gorgas would make his working day longer than usual, visit his forces, and make the men feel that the task to be done was worth the fight.

He made personal visits to the fever wards to encourage and cheer the patients. Notwithstanding the depleted hospital staff, the doctors and nurses maintained their cheerfulness. A steam-shovel man was sent to the hospital with an "awful headache," and was so sick he didn't care whether he lived or died. "In the morning," he said, "a cheerful-looking doctor came to my bed and asked me how I was coming on. He promised he would have me out on the work before I knew it. I asked the nurse who he was. 'Colonel Gorgas,' she said, and told me that he made a regular practice of rising early in the morning, so as to have time to drop in and cheer us up before starting his day's work. I felt it was up to me to do my share, too, and get well as quickly as possible, and I really did feel better. I used to wake up in the morning and watch to see him come in our ward, bright and smiling, and all the other fellows did, too, and we surely thought a lot of him, taking so much trouble for us rough-necks."

One day in the winter of 1905-06, a man ill with typhoid fever was brought into Ward 11 of the Ancon Hospital. Gorgas ordered the case into bed number 13. "Don't you know, Doctor," said the patient, looking pitifully at Dr. Gorgas, "I am from Tennessee and I couldn't get well in bed 13?" Instantly Gorgas turned to the orderly with a smile, saying: "Number that bed 12 and a half."

"For a few months during the winter of 1905," writes Dr. Pierce, "I was executive officer for Gorgas, and had an opportunity that comes to few of observing a great man at close range. The most distinct impression I have of those busy days was his constant patience and gentleness. Under all sorts of trying conditions he quietly worked on and on, seeming to know that ultimately everything would be all right, and that he would make the Panama Canal possible by sanitating the Zone and the two cities under his jurisdiction. I recall one doctor on the staff who wrote many long letters of complaint about the difficulties he had in administering his small part of work. I handled this correspondence, and finally, my patience exhausted, prepared a letter for Gorgas's signature to this doctor, which would, I thought, make him bear some of his own burdens and solve his own problems a little better before bothering his chief. Gorgas cancelled the letter, and wrote one of his own kindly letters to replace my impetuous effort. His natural gentleness caused him to explain to me, his subordinate, that he re-wrote my letter because he did not want to hurt the doctor's feelings. That incident is the key to Dr. Gorgas's character. He would never do anything that could hurt another in any way. He evidently followed that rule consistently, yet he had an esprit de corps among the personnel of the Sanitary Department that was splendid. All of us, from the chief assistants of Gorgas to the humblest employees of the department, were proud to serve under his kindly and intelligent direction.

"Upon one occasion I went aboard a ship at Colon wharf with Gorgas, and on deck, while I was engaged in some task, I heard Colonel Gorgas introduce himself to the captain of the ship as Dr. Gorgas. He chatted awhile with the captain. Later I was asked if Dr. Gorgas was the brother of the famous Colonel Gorgas of the army who had charge of the sanitation of the Canal!"

II

And in this way the Canal was built. It was a triumph of sanitation and of engineering, and it was also a triumph of character. Gorgas's supreme patience and resolution in the face of official difficulties had their final reward. The Canal Zone, after ten years of his ministrations, became a place completely transformed. The French, who had spent such disastrous days in the same region, would not have recognized it after the Americans had been there for a few years. The gaieties that marked the social side of Panama would have been quite impossible to the French, for the most common sight in the old De Lesseps days was an almost continuous procession of funerals. The fact is, however, that, by the time Gorgas had finished his work, the death rate at Panama, from all diseases, was lower than that of any American city or state. In 1914, the year the Canal was opened, the general death rate of the United States was 14.1 per thousand. The death rate of the Canal Zone in the same year was six per thousand. There were only three American states that had a lower rate than 10 per cent.—Washington, with 9.5, Minnesota, with 9.4, and Nebraska, with 9.2—and these three banner states, it will be observed, had a considerably higher rate than Panama. In other words, the Isthmus, which for four centuries had had an evil fame as almost the deadliest place in the world, had suddenly become almost the healthiest. It was a far safer place in which to live than any American state or any American city. This was the miracle of Gorgas's work—a performance in improving conditions of human life without precedent in history.

It was entirely fitting that Gorgas should be the first to take a boat through the Canal. It was a modest vessel—a canoe—and Gorgas had, as companions, Colonel Charles Mason and Mr. J. A. Le Prince of the Sanitary Staff. The trip was both profitable and amusing, as is shown in Mr. Le Prince's account.

"As we paddled through the canal bottom to Gaillard Cut," he says, "an Irishman called down to us from the top of the high, cliff-like embankment. He wanted us to stop, which we did. Then coming nearer to us, he shouted, 'Wait a minute! Wait a minute! There's something I want to know! I never drimpt I'd live to see the first ship go through this cut! Tell me, where be ye goin'?

"We told him that we were on our way to the Atlantic, whereupon he exclaimed: 'The Lord be praised! It's wid me own eyes I've seen the first boat go acrost, and now I believe ithers can go—but it'll be later, I'm a-thinkin'!'

"Beyond that point we paddled a distance northward, much to the admiration of our Irish friend, and then lifted the canoe up the steep side of the canal cut. I've always known that Gorgas had plenty of push and drive in him, and I certainly appreciated his upward push as we lifted that canoe up the steep sides of Gaillard Cut!

"We reëmbarked at Obispo Diversion Channel, at the top of the cliff, dripping with perspiration, but laughing and enjoying it immensely. Soon we reached some deep pools and got into the water to cool off. We then went on down the Chagres River toward Bohio, now under Gatun Lake, and at what was then called Tabernilla. Here a surprise awaited us. The river was up and the current very rapid. It was all we could do to steer clear of the boulders. We saw a number of men waving their arms and foolishly suggesting that we turn back, but we were in the grip of a strong current and too busy dodging obstructions to pay much attention to them. In another moment there was a terrific crash, and rocks were flying in every direction.

"Colonel Gorgas had the rear paddle and I the forward one. As coolly as possible he called, 'A little more steam forward!' and if ever I distinguished myself by rapid obedience to orders, it was at that moment! We knew in a flash that the reception committee we had noticed a few seconds earlier had been trying to warn us that the fuses were lit and a blast about to go off at the point toward which we were directly heading. Rocks, stones, and dirt rained about us, as we went full speed ahead in the rapid, boulder-strewn channel. We had intended to follow the river bed, but the swifter channel through a diversion cut suddenly caught our boat and whisked us through. It was a thrilling and exciting moment, with everything in action, including our imaginations and expectations, but we travelled too quickly to allow of any verbal expression of our sentiments to those who had started the barrage. Colonel Gorgas remarked simply, 'A rather warm reception!' but the forward paddle wanted to return as a committee of one for a sudden and active interview.

"On our way down the river we had a head wind against us, between Bohio and Gatun, with no river current, and my arms were all full of aches, for we had been paddling since sunrise, and I wondered if we should ever reach Gatun; but Colonel Gorgas was doing such noble work at the rear paddle that I was ashamed to give up or complain. When asked for the time, I had to explain that my watch had stopped permanently and stayed up in the Obispo Diversion. Finally we saw a *cayuca* with a sail coming toward us, and were temporarily encouraged by the hope of finding out approximately where we were. Ever since that day I have been wary of approximations. The *cayuca* passed close to us, and in it were two Jamaica Negroes. The Colonel bade them good afternoon and asked them how far it was to Gatun. They discussed the matter together and much to our amusement one of them replied, 'Not *too* far, Boss!' Hoping for a clearer approximation, while the Colonel smiled, I snapped out, 'Just how long do you think it will take us to get there?'

"The big Negro in the boat sized us all up very carefully, conferred with his partner, and after awhile his mental machinery operated, and back came the slow answer: 'Not too long, Boss!'

"Too much laughter might have rocked the boat dangerously, so we did not ask him how many hours, knowing the answer would be 'Not too many!' Seeing us laughing heartily, the Negroes thought it proper to grin also, but not too much.

"When we reached Colon, friends asked us where we came from, and thought we were joking when we replied that we had made the trip from the Pacific to the Atlantic in that canoe. About two years later I was invited to see the first (so-called) boat go through the Canal, and was amused that the large concourse of people who lined the Canal's banks were under the impression that they were watching the first boat go through the Canal from one ocean to another."

The whole trip, however, was not devoted to fun. During this first crossing of the Isthmus, Gorgas had his more serious moments; the thought that this was the first time men had traversed this neck of land by water naturally produced sober reflections. The dream of four centuries had thus become a reality. But it was not this sensational fact that chiefly occupied Gorgas's mind; his thoughts were upon the future—the meaning of the accomplishment in the centuries ahead. The effect of the Canal upon the world's commerce and the movement of populations—that was important, but even that was not the conception that was foremost in Gorgas's imagination. The successful sanitation of the Isthmus, he told his companions, really meant a revolution of human history. What it would accomplish, only our successors, ages hence, would completely understand. The accepted truth that white men could not live in the tropics—what would this experiment do to that great fallacy? The Canal had already proved it untrue. Nearly fifty thousand strangers, many of them white, were at that very moment living in the Panama Zone and enjoying health conditions much superior to those of their native countries; they were strong, happy, prosperous, and full of energy—witness the beehive of industry the Canal had become. What had suddenly made this tropical land so desirable as an abiding place of white men? Only one change had taken place: disease had been driven from the Isthmus, especially yellow fever, malaria—in large measure—pneumonia, the bubonic plague, and the like. Gorgas had demonstrated that the tropics, far from being inaccessible to white men, in reality provided a most desirable place of settlement. That these hot countries were the original headquarters of civilization, there was little doubt; indeed, it was inevitable that they had been, for the first men had no fire and no clothes, and so must have necessarily lived in warm climates. The penetration of the temperate zones was unquestionably a slow and tedious process, for it was only as human kind developed protection against cold that they could have lived in such regions. What, then, drove men to leave their pleasant tropical homes and seek living quarters in lands that were cold and uninviting nearly half the year? The reason, Gorgas believed, was simple enough. The pressure of disease drove them into less destructive parts of the earth. Disease naturally flourishes in hot areas, for all kinds of animal life, particularly disease germs and the conveying insects, are stimulated by the heat. Similarly, the cold of the temperate zone killed these malevolent forms of life, or at least many of them, with the result that life, even though it was more difficult, was far safer. This is the reason that practically all great civilizations have arisen in the temperate zone. Mesopotamia, Egypt, Asia Minor, Greece, Rome, Europe, and the Mediterranean littoral, northern and southern China, Japan and northern India—these countries, the seats of past and present civilization, were all located in the temperate zone. Two civilizations developed in America before the arrival of the white man—Mexico and Peru; the fact that neither flourished in the temperate zone may seem at first to refute this generalization, but not so; for both came into existence on high tablelands, several thousand feet above sea level, and therefore in regions as cool in climate and as resistant to disease as the countries farther north and farther south. The colonization of the Americas demonstrates the same thing. The earliest colonizers were the Spanish, but they, for the most part, made the mistake of settling in the tropics, with the result that the nations founded by them have not flourished. Only when white men began settling the colder zones did great success come. The chief reason for this was the fact that life in tropical America was a constant struggle against tropical disease. Was this not the reason that Africa had for ages been known as the Dark Continent?

The subject then, and afterward, was a favourite one with Gorgas, and he became eloquent as the conversation went on. From every possible standpoint except disease, he declared, the tropics were far better adapted to civilization than the temperate zones. The belief that heat in itself was a deterrent to work and energy had been disproved. The ten years' building of the Canal had shown it to be a mistake. Certainly men had never worked harder and to greater purpose than the labourers who had constructed this mighty ditch. Who ever saw more ruddy and vigorous children than the thousands who were at that moment swarming on the Isthmus, daily attending school, playing with all the heartiness and enjoyment of childhood? The white workers were as rugged and as sunburned as farmers in our Northwestern States. There was nothing in the belief that a tropical country necessarily bred laziness. The present inhabitants were unquestionably slothful: but here was again apparent the inevitable working of biological law; in the age-long struggle for the possession of the earth, the most energetic races seize the most desirable parts, while the less capable peoples take what is left. That, and the constant presence of disease, explain the lack of industry in the tropics. But Nature otherwise intended the warmer places as the headquarters of the highest civilizations. Here she worked for man most assiduously and most successfully. She does not work for him six months in the year, as in northern countries, but for twelve months. There are not one or two crops, but an unending succession. In no parts of the world does human effort produce such great results. But look at the vast stretches of the earth's surface that are now unused! The valleys of the Amazon, the Orinoco, the Congo, and the Nile could support great nations of white men. Only one thing deterred —disease; once remove this horror, and these fruitful areas could be transformed into vast garden spots and the miracle of the Mississippi Valley would be duplicated in each. Art and industry and all the attributes of high civilization would gather around the Caribbean Sea, as in ancient times they gathered around the Mediterranean.

This then was the real meaning of the canal work, as Gorgas saw it and explained it to his associates in that first trip across the Isthmus. He had restored to white civilization untold millions of acres of which disease had robbed it. To bring these extensive territories within the purview of modern life must necessarily be the task of the future. Yet the rest of Gorgas's days were to be devoted to this great work. He was sixty years old when the Panama Canal was finished. In the main, life had dealt gently with him, but his once black hair had become silvery white, though his eyes had lost nothing of their sparkle nor his skin its freshness. He looked forward cheerfully to many years of labour in his chosen field—the extension of the lessons of Havana and Panama to South America, South Africa, Asia, and other sections where disease had abruptly arrested human progress. His vocation was now to help bring about the great change in the habitable world which he had outlined to his friend and comrade in that first canoe trip through the Canal for the construction of which he was mainly responsible.

CHAPTER IX

CARRYING THE PANAMA LESSON TO OTHER LANDS

I

THE opportunity to begin this new task—the application of the lessons of Panama to all parts of the world—came even before the completion of the Canal. In the autumn of 1913, a death-dealing blight fell upon the Negro workers of the Rand in South Africa. Pneumonia, to which these black men were not accustomed, began to sweep them away by the hundreds. The use of the unfortunate creatures of the jungle for the exploitation of the gold and diamond mines had for years been a blot upon civilization. But the mortality that now descended upon them—a death rate, chiefly from pneumonia, of thirty-five per cent—gave especial emphasis to this long-standing evil. The British Government declared that, unless the disease were checked, the recruiting of Negroes for this purpose must come to an end. The owners of the mines were face to face with the problem of shutting them down. Was there any way in which the plague could be checked?

It is perhaps not surprising that, under these conditions, the mine owners turned their thoughts to the sanitary work that had just been brought to so successful an end at Panama. About this time, Mr. Samuel Evans, of the Transvaal Chamber of Mines, happened to read a lay sermon on "Man's Redemption of Man" recently delivered in Edinburgh by Sir William Osler, Regius Professor of Medicine at Oxford. His attention was particularly arrested by this paragraph concerned with Gorgas's work at the Canal:

"There is nothing to match it in the history of human achievement. Before our eyes to-day the most striking experiment ever made in sanitation is in progress. The digging of the Panama Canal was acknowledged to be a question of the health of the workers. For four centuries the Isthmus had been the white man's grave, and during the French control of the Canal the mortality once reached the appalling figure of 170 per thousand. Even under the most favourable circumstances it was extraordinarily high. Month by month I get the reports which form by far the most interesting sanitary reading of the present day. Of fifty-four thousand employees, about thirteen thousand of whom are white, the death rate per one thousand for the month of March was 8.91. Here is a chapter in human achievement for which it would be hard to find a parallel."

Here, then, not improbably was the very man the South African mines needed. Mr. Evans decided to investigate the matter personally and in a few weeks took sail for Panama. He spent several weeks on the Isthmus in almost daily association with Gorgas. The two men became close friends; Mr. Evans not only studied Gorgas's work at first hand, but he made a complete examination of documents and statistics, as a result of which he said that he had been much impressed. It so happened that Gorgas had met and solved the very problem that was then causing so much havoc in the South African mines, pneumonia among the Negro employees. This was one of the minor sanitary achievements of Gorgas, accomplished as far back as 1906; in the more spectacular conquests over yellow fever and malaria it had attracted little public notice. When the work started on the Canal, however, pneumonia was just as destructive among the Negro workmen as yellow fever among the white. For the most part, West Indian Negroes, who made up the bulk of the coloured population, exposed themselves to yellow fever with impunity; it was a disease with which they had lived for centuries and from which they had thus become immune. Pneumonia, however, was a malady as strange to them as measles and smallpox had proved to the original American Indians; they had, therefore, developed no protection against it; once exposed to its ravages, the poor creatures died at a shocking rate. Living and working conditions, Gorgas discovered, ideally facilitated this destructive process. The French had left in the Culebra region a large number of wretchedly constructed huts, which, hastily repaired and made mosquito proof, were now used as headquarters for the West Indians. At Panama the rainy season lasts for eight months; the Negroes were therefore wet for the larger part of the time. They were too poor, in these early days, to afford more than one set of clothing; in this they worked in the rain, and at night they retired to their cold cabins, sleeping in their wet garments. This kind of human material proved ideal for the pneumonia germ. The fact that the Negroes slept in bunks alongside the wall, packed closely against one another, made infection inevitable. A single pneumonia victim, under these conditions, rapidly communicated the disease to his entire group. The atmosphere of each hut became fetid with contagion; more Negroes died of pneumonia than from all other troubles combined; the news went back to the West Indies, and, unless the plague were conquered, it was certain that the Government would prohibit recruiting. Gorgas, however, found a simple solution. The whole trouble, he insisted, was the crowded condition in which the Negroes lived. If they could be dispersed and any pneumonia victim segregated, there was every likelihood that the disease would disappear. And so the event proved. Government land was set apart and the black workers encouraged to build houses, separated from one another by a safe distance. At the end of a few months Negro cabins, commodious and neat, were scattered all over the reservation; the Negroes, now comfortably housed, brought their wives and children to the Isthmus, and a contented and prosperous community supplanted the wretched settlements. Pneumonia, as an epidemic, disappeared instantaneously.

This demonstration convinced Mr. Evans that the South African problem was not a hopeless one. Returning home, he recommended that the Chamber of Mines invite Gorgas to come to the Rand and advise on sanitary problems. That the climatic difference between Panama and the Witwatersrand was great Gorgas well understood; for this reason certain friends advised him not to accept the invitation; fundamentally, however, Gorgas declared that the problem was the same.

Meanwhile, recognition of Gorgas's life work came from numerous other sources. In 1908 the American Medical Association had put the seal of its approval on his career by electing him President; honorary degrees from several universities—Pennsylvania, Harvard, Brown, the University of the South, and others—had emphasized still further the estimation in which his work was regarded in intellectual circles. Perhaps the judgment of the medical profession was best expressed by Dr. William H. Welch, the dean of American physicians, in conferring on Gorgas the degree of LL. D. from Johns Hopkins. In this tribute Dr. Welch did not hesitate to point out that the Panama achievement had been beset with great difficulties:

"In behalf of the Academic Council, I have the honour to present for the honorary degree of Doctor of Laws, Dr. William Crawford Gorgas, Colonel in the Medical Corps of the United States Army, member of the Isthmian Canal Commission, and Chief Sanitary Officer of the Isthmian Canal Zone, formerly president of the American Medical Association, physician and sanitarian of the highest eminence, who, by his conquests over pestilential diseases, has rendered signal service to his profession, to his country, and to the world.

"With high administrative capacity and with full command of the resources of sanitary science, Colonel Gorgas has given the world the most complete and impressive demonstration in medical history of the accuracy and the life-saving power of our new knowledge, concerning the causation and mode of spread of certain dreaded epidemic and endemic diseases. He it was who, by application of the discoveries of Major Reed and his colleagues of the Army Yellow Fever Commission, was mainly instrumental in freeing Cuba of yellow fever, and he it is who, in spite of obstacles and embarrassments, has made the construction of the Isthmian Canal possible without serious loss of life or incapacity from disease—a triumph of preventive medicine not surpassed in importance and significance by the achievements of the engineer.

"In the conquest of science over disease, in the saving of untold thousands of human lives and of human treasure, in the protection of our shores from a former ever-threatening scourge, in the reclamation to civilization of tropical lands, in results such as these are to be found the monuments of our laureate, his victories of peace, to which this University would now bear testimony by such honour as it can bestow."

Two honours of particular interest came to Gorgas about this time. His father, General Josiah Gorgas, had spent his declining years as President of the University of the South at Sewanee and President of the University of Alabama at Tuscaloosa. Gorgas was therefore much touched and flattered when both these institutions—Alabama in 1911 and Sewanee in 1913—offered him the position that his father had filled. Gorgas's mother was living in 1911, at an advanced age; the affectionate relations that had existed between the two in Gorgas's youth and early manhood had only grown stronger as years went on; naturally the growing fame of her son had added to the happiness of the mother's declining years; and nothing would have delighted Gorgas more than to retire from Panama to Tuscaloosa, where his mother was living. A few letters written by Gorgas at this period show that he had reached the mature period of life when an academic existence would have been far more congenial than those new adventures in foreign lands that duty was apparently making inevitable:

To Miss Jessie Gorgas[1]

DEPARTMENT OF SANITATION,
ANCON, CANAL ZONE

February 20th, 1911.

DEAR JESSIE:

I have been in your debt for some time and more particularly for your birthday letter of last October.

Yes, indeed—I have been very fortunate in life in that I have been given the opportunity of serving and still more so in living to see my work so liberally recognized. The life is very pleasant to me down here. The work is congenial and of endless variety. While I anticipate with pleasure my retirement, I expect that I shall miss the work, as do most retired officers whom I meet, though I am very fond of reading and look forward to getting a good deal of pleasure in this way when that time comes. As it is now I do not get much time for reading. I manage to keep a couple of books on hand always to read

[1]Of Tuscaloosa, Alabama, Dr. Gorgas's sister.

at such odd time as I can. One solid and one light. My solid book at present is Bryce's "American Commonwealth" and my light book one of De Morgan's—"Alice-for-Short." I have been reading Bryce's book ever since he was here. So you see that I do not get along very rapidly. But I find it very interesting and it soaks in. Have you read any of De Morgan's books? He makes me think of Thackeray. I have stopped paying any attention to my eyes as far as use is concerned. My left eye is useless but the right seems to be useful enough.

We are having crowds of people come to the Isthmus. The Tivoli Hotel is full all the time. Among these are a great many people who bring us letters, and in this way we meet many pleasant people.

With dearest love, I remain,
Affectionately your brother,
WILLIE.

To Mrs. Josiah Gorgas

DEPARTMENT OF SANITATION,
ANCON, CANAL ZONE

August 1st, 1911.

DEAR MOTHER:

I inclose your correspondence with Mr. Johnson concerning the presidency of the University. I have never given up an idea with more regret. I had never thought of such a thing till I got Jessie's letter in New York the day I sailed. And then it made no particular impression upon me. But the more I thought of the matter the more attractive it seemed. I could not have a position that I would like better. To have lived near you and been able to see you every day was the greatest attraction of it all. And then to have renewed the ties with Alabama which our family has held for the past three generations would have been delightful. Marie was charmed with the idea of living in the old house and filling it up and living in real old Colonial style for the rest of our lives. The salary with our retired pay would have allowed us to entertain very nicely. And then the whole romance of the thing appealed very strongly to our sentimental side. I hesitated a long time over the matter. Consulted my friends. Among others the Secretary of War and General Wood. Advice was variable, some said "yes" and some "no." We wanted much to have the family to consult. But it seemed to me that this was my life work on which my scientific reputation rested. That if I separated from the work before the Canal was opened I would lose a good share of this reputation. So very reluctantly I declined. But if it should ever come up again after the Canal is finished I would jump at it.

Life has been very gay since we have been back, the Secretary of War and his party and General

Wood and his party being here at the same time. Marie entertained them all.

I came down on the same steamer from New York with the Secretary and his party. He impressed me very favourably.

We have had a grand olive-branch shaking with X. Y. Z.[1] since we have been back. He came to our house to lunch when we entertained the Secretary, and we went to his house when he entertained. I inclose some letters that may interest you. Marie joins in love.

Fondly your son,

WILLIE.

To Mrs. Josiah Gorgas

DEPARTMENT OF SANITATION,
ANCON, CANAL ZONE

October 3rd, 1912.

DEAR MOTHER:

I am fifty-eight years old to-day, and a very happy and satisfactory fifty-eight years they have been to me. I wish that I had given my relatives and friends equal satisfaction during these years. But children never know how much thought and care they give their parents till they themselves are grown and have children of their own.

Father mentions in his journal[2] how sorry he is to

[1]General Goethals.

[2]The journal kept by General Josiah Gorgas, now in the Library of Congress.

see me so set upon getting to West Point when I have such an excellent opportunity in Uncle Tom's office. But later he is entirely satisfied at my turning my attention to medicine.

Father, in 1874, reviews his life by decades. And after considering the past decades he wonders what the next decade has in store for him and his little family. He is in perfectly vigorous health then and fifty-six years old. Two years younger than I am now! He writes that whatever he accomplishes in the way of caring for his family must be done in the coming decade. And he was right. When the end of the decade rolled around he had gone into the next existence. And it is more than probable that the same will occur to me. Reading the journal has been fascinating to me. It has been just like talking to Father. His last entry was made in 1878 and was very happy and cheerful. He had just been offered the position at Tuscaloosa, and at the same time a position in the University of Georgia. Everything is running along smoothly with us. Minna and Aileen are having a very good time. They sail for New Orleans on the 10th. Marie looks and feels well.

It looks more and more as if we are to have a Democratic President. I hope so. And that he will make a President of whom we can be proud.

Your son affectionately,

W. C. GORGAS.

To abandon all these cheerful and profitable prospects for rough travelling in South Africa—and afterward in South America—in pursuit of the plagues that afflict mankind, naturally demanded considerable force of character, but Gorgas did not hesitate. He was approaching his sixtieth year, but the world was full of misery which he might lighten. He therefore accepted the invitation from South Africa and sailed for England in the fall of 1913. The fact that the British authorities felt constrained to find their scientist in the United States caused some comment in English medical circles, which certainly did not lack experienced sanitarians, but there was a generous and whole-hearted recognition of the wisdom of the selection. "Probably the best estimate I have heard of the scientific administrative ability of General Gorgas," said Colonel Joseph H. Ford, U. S. A., "was voiced by Sir Arthur Slaggett, then Surgeon-General of the British Army, when I was his guest in London, July, 1914. Referring to General Gorgas's mission to improve the health of the miners of South Africa, General Slaggett said in effect: 'After we have accomplished so much in preventive and tropical medicine, we cannot but feel disappointed that the mine owners have gone outside of our service and even out of the Empire for a consultant. Yet we feel, too, that they are right. On those subjects which he will study there.

General Gorgas is the greatest authority in the world.'"

Arrived in London, Gorgas devoted his time to the collection of data and interviewing medical men familiar with conditions on the Rand, and officials of the Rand who were living in London. And then, November 15th, Gorgas, Major Noble, and Dr. Darling sailed on the steamship *Briton* of the Union Castle Line, for Capetown. "We had a very pleasant stay in London," wrote Gorgas from shipboard, "and met many of the distinguished medical men with whom I had formerly come in contact, or corresponded. Marie, Noble, Darling and I lunched with Sir William Osler at Oxford. I dined with Sir Ronald Ross, who had visited me at Panama. He was given the Nobel prize for discovering that malaria is transmitted by the mosquito. Another distinguished doctor with whom I dined was Sir Almroth Wright, and Marie and I lunched with Dr. and Mrs. Sandwith. He is a well-known practitioner whom we met in Egypt. We also dined with Mr. Sydney B. Williamson with whom we were associated for many years on the Canal Zone, and went with him to the theatre.

"But the greatest enjoyment I had was going around with my dear old friends whom I knew and loved so well. Think of the memories that come thronging when one looks at the very house in which Henry Esmond lived, or where dear old Colonel

Newcome spent his declining years, and where he finally answered 'Adsum' when the last roll call came; or the home where David Copperfield suffered and finally triumphed. I love to wander among the tombs where are laid the bodies of the great men we have known in history. I get so wrought up and enthused I scarcely can contain myself."

The travellers reached Capetown December 2d, after a pleasant but uneventful trip, and took the train immediately for Johannesburg, nine hundred and fifty miles distant. At the Johannesburg station, Mr. Evans and a committee from the Chamber of Mines met them and took them to the Carlton Hotel, where a suite of rooms had been reserved. In these rooms offices were established. The next morning the Chamber of Mines held a meeting and generally discussed existing conditions. Afterward, from the medical officers of the mines and health officers of the city located on the Rand, an insight into the medical problems was obtained and a programme mapped out for visiting the scenes of their labours and inspecting hospitals.

"We went with Mr. Evans to the National Observatory," wrote Gorgas, "looked over the war records, and had a pleasant view of the city and surrounding country. We lunched with Mr. and Mrs. Honnald. He is an American engineer. In the afternoon we called on Sir Lionel Phillips. There were some twenty-five or thirty people there taking tea, and we listened to beautiful music from his great organ. Sir Lionel is a highly cultivated gentleman and a fine fellow. I called on Mr. Williams at the hotel. He is the son of the Mr. Williams we met at Panama, and is the superintendent of the Kimberley Diamond Mines. He gave me a great deal of information about the way they care for their labourers, which is quite different from the way they are cared for at the gold mines. We were out all day with Dr. Porter, the health officer of the city, and dined with him and a party of fourteen at the Rand Club. We are invited by Viscount Gladstone, the Governor-General, to lunch with him next Friday. Mr. Evans will take us the fifty miles to Victoria in his motor."

More than fifty hospitals of the Rand were visited. The barracks were inspected and information was obtained as to the square area allowed each occupant as well as the cubic air space provided. The question of food supply, its character, preparation, and quantity, was also carefully studied. Gorgas was inclined to think that pneumonia could be controlled by placing the natives in little villages about the mines rather than in the barracks. Conditions were much the same on the Rand as at Panama, when pneumonia was making such havoc there. As soon as the Negroes were allowed to scatter at Panama and live in their own houses, pneumonia disappeared. Gorgas believed that in the barracks the Negroes became infected at once, and that therefore many cases of pneumonia developed. In single huts the infection was slower, and the workers gradually became immunized.

Recruiting labour for the mines of the Rand was one of the great outstanding problems. All labour, except a few natives living on the location in permanent small cantonments, was short-time labour for periods of about six months. This meant that, to maintain a working force of about two hundred thousand men, it was necessary to recruit approximately four hundred thousand every year. Every man who was disabled by accident or sickness, or who died, was an economic loss, not only to the mines, but to the productive wealth of the country, for it was upon the native labour that the Union of South Africa depended for industrial development.

Deeming it necessary to investigate the method of recruiting a labourer at the source of supply, and to follow him on the journey from his home to the receiving compound, it was planned to have Major Noble and Dr. Darling go to the town of Inhambane, Portuguese East Africa, about three hundred miles north of Lorenzo Marques. They were to leave Christmas night.

On Christmas Day, Dr. Gorgas wrote as follows:

"We reached Johannesburg three weeks ago to-day. Darling and Noble are studying my commercial code, trying to send Christmas greetings to their wives. Unfortunately this kind of code does not lend itself to love letters. Darling has triumphed. He has found two code words that mean 'Love in carload lots!' He thinks this will satisfy Mrs. Darling.

"I breakfasted at the Y.M.C.A at 8 o'clock, and made an address to the two hundred men present. Then Mr. and Mrs. Evans took a party of fifteen forty miles out on the veldt, where we picnicked and had a real good time.

"It is hot and dry to-day, very much as it is in Panama at this time of the year. A dust storm has just begun and the air is filled with blowing dust (just as used to be the case in Oklahoma in the fall). All the doors and windows are tightly closed to keep out the dust.

"Noble and Darling are about to start on their trip to Inhambane."

On January 8th he wrote:

"I have just got in from Kimberley. Just missed being held up on the road by a rail-road strike which is to go into effect to-day. Mr. Evans was with me, and Noble and Darling, who returned from their trip to Inhambane in time to go with me. We had a most interesting visit, and were the guests of the De Beer mines, where we were shown everything. Diamonds of all sizes being sorted and prepared. We saw on the table three weeks' produce of the mines, valued at $500,000."

As a result of their trip of inspection, Major Noble and Dr. Darling found that the labourers enrolled at Inhambane were transported by ship and rail to Rosanna Garcia, where they were held until twelve hundred were recruited. Then, scantily clothed, they journeyed by train from sea level to five thousand five hundred feet. Food was given them, and a blanket, but the marked change in temperature, with crowding on board ship, at the collecting station and on the train, provided opportunity for infection. A few of the labourers on each train arriving at the recruiting compound were ill with pneumonia, and an additional number became ill while in the receiving compound before they were transferred to the mines. In the mines themselves, working conditions were excellent, but merely the passing from the warm air underground to the high altitude caused a sudden chill, which resulted in a lighting up of any latent infection. The labourers in the barracks were also a source of contamination to one another; as a considerable number were housed in one room, infection was bound to spread, even though only one case of a respiratory disease was introduced. Gorgas found that the labourers fell ill even before they reached the Rand, and that their infection increased for some time thereafter; after a few months, however, the susceptibility of the individual labourers decreased, the decrease being in direct proportion to their length of service. In other words, what was termed a "new boy" was far more susceptible than the "old boy."

About the middle of January the European miners and railway employees of the Union of South Africa declared a strike. As the strike would put an end to the work of investigating the conditions on the Rand, it was decided to accept the invitation of the Government of Rhodesia to visit Salisbury, the capital, and advise as to the methods for the control of malaria, a disease that was taking a large toll from the European colonies.

At Salisbury they met many interesting people, and were delightfully entertained. The night of their arrival a dinner was given by Mr. Watson, one of the executive body of the chartered company of Rhodesia, at which Gorgas was seated next to Sir Starr Jameson, the president of the company, the man who started the Boer War by leading a raid on the Transvaal. Doctor "Jim" was intimately associated with Cecil Rhodes at Kimberley, and in the development of Rhodesia.

A charming surprise came to Gorgas the next day when he called upon the Governor, Sir William Milton. He was a little astonished when Sir William presented him to Lady Milton as "General Gorgas." For several years Gorgas had held a colonel's rank and he made a deprecating move of the hand when his host so glibly promoted him.

"But I still think I am right, General Gorgas," Sir William insisted, giving the "General" a particular emphasis.

Gorgas again attempted to correct the Governor, and by this time everybody except the embarrassed American was smiling broadly.

"I am delighted, General," Sir William went on, "to be the first to notify you and congratulate you."

And with that he handed Gorgas a news bulletin he had just received. It contained cablegrams from Washington saying that President Wilson had that day appointed Gorgas Surgeon-General of the United States Army.

The following letters will give an idea of what was done at this time:

Salisbury, Rhodesia,
January 22.

We left Monday for a three-day trip into the country, going north about one hundred miles to the end of the railroad and coming back in a motor car. It was like a political campaign. We had the private car of the Governor. I received the farmers and gave them a sanitary talk, or if the crowd was too large for the car, we would have the talk outside. We reached the end of the road, Shamon, at 9 P.M. Here I made an address in the town hall and showed lantern slides of sanitary work. Monday night we slept in the car. Tuesday we took the motor car and ran back toward Salisbury down a most beautiful valley of great agricultural possibilities, well dotted with farms. Dozens of these places were visited, and we talked with the people about anti-malaria work. Our car had been run down the railroad about halfway to Salisbury and left on a siding. It looked lonesome—not a dwelling in sight. As I went to sleep I could not help thinking of the time a few years ago when a lion came into the sleeping car and carried off one of the occupants. But no lion disturbed us. Wednesday we continued our motor trip into Salisbury.

January 25.

Last night I addressed the people of Salisbury in the theatre. The building was filled—about a thousand people. I talked for forty-five minutes, and showed slides for about thirty minutes afterward. Noble presided over the slides and Darling took post at the back of the theatre, so as to let me know whether or not I was speaking sufficiently loud. The audience was appreciative.

January 27.

I worked hard all day yesterday on my report and finished it about six o'clock, stopping just long enough to go to church. Sir William Milton asked me to make a written report, so that the Government can publish it. We got off this morning at nine-thirty, and said good-bye to our friends in Salisbury with regret, for they have been very courteous to us. Doctor and Mrs. Fleming were down at the depot to say good-bye. Mrs. Fleming gave us a basket of figs. Noble, Darling, and I have just finished them. I wonder if I am Surgeon-General, and if I am still on the Commission, and who has taken Gaillard's place.

January 28.

Reached Buluwayo after twenty-four hours' trip from Salisbury. The sleeping cars were good. Buluwayo is the principal town of Rhodesia, about fifteen thousand people. The Government House is located where Lobengula, twenty years ago, had his corral. Lobengula was the last king of the Matabeles. The Government House has a broad driveway some three miles long leading up to it. The tree under which Lobengula held court is still standing. It filled me with sadness to think of the slaughter and execution and human suffering that had taken place there.

In the afternoon we went out fifteen miles to the

Khami ruins. These are the ruins of a prehistoric city which must have accommodated fifty thousand people. The whole country is filled with old gold mines. Archæologists think that this is the Ophir of the Bible, and that this is the country from which Solomon and the king of Tyre got their gold. We spent two hours walking about the ruins, where now there is not a human being living within miles. We came across a large troop of baboons among the ruins. They did not seem particularly shy or unfriendly. We did not do anything to provoke them. This morning I went up to Government House to call on Sir William Milton, the Governor, who has been exceedingly kind and attentive.

January 29.

We spent the day yesterday at the Matapos Hill, where Cecil Rhodes has his lonely tomb. We left Buluwayo at ten in a motor, rode thirty miles through an uninhabited country as wild and rugged as nature could make it. Dr. Eaton, the health officer, took us as the guests of the Governor.

Cecil Rhodes was buried on the top of a granite hill some six hundred feet above the valley. The formation is peculiar; I have never seen it before: a dome of solid granite makes the mountain just the shape of the dome of our Capitol, only ten thousand times as large. Not a particle of earth anywhere upon it—only smooth granite just as it bubbled up in its molten condition. As far as the eye can reach, hundreds of hills in the same condition. We disturbed a herd of thirty baboons on the hill, and saw deer several times.

We returned to Buluwayo and took the train at six-thirty. We said good-bye to Sir William and other friends at the station.

On the return journey to Johannesburg, Sir Starr was a fellow passenger from Buluwayo to Mafeking. Gorgas had several conferences with him concerning health conditions in Rhodesia and South Africa. Sir Starr was a man of magnetic personality, and, said General Noble, it was easy to understand why men would follow him on a forlorn hope such as the Jameson Raid.

It is an interesting fact that Gorgas, in this South African expedition, frequently trod the same path which David Livingstone had passed nearly three quarters of a century previously. Dr. Livingstone, the Medical Missionary, belonged to the same profession as Gorgas; a profession which, as he himself said, "is preëminently devoted to practical benevolence, and which, with unusual energy, pursues from age to age its endeavours to lessen human woes."

"It is in the Anglo-American race," Dr. Livingstone said in 1856, "that the hope of the world for liberty and progress rests."

It is perhaps not strange that Gorgas's friends see, in his own labour in that Africa which Livingstone did so much to open to white civilization, a fulfillment—in part at least—of the Livingstone prophecy.

II

Gorgas and his two companions sailed from Capetown on the twenty-eighth of February. Besides short visits to the diamond mines at Kimberley, and to Southern Rhodesia, they had been on the Witwatersrand about three months. They left having, as Mr. Evans said, made many friends and inspired a sanitation policy which has saved a large number of lives. The day before leaving, Gorgas handed in his report and recommendations to the Transvaal Chamber of Mines. It aroused great interest. A number of recommendations were made, many of which have since been put into force, largely under the able direction of Dr. Ornstein, one of Gorgas's lieutenants on the Canal Zone, who in April, 1914, became the chief sanitation adviser of the Central Mining Company. None of the recommendations were novel or revolutionary in character; yet the results have been astonishing. Within four years the mortality from pneumonia dropped to about three per thousand, and the mortality from all other diseases to six per thousand. "It has been asserted," writes Dr. Ornstein, "that the introduction of prophylactic inoculation against pneumonia was the great deciding factor. Aside from the fact that prior to 1918 inoculations were carried out on only a portion of the natives, and that it is now known that the dosage used was inadequate and consequently the influence of the inoculation on the pneumonia mortality could not have been very marked—the fact remains that the mortality from the *other diseases* was reduced from 13 to 6, and on these the inoculation against pneumonia could have no influence whatever."

"The success of any system of sanitation," says Gorgas in this report, "which is more or less new to any locality, will depend a great deal upon the choice of the man who has charge of carrying it into execution. If he believes in it, has tact, is enthusiastic and persevering, it will succeed. If he is discouraged by difficulties and opposition he will fail, even if his system is correct."

Unconsciously Gorgas in these few words exposes the mainspring of his character; his fixity of purpose, his reasonableness, and his resourcefulness. Dr. William H. Bell, U. S. N., writing of Dr. Gorgas and his work in Panama, said: "His own system won out, not alone because of its proven correctness, but because of his confidence in it from the first, and the firm action which that led to, even the elimination of important subordinates, and because of his wonderful personality and his ability and readiness to find reasonable means for meeting reasonable obstructions. The gentleness and patience with which he brought the strength of his scientific position and the force of his character to prevail won the day in concrete results, and brought him ardent, loyal support everywhere. It is all very subtly explained in the above quotation."

Great honours were meanwhile in preparation for Gorgas on his arrival in England. Just as he was leaving Johannesburg he received the following letter from Sir John MacAlister:

DEAR COLONEL GORGAS:

Our friend Osler tells me where you are just now, and that you are sailing for England on February 20th.

I am writing to ask on behalf of the president, Sir Francis Champneys, the Council and Fellows of this society [Royal Society of Medicine], that you will honour them by lecturing before the society during your visit to London, and accept a reception by the President, Council and Fellows, and dine with the Council the same evening.

At the foot of this letter I give a list of most convenient dates for us, and shall be greatly obliged if you will select one of them and let me know at your earliest convenience.

"We are steaming up the English Channel," notes Gorgas, March 16th, and a little later he writes:

"Sir William Osler tells me he hopes I will be able to fall in with the somewhat active programme which has been arranged, and that MacAlister, the secretary of the Royal Society of Medicine, will give me full particulars. That the Colonial Secretary, the leading members of the profession, the Archbishop of Canterbury, Lord Bryce, Lord Moulton and others will be there."

Sir William Osler said that in his opinion the greatest ovation ever given a medical man in England was on the occasion of General Gorgas's visit to London in 1914.

The leading medical scientists of Great Britain, the universities and the press all did him the highest honour. This quiet and unpretentious American was almost overwhelmed by the interest his visit aroused. "Perhaps of all living Americans," said the *Daily Mail*, "Dr. Gorgas has conferred the greatest benefit on the human race. The whole world, particularly the British Empire, with its large tropical possessions, owes him a debt which Britons are proud to acknowledge. Entertainments on a lavish scale have been prepared for the American army surgeon who cleared up Panama from the tropical diseases which made the building of the Canal for years an impossibility. The British Society of Medicine will give a banquet in General Gorgas's honour on Monday next."

Perhaps the one man most keenly interested in Gorgas and his work was Sir William Osler, the great professor at Oxford. On his representation Oxford University held a special convocation to confer on Gorgas the honorary degree of Doctor of Science.

"Dear Gorgas," wrote Sir William, on his arrival, "I have sent word to the Vice Chancellor that Tuesday will do. You will have official notice from the Registrar. All will be arranged about your gown. Have you your uniform with you? I am asking the Ambassador to come to the ceremony, and Squier. As it is out of term we have to hold a special convocation for you. I shall see you to-morrow evening. I hope we have not arranged a too strenuous programme."

The Oxford Convocation, which took place on March 23, 1914, was an impressive spectacle. The position which Gorgas had acquired in the estimation of British scientists was well brought out in the address of the Public Orator, Mr. A. D. Godley, of Magdalen College:

"Those are most to be honoured by us who have increased knowledge and thereby promoted the welfare of the world. Such are many students of medicine; it is a fine thing to have the scientific knowledge which can cure disease: but theirs is a still finer if more dangerous task who can extirpate the causes from which disease springs. It is such men who destroy the seeds of death which are bred in swamps, risking their health and even their lives to save their fellows. These heroes are a modern realization of the legend of Heracles, the cleanser of foul places and the enemy of evil beasts.

"The eminent American whom you see to-day has like many of his countrymen fought in the forefront of the battle. His achievements are too numerous for me to relate in detail. Suffice it to say that it is he who cleansed Havana; it is he who put fever and pestilence to flight in the Isthmus of Panama, and made possible the long-thwarted construction of the great interoceanic waterway; it is he who has recently improved the sanitary conditions in the South African mines. He purified foul air; he waged war on the myriad swarms of death-disseminating mosquitoes. The result has been an amelioration of the conditions of human life in plague-haunted districts, where once 'in silent fear the helpless healer stood,' and it is now possible to live in comfort and to work with advantage. There can be no better example to those 'Whose skill hath served the human lot to raise, and won a name that endless ages praise.'"

"Preëminently distinguished," said the acting Vice Chancellor, Dr. T. H. Warren, in admitting the candidate to the Degree of Doctor of Science, "sagacious, health-bringing, the modern Machaon of the American Army, whom indeed I should wish to salute not only in Latin prose but also in Greek verse thus:

"Hail Router of the Plague of flies! hail Isthmian
Conqueror true!
Gorgas, to that wise Goddess dear, the Gorgon
death who slew!"

"I, by my authority and that of the whole University, with special pleasure admit you to the Honorary Degree of Doctor of Science."

CHAPTER X

CLEANSING SOUTH AMERICA—THE WORLD WAR

I

AFTER the completion of the South African work, Gorgas assumed, at Washington, the duties of the Surgeon-Generalcy. In recognition of his services at Panama, Congress raised his rank to that of Major-General, an almost unparalleled honour for the medical corps of the army. However, the new Surgeon-General had little opportunity, at this time, to give to his official labours. The call for his services in the field that he had made his own became insistent.

A year or two before an organization, unique in history, had come into existence. Mr. John D. Rockefeller had placed a large part of his great fortune at the disposal of the recently incorporated International Health Board. This body, originally brought into being for the purpose of fighting the hookworm in the Southern States, had now extended its operations into a battle against disease in all parts of the world. It was seriously attempting to make practical application of the discoveries of preventive medicine. The labours of Pasteur, Lister, and their followers had clearly demonstrated that contagious disease was not necessarily the heritage of human kind. A community submitted to these misfortunes only because it lacked the intelligence or the means to free itself. The greatest demonstrator of this great truth, so pregnant in meaning for the future of civilization, had been Gorgas himself. It was therefore not strange that the International Health Board, making its plans for this world-wide onslaught on disease, should seek to enlist Gorgas's services. Yellow fever naturally loomed before it as one of its greatest tasks. It was the one malignant disease which it seemed a comparatively simple matter to destroy. The rapidity and certainty with which it could be done Gorgas had demonstrated in Cuba and Panama. The possibility of chasing down the last yellow-fever germ, of making the disease as extinct as the animals of the pre-glacial period, now dawned upon humanitarians, not as a dream but as an exceedingly practical matter.

Yet only the most persistent efforts could accomplish this great end. The United States had taken the lesson of Panama to heart; by 1914 the places in the Southern States that yellow fever had periodically visited had abolished it, apparently for ever. The city of Rio de Janeiro had enforced the same lesson. Other cities and countries, however, had not profited, to any great extent, from the American demonstration. Mexico, Yucatan, the Central American and South American countries still harboured the disease in endemic form, and there were many signs that it prevailed on the west coast of Africa. Moreover, there was the greatest anxiety lest it spread to parts of the world that had previously been free. The Panama Canal, which had seemed to be the greatest enemy that yellow fever had ever had, might develop into its greatest friend. Sanitarians everywhere regarded its opening with dismay. That it would promote the world's commerce was apparent, but the apprehension was that, in accomplishing this great end, it would also disseminate disease. When Dr. Wickcliffe Rose, the President of the International Health Board, visited certain Asiatic countries in 1914, he found them almost in a state of panic. These countries had never suffered from yellow fever, but he found Singapore, Hong Kong, and Colombo waging a war of extermination against the Stegomyia mosquito, which they had in plenty. They were doing this, he was informed, as a measure against an expected onslaught from yellow fever. The opening of the Panama Canal would place all China and the Far East in immediate touch with the Gulf ports. Commerce had always been the way in which yellow fever had been carried from country to country. A hundred years ago ships sailing from Cuba and Central America had carried the disease into Spain,

Italy, and even northern Europe. Was it not likely that the establishment of direct sailing routes between the Gulf and the Far East would prove a similar bane to that region? And the result would be something frightful to contemplate. There were hundreds of millions of human beings non-immune from the disease, not accustomed to sanitary measures of any kind; once the yellow-fever germ obtained a footing, they would die by millions. The epidemic that would result would probably be the worst since the Black Death had swept across Europe in the 14th Century, destroying a fourth of its population. This was what the Panama Canal might do to these unprotected countries unless the danger were checked. What was the most satisfactory way of combating the threatened evil? Obviously there was only one way. The thing must be eliminated at its source. The remaining foci of yellow fever, in Central and South America, must be destroyed. Only the quenching of the fire in these areas could prevent its being transmitted to other parts of the world.

This phase of the problem Dr. Rose presented to Gorgas, asking his advice.

"Is there anything to be done?" he asked.

Gorgas did not hesitate. He was in one of his most enthusiastic moods. The solution was simple.

"Of course! Eradicate yellow fever!"

And then he described the devastation caused by

certain historic yellow-fever epidemics, and the menace of such hotbeds of the disease as Manaos, Guayaquil, and Merida in Yucatan. He gave the complete stories of the work of Oswaldo Cruz in Rio de Janeiro, of Liciago in Vera Cruz. What did these experiences prove? Were they not clear demonstrations that the disease could be stamped out wherever it showed its head? Was the complete eradication of yellow fever possible? On that point Gorgas entertained not the slightest doubt.

"I hope," he told Dr. Rose, "to have the privilege of writing the final chapter in its history. To this I propose to give up the rest of my life."

Dr. Joseph H. White and Dr. Henry R. Carter supported these same views. The number of endemic foci of yellow fever, they declared, were few; these centres were the sources from which epidemics spring; the extermination of infection at these points is feasible; and if these seed beds were destroyed, the disease would necessarily disappear. They were eager to see it undertaken. These three men held not only a positive conviction as to the possibility of freeing the world of yellow fever, but also a crusader's zeal for the adventure. Their enthusiasm for the enterprise was contagious—as contagious as yellow fever itself—and communicated itself to Dr. Rose and the entire Health Commission.

After repeated consultations Dr. Rose presented

to the International Health Board a memorandum embodying the results of these discussions. General Gorgas, Dr. Carter, and Dr. White were invited to meet the executive committee at New York. At its meeting in May, 1915, the Board voted to enter the field of yellow-fever control, and approved a general plan of operation involving international concert of effort in the warfare on the disease.

The war, by decreasing commerce, somewhat protected oriental countries from contamination, and also tended to delay the programme. Before any elaborate work could be undertaken, Dr. Rose and his associates wished to have complete and accurate information. At that time no one knew, from first-hand observation, what were the permanent headquarters of yellow fever. Gorgas was therefore invited to spend several months visiting suspected countries, seeking out the hiding places of the disease, and thus providing material for a comprehensive campaign. In June, 1916, Gorgas started on his travels, taking with him Dr. Carter, Dr. Juan Guiteras, his associate in the old Havana days, Major Eugene R. Whitmore, and Mr. William D. Wrightson. The next four months were among the most delightful and enjoyable of his life. Inevitably the trip became for Gorgas something of a triumphal progress. The party visited Ecuador, Peru, Colombia, Venezuela, Brazil, and, afterward, Mexico and several of the Central American states; everywhere Gorgas's reputation had preceded him, and everywhere all classes turned out to do him honour. Presidents, governors, and mayors met him at the stations; banquets and public meetings were held to celebrate his arrival; universities conferred their degrees and important public bodies endorsed his sanitary plans. Gorgas was by nature a social being, and he entered into these entertainments with the zest of a schoolboy. His genial manners, his approachableness, his constant good humour and sympathetic interest in existing difficulties and problems at once put him on terms of practical coöperation with his new friends. From the standpoint of the International Health Board this was the most valuable result of the Gorgas trip. The plan of searching out the seed beds of the disease and mapping a plan of campaign was important, but still more important was the establishment of satisfactory personal relations with these communities. The enterprise was a delicate one and could easily wound the sensibilities of proud peoples, and the South American populations have the quality of pride well developed. If representatives of some South American Health Commission should land in the United States with plans for making American cities cleaner, more sanitary, and less of a menace to the outside world, the wrath of Americans can well be imagined. In certain respects medical science is as far advanced in Latin America as in the United States; and a resentment at such an intrusion as that planned by the International Health Board might reasonably be expected. The outcome, how-

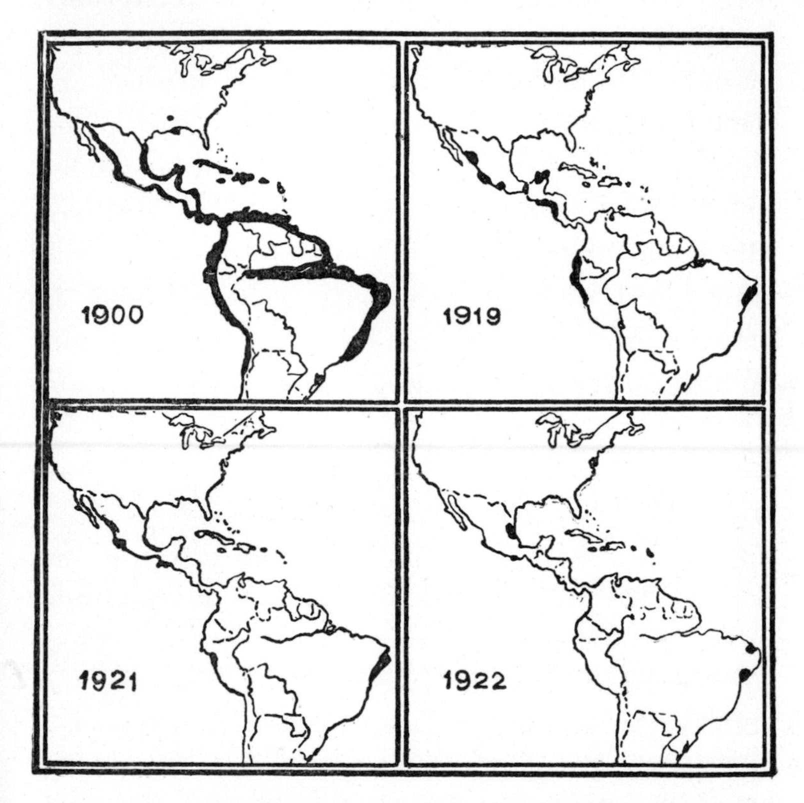

This map graphically illustrates Gorgas's life work. The shaded parts show the sections of the western hemisphere in which yellow fever was prevalent at the indicated dates. In 1900, before Gorgas's work in Havana, this disease was a commonplace in the Gulf cities of the United States, in Mexico and Central America, the Carribbean region, and tropical South America. In 1922 the disease was known only in one or two cities in Mexico and in Brazil.

ever, was a diplomatic triumph for Gorgas. His great fame as the conqueror of yellow fever gave him a personal authority that no one else could have brought, and the tact with which he explained the purpose of his errand disarmed all criticism. Everywhere public officials hailed him as the promised restorer of good health. Everywhere full coöperation with the International Board was promised. The result of Gorgas's visit was that practically the whole of South America was opened to the International Health Board. It formed the basis of the very successful campaign which began soon afterward and which is now approaching a triumphal end.

II

Returning to the United States, Gorgas laid before the Board a plan for the elimination of yellow fever. He was made director of this work, but the war for a time necessarily postponed operations. The United States was now engaged in the greatest military undertaking in its history. Gorgas suddenly found himself at the head of the Surgeon-General's office at a time when this was almost the most important branch of the service. The military ardour of his youth had not quieted down, his love of adventure was as keen as ever. His diary of his South American journey manifests almost as lively an interest in Pizarro and the Incas as in yellow fever, and now that his country was at war with Germany Gorgas would doubtless have felt a greater joy leading a regiment than in fighting the battle against disease. However, he was sixty-three years old, and had suddenly become the man on whose work the health and efficiency of several million young men depended. In every American home Gorgas was the man whose labours were of chief importance to American mothers and fathers. To describe his work in this crisis—the last important work of his life, as the event proved—would be to recount the history of the medical corps for the years 1917–18. Fortunately Gorgas began his reorganization before hostilities were declared. He was far from being a Pacifist; like many other Americans he foresaw the probability of American intervention, and, soon after becoming Surgeon-General, he began preparations. He amplified the Medical Reserve Corps so that, when war began, more than two thousand civilians had been enrolled, and the machinery had been established that enabled him within a year to add at least 30,000 civilian doctors. Similarly Gorgas had made plans for amplifying his enlisted personnel, bringing it to a great size the following year. In the spring and summer of 1916, Gorgas appeared almost daily before the Military Affairs Committees of the Senate and of the House, and personally advised in the preparation of the revised Army Bill. He was entitled to the courtesies of the floor of the Senate Chamber as the authorized head of the Medical Corps of the United States Army.

The result of his work appeared when the Medical Corps went from a peace to a war basis. At the beginning there were 435 regular Army Medical Officers, and between 2,000 and 2,500 medical men in the Medical Reserve Corps—that is, lay medical men. In 1918, at the time of the Armistice, there were more than 32,000 medical officers in active service and more than 35,000 civilian doctors enrolled in the Medical Reserve Corps. There were, besides, approximately 250,000 men in the enlisted personnel, and 22,000 nurses, probably the largest corps, in the aggregate, that was ever under the command of one major-general. The Medical Corps, at the end of the war, was larger than the entire standing Army of the United States before the outbreak of hostilities. Great success also followed Gorgas's effort to reorganize the hospitals and the hospital staffs of the Army. He was responsible for sick soldiers wherever they were. There were only seven Army hospitals in the United States when the war began, but these were increased to more than one hundred, including three embarkation hospitals and two base hospitals. Gorgas established a fully equipped hospital at each of the army camps and cantonments, more than thirty-two in all. In France he provided accommodations for 25 per cent. of the American soldiers in the field. He constructed one hospital with 27,000 beds and many smaller hospitals. In pre-war days, the army hospital capacity in the United States, outside of the limited facilities at army posts, was for 3,843 men. When the war ended, Gorgas provided hospital accommodations in this country alone for one hundred thousand men.

Under his direction in the neighbourhood of six million men received medical examinations, of which approximately one third were rejected, leaving an accepted personnel of practically four million men. It was the business of General Gorgas's department not only to examine these men, but to see that they were kept well, provided with prophylaxis, and, when they became ill, to see that they were properly cared for. It was his duty to care for the wounded and sick overseas in the most scientific manner; and, finally, to make a record, at the end of the war, of the health condition of the soldiers retiring to private life.

Gorgas used liberally all modern preventive measures, including vaccination against typhoid and paratyphoid, antitoxin for diphtheria and tetanus, serums for influenza and other infectious diseases. He urged suitable and sufficient clothing for the men, ample air space in barracks to insure proper ventilation, exercise and recreational sports to keep the men fit. He did not enforce regulations for the protection of the men in a perfunctory or routine manner, but was personally interested in their welfare. His testimony before important investigating committees demonstrated his keen appreciation of his responsibility and his deeply sympathetic interest. Indeed it was commonly said that his attitude toward the boys was that of a sympathetic father. Gorgas also showed great ability as a councillor. In his war work his real efforts were necessarily concentrated on big problems, where he, as councillor, had the final decision in matters pertaining to his department. As one of the surgeons-general in attendance on the General Medical Board of the Council of National Defense, and as a member of the Executive Committee of that body, he was one of the most valuable councillors and advisers. He was a regular attendant at the weekly or bi-weekly meetings of the Executive Committee, and assisted in the formulation of new policies involving not only his own department but all of the activities of the Government which had to do with medicine, surgery, and sanitation. The Executive Committee, which did most effective work under the chairmanship of Dr. Franklin H. Martin, was representative of the highest medical genius in America; its other members were Doctors Welch, Vaughan, Simpson, Mayo, Admiral Grayson, besides the three Surgeons-General—Gorgas, Braisted, and Blue.

Gorgas was also an effective administrator. He

selected and depended upon strong men for his aids, and when he had chosen them, his faith in their honesty and integrity was unshaken, even if they were criticised. He had the courage of his convictions, and stood by his judgment when once formed. "While he was the mildest of men in dealing with his associates," says one of them, "occasionally he was thought to be stubborn because he failed to yield on some line of action upon which he had determined. He was always ready to discuss all sides of any question but he finally made his own decisions, and on these he was definite in action. He was dependable to a fault."

To an unusual degree Dr. Gorgas had the confidence not only of the public but of the American medical profession. The problem, therefore, of interesting the professional medical men in the medical need was not particularly difficult. With the quick decision that directed all his acts, Gorgas grasped and provided for the needs of the conflict. He called to his aid the most distinguished medical men of the country—such men as William H. Welch, Dr. Victor Vaughan of Ann Arbor, Dr. Frank Billings of Chicago, Dr. E. G. Brackett, and Dr. Samuel Mixter of Boston, Dr. A. J. Ochsner of Chicago, Dr. William H. Logan of Chicago, Dr. George B. de Schweinitz of Philadelphia, Dr. Charles W. Richardson of Washington, Dr. Theodore Janeway of Baltimore, Dr. Wakefield Longcope of Baltimore, Dr. Pierce Bailey of New York, Dr. Stuart McGuire, and other leading surgeons, internists, and men skilled in all lines of medical work. Through the general response of these medical leaders such material as had been unknown in previous national crises was offered the Government. Their coöperation made possible the splendid medical organization that trained in less than a year the great army of doctors, nurses, and hospital attendants who cared for the American sick and wounded in France as well as for the recruits in the training camps in the United States. One of the first to come to Washington was Dr. Will Mayo, to whom Dr. Gorgas had written in the first days of the war. His prompt response gave Gorgas great satisfaction and pleasure. Throughout the war either Dr. Will or Dr. Charles Mayo, and sometimes both, had a desk in the Surgeon-General's office.

"Without the opportunity of watching the varied work and rapid extension of the medical service in the army during the earlier months of hostilities," writes Dr. Brackett, "one could hardly realize the size of the task, the rapidity of movement, and the necessary devotion required to meet the daily emergencies and complications incident to a state of war; and at the same time plan for extended operations in a field entirely new. In such an exigency one may imagine the difficulty of carrying on any definite policy, however well formulated and however clearly held in mind. Yet although too near the centre of authority to be untrammelled, Dr. Gorgas always had a definite policy which he attempted to carry out, and this was evident to those who came in contact with him, and who had the opportunity of discussing his plans with him.

"One must remember that in the larger national organizations the development of medicine into specialties had not been recognized in a practical way. The new demands, however, made upon the medical department by the war necessitated just this development into specialties which had taken place. Without the services of men especially trained in their particular branches, the emergency which arose from the massing of great numbers of men together under war conditions could not have been met. At the same time it was necessary to recognize that these men with special training and possessed of skill in their departments, were in consequence less fitted to take up general lines of work. As a result of this situation Dr. Gorgas established bureaus in his central office to organize special medical and surgical groups, and he put in charge of these bureaus men who were recognized by the medical community. These men called their confrères into service, and organized their departments. As a result the response by medical men all over the country was rapid and generous, and practically at no time during this period was it necessary to urge men who were actually needed to enter the military service."

When the epidemics of influenza and pneumonia swept the country, devastating our camps, the medical profession, almost to a man, stood back of Gorgas. He personally inspected all the camps. "A notification," said Dr. Vaughan, "that any camp had an undue amount of sickness was sufficient to bring General Gorgas to it with the greatest speed. In making these inspections he insisted that he and those who accompanied him should take at least one midday meal in the hospital unannounced, and with the purpose of ascertaining by personal experience how the patients were fed. He not only adhered to this rule himself, but insisted that all inspectors should do the same. The skill and devotion of General Gorgas to the welfare of the enlisted man resulted in the mobilization of a great army with a smaller death rate than had hitherto been known in the annals of military medicine."

With the exception of one disease, influenza, which ravaged cities the same as camps, preventable diseases were either eliminated or reduced far below the rates prevailing in civil life.

When the influenza epidemic raged at Macon, Georgia, Dr. Gorgas and a dozen of the leading

General Gorgas as Surgeon General at his desk.

physicians of the country went to the camp. When conditions had improved, the officers of the Alabama brigade gave General Gorgas a dinner. He responded to the compliments paid him by a happy speech, in which he said: "I have had every honour my profession could give me. My government has given me every honour that it could bestow upon any physician in its medical service. Yet I am not satisfied. I still have one ambition to realize before I can count my life happy and rounded out. I wish it were possible for the President to reduce my rank as Major-General to that of Brigadier-General and put me in command, in active service in France, of that brigade of splendid Alabamians whom I have seen here."

Gorgas offered freedom to the men working under him, and then held them to their responsibilities. This method was one of the things which largely contributed to his success. One episode illustrates this. Having prepared a draft of a certain organization, its general plans having been already discussed and decided upon, Colonel Brackett took it to Dr. Gorgas for his signature, necessary to put it in active operation. Turning to the place on the last page reserved for his name, Gorgas took up his pen, turned to Colonel Brackett and said:

"This is all right, Colonel Brackett?"

"Yes, sir," said the Colonel.

"For," Dr. Gorgas said, "if it isn't, it comes back on me."

In this action one can realize not only the trust but the responsibility which he placed upon those to whom he delegated authority and action.

But trouble was the lot of all those who sought to pilot this nation in the great war, and Gorgas had his share. "In company with General Gorgas," says Dr. Franklin H. Martin, of Chicago, "I was called several times to appear before the Military Affairs Committee of the United States Senate to report upon the conduct of our activities. General Gorgas's attitude upon these occasions was always most admirable. While meeting with perfect candour the issue under discussion, his simplicity of manner and his frankness won the immediate approval and sympathy of his audience.

"Unlike most line officers, and some of the officers of the regular Medical Corps, General Gorgas recognized and advocated the importance of modifying the law and thereby making it possible to confer higher rank on the officers of the Medical Reserve Corps. To accomplish this, an amendment to the existing law was necessary, and this involved the preparation and passage of a bill through both branches of Congress, and the signature of the President of the United States. All of this had to be preceded by a propaganda that would overcome the indifference and definite opposition of many influential factors, and that would stimulate the legislatures to action. On several occasions General Gorgas appeared before the committees of Congress and made his plea so convincingly that in spite of much opposition the bill was at last made a part of a General Appropriations Bill, and the prospect of its passage seemed assured.

"At this critical juncture, due to a peremptory summons, General Gorgas and I found ourselves, one morning, face to face in the waiting room of the First Assistant Secretary of War, Mr. Benedict C. Crowell (Secretary Baker being in Europe). We were ignorant as to the reasons for our summons. Upon entering the office of the Secretary of War, we were surprised to find the Chief of Staff of the Army also present. As we were seated, with the Assistant Secretary of War acting as interlocutor, it became apparent that we were under censorship because of our activity in advocating or lobbying for the bill which would provide higher rank for officers of the Medical Reserve Corps. With the Chief of Staff apparently an amused onlooker, the Assistant Secretary proceeded in a rather brusque fashion to quiz General Gorgas regarding his activities in advocating legislation concerned with the Corps, the uniform of which he wore and of which he was the head. It was even intimated that he had in public addresses urged men to write to their Congressmen and Senators, instructing them to vote in a certain way. When General Gorgas was asked directly if he had committed these indiscretions he answered that he could not remember that he had done the particular thing of which he was accused. 'But,' he said, in his direct and outspoken manner, 'you know, Mr. Secretary, I am in favour of the passage of the Owen-Dyer Bill, and I would consider myself disloyal to my corps if I did not do everything in my power to bring about its passage.'

"The Assistant Secretary was disarmed by this frank statement, and evidently forgetting to make the point that it was contrary to regulations for an officer to interest himself in legislation, he began to argue the merits of the bill for increased rank. He asked General Gorgas if he was not inconsistent in urging higher rank for members of his Reserve Corps when there were other reserve corps for which such higher rank would be just as desirable.

"'Not at all,' the General replied. 'I have no definite knowledge of the requirements of the other corps, and I should never think of interfering in their organization. I do know the needs of my own corps, and I feel that I must favour such a change in the law as will meet its needs.'

"General Gorgas was then asked to explain just how the passage of this law would benefit his corps.

In his quiet, convincing manner he responded by drawing a mental picture of his vast corps with its service in the camps of this country; its service overseas where the distinguished members of our medical profession, serving as majors, were working side by side with their distinguished confrères of Europe, who, while performing the same duties, were colonels, brigadier-generals, and major-generals, thus outranking our own men and bringing many unnecessary humiliations to bear upon them. The story was so convincing, so unanswerable, and so pleadingly told (the names of well-known civilian doctors serving as illustrations) that the General obviously had won his case. Even the silent listener, the Chief of Staff, was apparently satisfied that the distinguished officer, although a medical man, had turned the tables on the civilian Assistant Secretary, and was ready to allow further discipline to remain in abeyance.

"Another incident occurs to me which exhibited not only the General's good nature, but his adeptness at successful repartee. On an occasion when we were being dismissed from a hearing of a Senate Committee and had risen to go, one of the senators asked me why the Medical Corps of the Army and Navy were prejudiced against the irregular practitioners of medicine, mentioning a well-known cult, and why we refused to allow them to enroll as medical officers. I referred the question promptly to General

Gorgas, the executive head of the Medical Corps of the Army.

"The General said, speaking the name of the well-known Senator, 'Why, no, Senator ——, we are not prejudiced against any qualified medical man. In fact, we need all of the aid we can get.'

"'But,' replied the Senator, 'you refuse to enroll osteopaths.'

"'Yes, Senator, that is very true; but the law does not authorize us to enroll these practitioners as medical officers. If, as a member of the law-making body, you should change the law, it would be my duty to obey it.'

"And then he added, with a twinkle in his eye, 'Will you change it?' The distinguished Senate Committee dismissed the Surgeon-General with a laugh, and he bowed himself out, taking with him all of the honours.

"But it was late in 1917, or early in 1918, when the famous investigation of the conduct of the War Department was on, and when the Department was being rather roughly handled, that General Gorgas definitely changed the drift of criticism and did much to save the situation by placing things in their true light.

"There had been much suffering on the part of our newly recruited soldiers, especially in some of the partially constructed camps in the South. Particularly was this true among the sick because of inadequate hospital facilities. The policy had been to hasten the completion of the living quarters for the men, and to leave the construction of the hospitals until the last. There was much complaint, too, on account of an insufficiency of clothing and blankets. The death rate among the sick was considered appallingly high and the whole country was aroused. The question was being asked, 'Are we to have another falldown in this war of the medical administration similar to the notorious failure in the Spanish-American War?' This was a direct charge aimed at the War Department, and a serious reflection on all in authority, from the President down.

"When the investigation, which is the inevitable result of such an arousing of public opinion, was started by the Committee on Military Affairs of the Senate, General Gorgas, as Surgeon-General of the Army, was called upon to testify. Instead of attempting to explain away or to excuse the obvious lack of perfection of organization or administration of the affairs in those early days, in his characteristically dignified and patient manner he presented an outline of his department in peace times, and its sudden expansion from a personnel of less than five hundred to twice as many thousands in three quarters of a year; its transition from a group of trained military medical officers to this large corps, ninety per cent. of whom were six months before untrained civilian doctors; the expansion of his field organization, including transportation, hospitals, medical supplies, nurses, orderlies, and an enlisted personnel of thousands of untrained men; and his own camp equipment which, while providing for its own expansion and reorganization, had also to care for the sick among two million men who had been transferred from all kinds of environment and brought together to be converted into a homogeneous army.

"For one whole day, January 25, 1918, General Gorgas was subjected to a running quiz by the different members of the Committee on Military Affairs of the Senate. He explained patiently the efforts that he had put forth personally to complete his organization, and also cited how he had personally visited many camps. He outlined the architectural construction of the many camp hospitals; the effort that had been made to obtain the required number of cubic feet of air space for each man, etc., *ad infinitum.* He was asked if he could tell the exact number of windows in a certain structure that had been inspected. He admitted, with patience, that he could not say definitely from memory what the arrangement of the windows was, but that those details, of course, were familiar to his experts. One of the senators asked if he should not be required personally to know these details. General Gorgas caused a smile by saying that it might be convenient for him to know these things, but that he was convinced that he was already attempting to carry personally too many details.

"Finally he said: 'Gentlemen, it must be apparent that in such a great expansion of a small organization of experts to an organization of the size of this present corps, with inexperienced men, mistakes are inevitable. However, while we may have made mistakes and may make other mistakes, I can assure you that we will endeavour not to make the same mistake twice.'

"This all-day grilling succeeded in making a friend for General Gorgas of every member of that Senate Committee. It made for him a friend of every newspaper man present. This gentleman at the head of the most important corps of the Army, and in whom every father and mother who had sons was vitally interested, was pronounced a safe executive. The next day the confidence that this day's conversation with General Gorgas had created in the minds of his hearers was carried by the newspapers to the home folks of the whole country, and from that time on no breath of criticism was heard as to the medical conduct of the war; also the attitude of the people toward the Administration and the early conduct of the war was changed from violent criticism to admiration and profound confidence.

"General Gorgas, by his positive but winning

personality, and by a patience that assumed that the Senate and the people were willing to have their erroneous impressions corrected, quietly persisted in telling the whole story of the early days of that marvellous reorganization of our departments, and compelled his hearers to appreciate the bigness of the task, and finally sympathetically to appreciate that the men who were carrying on, while human, were men of patriotic devotion to their tasks who were endeavouring with all of their might to make good.

"The following incident will serve to illustrate how much General Gorgas was a man of peace, notwithstanding the fact that he was called upon to enroll, to organize, and to preside over as a soldier the largest and one of the most important corps of the great war. Once while he and myself were waiting for an interview in the office of the Secretary of War, we spoke of the horrors of the war in which we were both so busily engaged. I remarked to the General that it must seem to him that fate had pursued him pretty closely; after all the work he had done in sanitation to be suddenly called upon to raise an army of civilian doctors for the greatest war of history.

"'Yes,' he said, 'I wish the horrible war were over.' I said: 'What is the very first thing that you would do, General Gorgas, if to-morrow morning before arising you should receive a telephone message assuring you that the war was ended?'

"'Do you know what I would do?' he asked, while his eyes had a far-away, wistful expression. 'I would ring off, call New York City, and order a passage for South America. I would go to Guayaquil, Ecuador, the only place in which yellow fever is prevalent, exterminate the pestilence, and then—and then return to Panama, the garden spot of the world, and end my days writing an elegy on yellow fever.'

"And this was not the mere daydreaming of a man overwhelmed by a stupendous task, but the real yearning of a peace-loving man, who within a month after the armistice accepted a commission from the Rockefeller Foundation to go to Guayaquil, Ecuador, to do the very job that he wished to do."

CHAPTER XI

THE END

I

THREE days after the armistice was signed Gorgas laid down the duties of the Surgeon-Generalcy; he was retired for age. The spirit in which he took leave of official life is well brought out by an anecdote.

On November 14, 1918, Dr. Charles W. Richardson of Washington gave a dinner in honour of General Merritt W. Ireland, the newly appointed Surgeon-General of the United States Army. One of the guests on this occasion was the retiring Surgeon-General. Among the forty-two guests were Colonel Dercles, the French Medical Aid, the heads of the several divisions of the Surgeon-General's office, and other distinguished members of the medical service.

General Gorgas was called upon to describe the sensation one experiences upon reaching the age of retirement. After a few introductory remarks, in which he felicitated the new Surgeon-General, he began by saying that he felt sixty years young that night. He then told how when a very young man in his college days he had paid marked attention to an attractive young woman who was ten years or more his senior. At last the youthful William had decided that he was deeply in love, and the possession of the idol of his heart was indispensable for his future happiness. He sought a favourable opportunity to make known to the young woman his deep infatuation. The opportune moment came at last, and he eloquently poured out his loving message. She listened patiently to him. Perturbed and silently for a moment she observed him, and then rather pitifully remarked, "Willie, how insufferably young you are."

The General, with his winning smile, looked around at his auditors and stated, "and that is how I feel to-night."

The speech was short and simple, but those present will never forget the true genuineness with which he spoke, the brightness of his face, and the gleeful spirit which he displayed.

The signing of the armistice left Gorgas free again to take up the task entrusted to him by the International Health Board—the elimination of yellow fever. Even during the war great progress had been made. Soon after the cessation of hostilities Dr. M. E. Connor took charge of the work in Guayaquil, Ecuador, and in six months had delivered this pest hole of the disease that had made it a byword for two centuries. Thus the work which in four years was to free North America and practically all of South America from yellow fever was well under way. Gorgas had planned all this so well that it could be safely left in the very competent hands that have since carried it on so triumphantly. There was one serious problem, however, awaiting solution. Was the western hemisphere the only breeding ground of this disease? Did it exist in any of the other continents? That Europe and Asia were uncontaminated was certain. But many suspicious rumours had come to Gorgas about the western coast of Africa. These seemed to indicate that cases of yellow fever had broken out in points distributed over the vast region extending from Senegal to the Belgian Congo. A British commission had studied the situation and submitted a report that apparently confirmed these popular accounts. If yellow fever did prevail here it was certainly a serious matter. The one man to find out was Gorgas himself. Though he was sixty-six years old he did not decline the commission. On May 8th, with his wife and personal staff, he sailed for London.

It was a task which he was destined not to fulfil. His last days are well described in a memorandum prepared by his wife:

"On May 8th General and Mrs. Noble, Mr. Sullivan, Dr. Gorgas, and I sailed for London from

Quebec on the steamship *Victorian*. Dr. Guiteras expected to join the Commission in London. We were hoping that the *Victorian* would get us to London in time to reach Brussels for the opening of the International Hygiene Congress. Dr. Gorgas had been awarded the Harbin gold medal 'in recognition of his services to mankind.' It was to be presented to him by the King of the Belgians at the inaugural meeting of the Congress at midday, June 20th. Unfortunately for our hopes, our passage was rough and exceedingly slow. Though we lost no time in London, arriving at 1 A.M. and taking the train for Dover at eight o'clock the same morning, we missed the opening ceremony at Brussels by a few hours.

"Delightful rooms had been reserved for us at the Palace Hotel. From the windows we looked down on the green park below—an extensive park with magnificent trees, their lofty tops almost within reach. Beyond lay a vast sweep of rolling country.

"Can one be in Brussels and not feel the thrill of it? We had been reading 'The Spell of Belgium' by Mrs. Larz Anderson, in which she describes Brussels in previous wars when 'men and women, too, had led their armies to its attack and its defence; had fought and died by the thousands about its walls.' The same indomitable courage had just been shown by their descendants in the World War.

"We were eager to meet the Belgians. An opportunity came the next day, when General and Mrs. Noble, Dr. Gorgas, and I lunched with the Minister of Finance and Mme. Vandervelde. Besides the Belgians present were Lord Dawson (King George's physician), Lady Dawson, and Olga Nethersole.

"Mme. Vandervelde, a beautiful woman with titian hair and great eyes, looked charming. After meeting her it was easy to understand why she had been so successful in the United States in her efforts to raise money for the starving Belgians. Mme. Vandervelde had a soft speaking voice, a logical way of presenting a subject, and a magnetic personality completed the charm.

"While we were talking in little groups, just before luncheon, Dr. René Sands, physician to the Queen, was called to the 'phone. The Queen, he said, on rejoining us, was receiving the visiting ladies that afternoon at Laeken, the summer palace, and had sent us a special invitation. In order that we might reach Laeken on time, Mme. Vandervelde graciously hurried her luncheon a little. Such a delightful luncheon, with odd table decorations! The centrepiece and doilies were made from flour sacks embroidered in striking colours—the identical sacks which, filled with flour, had during the World War been sent to the destitute Belgians from the United States—largely through the efforts of Mme. Vandervelde. Queer, carved wooden animals were here and there on the table—giraffes, tigers, elephants, etc. They were made by the Negroes of the Belgian Congo. Mme. Vandervelde spoke of them as samples of 'nigger art,' which puzzled us at first as she gave the French pronunciation. Seated on my left was a distinguished professor from Liège—Professor Hutzeigt, who did not speak English. So I had a chance to see what I could do with French.

"Immediately after luncheon we started for Laeken, a beautiful drive, Mme. de la Croix, the wife of the Minister of Justice, taking us in her car. Alighting from the machine we found ourselves in a new world—a fairyland of glass-covered bowers aflame with pink azaleas, fuchsias, and climbing geraniums. They covered the sides and hung from the roof—an amazing pink glow. Passing through these galleries of bloom, about the largest in the world, the pride of old King Leopold who had planned them, we entered the palm room, with huge palms reaching up to the glass dome. This opened to the parterre, the mossy green lawn dotted with begonias. Here and there were grottoes and splashing fountains. We faced the palace, an impressive gray-stone building with great clumps of rhododendrons about it—the approach a beautiful vista.

"The women in their pretty gowns arranged themselves on either side of the path leading from the palace, the great trees overhead. General Noble and Dr. Gorgas were the only men in line. After a while an almost imperceptible stir indicated the coming of the Queen.

"Down the palace steps she came, and along the centre path, queenly and lovely in her summer gown of white. A long white cape hanging from her shoulders gave occasional glimpses of the rich yellow lining. On the Queen's head was a brown-and-gold affair that was neither a hat nor a cap—odd but becoming.

"Mme. de la Croix and Dr. Sands, who were to make the presentations, stepped forward. The gentlemen in waiting fell back. Taking our side first, before each in turn the Queen stopped and talked for a minute or more, seeming to know by instinct something interesting and pertinent to say to each. We were glad not to be the first in line, for we had time to notice the curtsies of the ladies ahead of us, and prepare to make our own as gracefully as possible.

"To Dr. Gorgas the Queen spoke of the sanitary work accomplished in Cuba and Panama, and also of his trip to the Rand. We were all impressed by the Queen's bearing, so dignified and poised, yet extremely gracious. After the audience was over, we strolled around the garden and through the greenhouses, with more leisure to examine the orchids and flowers. We left at last with reluctance.

"The day following our visit to Laeken we took

luncheon with Ambassador and Mrs. Whitlock in their attractive home—the Nobles also, and that night we attended a brilliant dinner given by another member of the cabinet.

"The Harbin Gold Medal was presented to Dr. Gorgas by Lord Sandhurst at a banquet which was the closing function of the Congress.

"The day after the Congress closed, General and Mrs. Noble and I left Dr. Gorgas and Mr. Sullivan at Brussels, and went off for a trip down the Rhine to Cologne and Coblentz, making a side trip by motor over the splendid roads to Wiesbaden; then on to Antwerp. We ran across old friends everywhere, and had a glorious trip. In Antwerp we met our Consul-General, Mr. Messersmith, and his wife, friends who had entertained us some years before at their home in Curaçao.

"Mr. Messersmith, advised of our coming, had arranged an audience for us with His Eminence Cardinal Mercier, at Malines. The interview was a memorable one. We found the Cardinal charming—tall, with stately bearing and a captivating personality. He gave us fully half an hour of his time. His trip to the United States was recalled with enthusiasm. I remember telling him how much I regretted not seeing him while he was in Washington.

"'Were you in the city at the time?' asked the Cardinal.

"'Yes,' I replied.

"'Well,' he said with a twinkle in his eye, 'then the fault was not mine!'

"Cardinal Mercier said that he was disappointed not to see Dr. Gorgas. He had followed his work with interest, and expressed for him a great admiration.

"When the Cardinal rose, to intimate that the audience was at an end, we took our leave in the proper manner, backing to the door. After descending to the ground floor, we turned and saw the Cardinal at the head of the stairs. He was looking down on us and with upraised hand bestowed his blessing.

"Many inquired for Dr. Gorgas on this trip and regretted that he was not with us. It was a disappointment to him, too, not to be able to go, but Ambassador Whitlock had arranged an audience for him with King Albert on the afternoon of the 22d. It was necessary to see the Secretary of Foreign Affairs with regard to the Commission visiting the Belgian possessions on the west coast of Africa.

"A few days afterward Dr. Gorgas left Brussels for London, meeting us at the Hotel Savoy. We spent an interesting evening talking over our experiences and planning for the West African trip. Dr. Gorgas gave us an account of his interview with King Albert and all that had happened after we left him.

"He was in happy vein that night, as he told us of his visit to the palace. King Albert was deeply interested in sanitation and had evidently read a good deal about the work against yellow fever in Havana and Panama. After about fifteen minutes' conversation with the King, Dr. Gorgas, thinking that politeness required them to withdraw, rose to make his adieux. 'But,' said Dr. Gorgas, 'the Ambassador looked so shocked and motioned me so decidedly to sit down, giving surreptitiously a violent jerk to my coat-tail, that I knew I had gone wrong. King Albert went on with the conversation as if he were absolutely unconscious of the little by-play.

"'The King was not aware that there had ever been any yellow fever in the Congo, and expressed a desire to have the ground looked over by the Commission, and a report made to him.'

"The conversation lasted for about an hour, Dr. Gorgas explaining the work and the results obtained in detail. And then the King indicated that they might leave.

"I have good reason to remember this conversation with my husband, for the following morning he was taken seriously ill. A few months before, in Peru, the Doctor had shown signs of exhaustion, and given cause for uneasiness to his friends. From this, however, he seemed to have completely recovered and this night particularly I thought his condition most promising. About three o'clock in the morning, however, the Doctor called to me and said in the calmest manner possible that he had just had a slight paralytic stroke. He showed no effects of it; his speech was unimpaired, but he had not the slightest doubt of the seriousness of his experience. Upon the advice of General Noble and Sir John Goodwin, the Surgeon-General of the British Army, he was taken to Queen Alexandra Military Hospital, Millbank. He stood the trip well. It must have been a keen disappointment to be so suddenly halted in the midst of his labours, at the very moment the promise of fulfillment was near—the fulfillment of his dream to rid the world of yellow fever and make the tropics safe for the white man. But his calm fortitude never forsook him. He was surprisingly cheerful.

"After the first week Dr. Gorgas had, I think, no hope of his recovery, though his attending physicians were optimistic. I said to him once when his vitality was at low ebb, rendering us all most anxious:

"'You're not going to give up. You will do your best to get well!'

"'Oh, yes,' he said, with a glimmer of his old humour. 'W. C. Gorgas is a fighter, you know.' And then, after a pause, his brave spirit shining through his dark eyes, 'I am going to fight to the very last. But this time I do not believe I shall win out. But—if this is dying, it is very comfortable.'

"He thought often of the future life, and pictured it with the simplicity and sweetness of a little child. His scientific training and turn of mind did not warp his spirit from its quest after God and His Kingdom.

"Dr. Gorgas liked his room—a cheerful room with windows facing the Thames, with the passing boats and busy river life. Everyone was kind. Almost daily flowers were sent, and his old friend Mr. Henry S. Wellcome spent much time and thought seeking delicacies to tempt his appetite. Colonel Robinson, and later Colonel Kennedy, medical consultant to the hospital, were in constant attendance. Lord Dawson, the King's physician, came in consultation.

"General Noble spent many hours at the hospital, and was a tower of strength to us both. Sir John Goodwin dropped in daily to see his friend.

"Usually visitors were allowed at the hospital only at stated hours, but for Dr. Gorgas all such rules were swept aside, and I was free to come and go as I pleased. No one can imagine what a comfort this was to us. Dr. Gorgas was greatly touched by this kindness—a kindness which seemed intensified as the days and weeks passed. Not once but many times he exclaimed: 'How fortunate I am to be here!' This was so characteristic of him, to look on the bright side of things. 'You know,' he said, 'I might have died at sea, or on the way to West Africa, and separated from you.'

"One morning on going to the hospital, the usual calm ordinary routine seemed a bit upset. An undercurrent of excitement pervaded the atmosphere, which roused my curiosity. Dr. Gorgas was steadily improving, and I did not associate him in any way with the stir and bustle. Later, the head nurse, Sister Erdley, beckoned to me from the hall. I went to her, and she told me with very evident pleasure that the King was coming that morning to see General Gorgas. Fearing to excite him, they had deemed it wise to say nothing to him until soon before the King was expected.

"'Will you tell General Gorgas now,' said Sister Erdley, 'that we are expecting the King at any moment?'

"I did so at once, and it did me a world of good to see the Doctor's look of surprise and pleasure. The disappointment he had felt in not being able to keep an appointment with the King was swept aside in a moment. To Sir John Goodwin the King had said, when he heard of Dr. Gorgas's illness:

"'If General Gorgas is too ill to come to the palace to see me, I shall go to the hospital to see him.'

"On that to me never-to-be-forgotten morning, the invalid, the dominant figure in the room bare to monastic simplicity, showed no trace of illness. There was a slight flush on his cheeks, the white pillows at his back and the faint touch of blue in his immaculate invalid's attire threw into relief the fine head capped by the heavy crown of snow-white hair.

"By special request of His Majesty, I was present at the interview. The King came in quietly, 'without fuss or feathers,' as he had expressed himself to Sir John Goodwin, accompanied only by Sir John and his Equerry in Waiting. The attending physicians followed the matron, Sister Humphrey, and Sister Erdley, the little group standing a few paces back.

"The King spoke to us in a delightfully simple way. His cordiality charmed us. The smile which always drew people to him hovered about the Doctor's lips as the King talked with him, expressing distress at his illness and earnest wishes for a speedy improvement in his condition.

"His Majesty talked at considerable length of the work which had been carried out in Panama and Cuba, and especially of the subject of yellow fever and the extermination of that disease. He thanked Dr. Gorgas for all the help which he had given the British Army in sending medical officers and nurses to work for the British forces, and assured him that this help had been of immense value and was deeply appreciated.

"Then, taking from his Equerry the insignia of Knight Commander of the Most Distinguished Order of St. Michael and St. George, the King presented it to Dr. Gorgas, saying: 'General Gorgas, it gives me very great pleasure to present you with the insignia of this Order; and believe me, I very sincerely appreciate the great work which you have done for humanity—work in which I take the greatest interest.'

"Nothing could have been more impressive, more touching, than this simple ceremony—all that Dr. Gorgas's illness permitted of the usual formal conferring of knighthood.

"A few minutes afterward, after talking of things in general, His Majesty withdrew with his staff, leaving us deeply moved by his visit.

"At that time we were all so hopeful of the Doctor's recovery that I even experienced a natural and undemocratic thrill at hearing myself called 'Lady Gorgas' and it pleased the Doctor greatly. Everyone continued to call him 'General,' as before, with one exception. The tall gaunt masseur, a Swede, thereafter never failed to give him full honours. He announced himself daily in the doorway with a bow and a ceremonious: 'And how does General Sir William Gorgas find himself this morning?'

"The day following the King's visit to the hospital a message was received to the effect that His Majesty hoped that General Gorgas was improving, and that no harmful effects had resulted from the visit and the bestowal of the order. In reply Dr. Gorgas said: 'The King's gracious visit has done me a world of good. I feel decidedly better for my decoration, and am ready for another!'—an answer, I was told, that amused the King. It certainly amused his attending physicians and Sister Erdley, who rejoiced to see her patient in such good spirits.

"The King subsequently kept in close touch with the War Office, and made constant inquiries regarding Dr. Gorgas's progress.

"Almost imperceptibly the Doctor grew weaker. Four weeks later the tender, passionate heart, that had never failed to respond to the appeals or the sufferings of others, was at rest.

"His faith in God and Eternity was absolute. Like Pasteur he believed that 'power for good given to us in this world will be continued beyond it.'"

On July 5th the following cable from His Majesty King George V, was received by Lieutenant-General Sir Thomas Goodwin at the War Office:

"His Majesty is so sorry to read in this morning's paper the death of General Gorgas, and wishes you to convey to his wife the expression of the deep sympathy of the King and Queen with her and her family in the great loss they have sustained. Please also tell her how pleased His Majesty is to think that he saw General Gorgas in the hospital, and was able personally to decorate him."

From President Wilson the following was received: "Allow me to express my profound sympathy with you in the loss of your distinguished husband, whose unselfish services to mankind can never be forgotten."

II

There were many tributes to the Doctor in the British press, and that from the London *Lancet*, probably the world's greatest medical journal, may be quoted as typical:

"The death, after a long illness, of Sir William Gorgas, Surgeon-General of the United States Army, took place on July 3d at the Queen Alexandra Military Hospital at Millbank. He was the best known and most uniformly successful medical administrator not of his age alone but of any age, and his work is comparable only with that recorded of Moses. No sooner were discoveries made tracing an endemic disease to a source removable by rigid hygienic measures than the services of this master-administrator were requisitioned to the farthest quarter of the globe to carry out such measures. And as if by magic—black magic, as it appeared to the slovenly, careless inhabitant; white magic to the admiring world outside—the areas were cleansed and freed. But there was no magic other than that wielded by a strong personality with only one idea in mind—the speedy accomplishment of the work of the moment. Havana, Panama, the Transvaal, the endemic regions of yellow fever in South America, are only the best-known sites of his activities.

"The story of the riddance of Havana from the curse of yellow fever has been told often enough but deserves to be recalled here; for it was typical of Gorgas's work. During the last forty-five years of Spanish rule on the Island of Cuba the number of deaths from yellow fever occurring annually in the capital, although varying greatly from year to year, was never below 50, and many times exceeded 1,000. The work of Major Walter Reed and his colleagues pointed strongly to the prevention of yellow fever being bound up with the destruction of the mosquito Culex (now called Stegomyia) fasciatus, or the prevention of its bites. Major Gorgas, as he then was, lost no time in putting this theory to a practical trial. As he himself tersely phrased it 'The only infected material from the towns looked after was the sick man, who was carefully sought out and screened from mosquitoes.' Havana was, and remained, in unrestricted communication with half-a-dozen infected towns; commerce was not interfered with and no restraint was placed upon the admission of clothing or bedding from infected localities; but under a purely anti-mosquito régime, during the year 1901–02 only five deaths from yellow fever were recorded. Seldom has a scientific discovery been applied so promptly and successfully to an administrative problem.

"The reputation of Gorgas as a scientist has been challenged in certain quarters, in view of the fact that he was not responsible for the actual discoveries without which his work could not have been done. For this he needs no defence. Science and art are at their greatest when they join hands, and the man who acts as a link between discovery and its application needs a combination of qualities as rare as those of the pure investigator. It has been too much the pride of the seeker after abstract truth in the exact sciences to care little as to its application. But even when research has been undertaken with the sole aim of finding the cause of an endemic fever or the source of an infection, the successful investigator would often cut a poor figure as the organizer of an expedition to stamp out the scourge in the light of his discoveries. It is not only as a scientist but as a leader of men, as a hero of at least two of the most successful campaigns ever waged, that the name of Gorgas will always be gratefully remembered. The formal procession with the body from Millbank under military escort to St. Paul's, and the ensuing ceremony in the Metropolitan Cathedral, are evidences of the reverence due to a great benefactor of humanity which in this case are amply called for."

The funeral, at the special desire of the British Government, took place in St. Paul's Cathedral. The American Ambassador, Mr. John W. Davis and Mrs. Davis, attended, and the King, Queen Alexandra, and the Duke of Connaught, sent representatives. A description, printed in a British periodical, eloquently gives the spirit of the occasion and forms a fitting end to this narrative:

"A riderless horse walked up Ludgate Hill the other day behind its sleeping master, and if a horse can feel and know what happens, its heart must have been breaking—unless there came to it new strength in the pride it felt in the sight of its master sleeping under the Stars and Stripes on his way to St. Paul's.

"For what was happening that day up Ludgate Hill was a rare and stirring thing. I looked down from the windows of the little House with Green Shutters in the very shadow of the dome, and I thought that here indeed was a public opinion of which our London, and our country, and all the entire world, might well be proud. For here was no great Englishman, no great Briton, going to his rest; here was a ragged, barefoot boy of Baltimore being carried to St. Paul's after his life's work was done.

"He had done for the world one of the greatest things that an American brain has ever done: he made the Panama Canal after thousands of people had died in the attempt.

"Now think how he began his life. This is what he told us:

"'I first came to Baltimore a ragged, barefoot little rebel, with empty pockets and empty stomach. My father had gone south with Lee's army. At the fall and destruction of Richmond my mother's house with all that she had was burned, leaving her stranded with six small children. She came to Baltimore and was cared for by friends. These memories are vivid with me, and can never be effaced.'

"And the other day he rode up Ludgate Hill, sleeping his last sleep on earth, wrapped in the Stars and Stripes. There were thousands of men and women and children standing still, there were hundreds of men in khaki passing by, there were ambassadors and other great people, and the lonely woman who was on her way with her hero to conquer disease in Peru when death took him from her. And there was the riderless horse.

"All these came up Ludgate Hill, and as the sun poured down on this ancient way, our hearts and ears throbbing with the solemn music of the Dead March, we knew that we were looking on the passing of a man whose name would shine for ages in the history of our race.

"It seemed good that death should find him here,

for so there came our opportunity to do a great man honour. He passed through the great door through which the sun streams into the nave of St. Paul's, and there he lay with Nelson and Wellington and all that mighty host who came this way and passed into the universe.

"They will take him to his own land, but in truth he belongs to us all. He was one of Life's great helpers, for he cleaned up foul places and made them sweet, and now, as they said of Lincoln, 'he belongs to the Ages.'"

This funeral of a British Major-General, in St. Paul's Cathedral, was the highest honour that Britain could pay a distinguished American. Its beauty and its solemnity will never be forgotten by those who witnessed it. But Gorgas's own country also gave him its greatest honours. The body lay in state for four days in Washington, and, at the services in the Church of the Epiphany, all branches of the Government and most foreign countries were represented.

The General was buried on one of the most beautiful slopes of Arlington—certainly an appropriate resting place for a man whose thoughts and activities, from his earliest days, had been associated with the American Army.

THE END

INDEX

5438